Hanging Out

Recent Titles in
The Psychology of Everyday Life

Working Out: The Psychology of Sport and Exercise
Justine J. Reel

Chilling Out: The Psychology of Relaxation
Christine L. B. Selby

Hooking Up: The Psychology of Sex and Dating
Katherine M. Helm

Filling Up: The Psychology of Eating
Justine J. Reel

Blowing Up: The Psychology of Conflict
Randi Minetor

HANGING OUT

The Psychology of Socializing

Valerie Hill and Tennille Nicole Allen

The Psychology of Everyday Life

An Imprint of ABC-CLIO, LLC
Santa Barbara, California • Denver, Colorado

Library of Congress Cataloging-in-Publication Data

Names: Hill, Valerie, 1975- author. | Allen, Tennille Nicole, author.
Title: Hanging out : the psychology of socializing / Valerie Hill and
   Tennille Nicole Allen.
Description: Santa Barbara : Greenwood, An Imprint of ABC-CLIO, [2018] |
   Series: The psychology of everyday life | Includes bibliographical
   references and index.
Identifiers: LCCN 2017034529 (print) | LCCN 2017038544 (ebook) |
   ISBN 9781440843938 (ebook) | ISBN 9781440843921 (hardcopy : alk. paper)
Subjects: LCSH: Socialization.
Classification: LCC HM686 (ebook) | LCC HM686 .H55 2018 (print) |
   DDC 303.3/2—dc23
LC record available at https://lccn.loc.gov/2017034529

ISBN: 978–1–4408–4392–1 (print)
         978–1–4408–4393–8 (ebook)

22 21 20 19 18   1 2 3 4 5

This book is also available as an eBook.

Greenwood
An Imprint of ABC-CLIO, LLC

ABC-CLIO, LLC
130 Cremona Drive, P.O. Box 1911
Santa Barbara, California 93116-1911
www.abc-clio.com

This book is printed on acid-free paper ∞

Manufactured in the United States of America

Contents

Series Foreword

Psychology is the science of behavior; it is the field that examines how and why people do, feel, and think the things that they do. However, in a very real way, everyone is a psychologist. Each of us observes and tries to understand the thoughts, feelings, and behaviors of people we are around, as well as trying to understand ourselves. Have you ever thought, "I wonder why she did that?" Or perhaps, "Why did I do that; it makes no sense." If you have, then you are asking psychological questions. Most people enjoy being "students of human behavior" and observing and thinking about people, human nature, and all of the variants of the human condition. The difference between "most people" and psychologists is that the psychologist has spent many years in school studying and learning about people.

In addition to studying and doing research, psychologists also work directly with people in many settings. For example, clinical and counseling psychologists work with people who are dealing with psychological disorders or are having problems in their lives that require professional assistance, but there are many other branches of psychology as well. Sport psychologists work with athletes and teams to improve performance and team functioning. Industrial/organizational psychologists help workers, managers, and organizations function more effectively and efficiently. Military psychologists deal with military personnel and organizations. Forensic psychologists work with police and other law enforcement organizations to help solve crimes and assist law enforcement personnel. In addition to all of the things that psychologists know about people, for any person, understanding psychology can help take advantage of what psychologists have learned to help all people live better and healthier lives and to deal more effectively with others.

The Psychology of Everyday Life is a series of books that will address many different and important psychological issues and areas, the goal being to provide information and examples of how psychology touches all of our lives on a daily basis. The series will also show ways in which psychological knowledge can help us. These books will address psychological concerns with the most up-to-date and relevant knowledge from the field of psychology. Information from the laboratories, classrooms, clinics, hospitals, and other settings will be brought together to help make sense out of some important and often complex ideas. However, these books will be directed toward readers who are not psychologists, but are interested in learning more about the field and what it has to offer. Thus, the language is not technical but is common language addressing "regular" people. There will be times when professional and technical language may be used, but only if thoroughly explained and related to the issues being discussed.

This series of books will focus on specific facets of our daily lives and show how psychology can help us understand and deal with these issues. A wide range of topics will be covered, from eating to exercising to relaxing to interpersonal conflict. Each book will consist of three distinct parts. Part I will answer the "who/what/where/when/why/how" questions related to the topic. These chapters will examine everything from how the subject manifests in our day-to-day lives and how it impacts our psychological well-being to differences across the lifespan and cultures to what famous psychologists have to say on the subject.

Part II in each book will focus on "real-life" examples and will address many of the issues that were introduced in each book in Part I, but will do so with examples and explanations that will make the issues even clearer. It is one thing to have knowledge, but it is an entirely different thing to be able to apply and use that knowledge, and this is what will be covered by the scenarios and interpretative analyses in Part II. When people read Part II they will begin to see many of the ways in which our daily lives are touched by psychology, and the many ways that psychology can be used to support and help people.

Part III in each book will address the controversial issues related to the book's subject. Like any academic and professional discipline, psychology has many areas where there are spirited disagreements among academics, practitioners, and researchers about important issues in the field. It will be very instructive for people to understand these issues and to see the careful and systematic ways that scholars think about and conceptualize various topics, and to see how they debate, discuss, and resolve some of their differences of opinion. For non-psychologists these controversial issues and how they are addressed will lead to a greater understanding of psychological matters, but also a better grasp of how scientists and professionals deal with differences and controversies and how these disagreements are addressed.

Psychology is a broad and diverse field with many different approaches, theories, methods, and ideas, and to capture this field in its breadth and depth would be impossible in a single book. This series of books, however, will serve as an introductory journey through psychology as it relates to the daily lives of ordinary people. I have been teaching, studying, and practicing psychology for many decades and I can hardly wait to read each of the books in this very exciting series, and I welcome readers to take this journey with me.

Rudy Nydegger, PhD, ABPP

Preface

"You are known by the company you keep." "Birds of a feather flock together." "It's not what you know, it's who you know." "She's my Twitter friend." Each of these familiar phrases points to the ways that we currently understand and value social relationships. This book looks at these and other aspects of something we regularly participate in but often take for granted—socializing. It applies theories and concepts from psychology and sociology to better recognize the functions, benefits, harms, and consequences of how we spend our free time and those we spend it with. Our aim is to offer a detailed examination of psychological and sociological thinking on socializing that uses both classical theory and a number of contemporary, cutting-edge studies.

In Part I, we look at how socializing works in our daily lives. Chapter 1 reveals a look at the multiple ways we socialize. As we see, the 21st century makes this possible in ways inaccessible and even unimaginable to us even in the late 20th century. This chapter helps us understand that socializing can include just hanging out and chilling, spending time with others that is unstructured or structured, and as a part of a crowd or a clique or a romantic relationship; that it can occur face-to-face or online; that its absence leads to the social, psychological, and physical harms of social isolation; that we can network with others, gaining chances for fun, support, and opportunities through socializing; and that our socializing is not limited to people who look like us as we explore socializing across racial, ethnic, gender, and class differences. In Chapter 2, we delve into why and how socializing is important for us. We focus here in particular on the psychological necessity and social impacts of socializing, how our social relationships are shaped, transformed, and sustained, as well as the role that social relationships shape our ability to get valuable resources through them, such as vital information and upward social mobility. Chapter 3 illuminates both what is good and bad about socializing as we consider its physical and psychological effects, the ways our minds respond to it, the impact of it on our life expectancy, its dark side, and what happens when do not have it—that is, when we are socially isolated. In Chapter 4, we offer a number of psychological theories to help us better understand and explain this concept. Some of the psychologists and theories we employ here include Vygotsky's Sociocultural Theory, Primary Socialization Theory, Social Learning Theory/Social Cognitive Theory, and Social Exchange Theory. Chapter 5 sees us illustrate socializing from a developmental perspective as we move through the life cycle. Here, we unveil processes of socializing in childhood, adolescence, and then as we experience emerging, middle, and later adulthood. We leave the cultural context of the United States for an exploration of socializing on a global level in Chapter 6. Here we highlight distinctions and similarities around socializing as we turn our attention to Norway, Japan, Brazil, Ghana, India, Mexico, and Saudi Arabia.

As we move to Part II, we turn our attention to concrete examples and applications of the concepts, theories, and data that we discuss at length in the first section of the book. Here, we present and interpret five scenarios related to socializing that many of us might expect to experience across our life span. In the first scenario, we look at what can be done to help a child wanting to make new friends. The second scenario finds us offering insight into supporting a teen trying to deal with peer pressure. External factors, like neighborhood and social characteristics that influence socializing, are investigated in the third scenario, while the fourth one reveals how one might cope with changes in friendships. In the last scenario, we offer insight into assisting older adults as they experience the shrinking of their social circles through their friends' moves, retirements, and deaths.

Part III allows us to go deeper into three areas of socializing as a number of social scientists explore enduring controversies and debates that are frequently associated with hanging out in general and with friendships in particular. In the first set of debates, two researchers ask whether race and ethnicity matter within friendships and if these do, then how. In the second set of debates, two other researchers inquire about friendships across gender as they analyze nonromantic relationships between women and men. In the last two contributions to this section, the complicated and at times contradictory role of technology in social relationships is examined by two researchers.

Though most people spend much of their free time with family, friends, neighbors, and colleagues, this is rarely looked at in detail. We seek to change that through the thorough examinations of social relationships we provide in the three sections of this book.

As a recent U.S. Census Bureau survey showed, when it comes to leisure time, other than watching TV, we spend more time socializing on an average day than anything else, we believe what follows presents a better understanding of socializing and how it influences our everyday lives.

Acknowledgments

This book would not have been possible without the love and support of my family and friends. I would especially like to thank my husband and mother for their constant encouragement and unwavering support. Thank you to my daughter, who is "my best girl" and who always brightens my day.

To my coauthor, Tennille Allen, thank you for agreeing to write this book with me. I am so glad we just happened to sit next to each other on our first day of work; these past years would not have been the same without you. I am truly fortunate to be able to call you "friend."

—Valerie Hill

First and always, thank you to my husband, James White, for making sure that I had time and space to write and for making sure that I had time and space to have some fun along the way. My dear sons, Allen and Langston, thank you too for being the best parts of my day, world, and life. I want to thank the rest of my wonderful family for all the love and encouragement you give.

Finally, I have so much gratitude for my coauthor, Valerie Hill. To say this would not have happened without you is a gross understatement. Thank you for the years of collaboration, conversations, and friendship.

—Tennille Allen

Collectively, we also want to thank our friend and colleague, Katherine Helm, for making this opportunity available to us. To our editor, Maxine Taylor, thank you for your patience and guidance throughout this process. Thank you as well to colleagues Jennifer Tello Buntin, Matthew Domico, Jacquelyn Manning-Dantis, Kristi Kelly, and Carlene Sipma-Dysico for your commitment and contributions to this project.

                —Valerie Hill and Tennille Allen

Part I

Socializing in Everyday Life

1

❖

What: The Many Forms
of Socializing

Socializing can be defined as mingling or associating with others. It takes many forms and is influenced by a variety of things such as our age, gender, and culture. This chapter will explore the many ways individuals socialize as well as their implications. We ask (and answer) the questions: what is socializing and what purpose does it serve?

HANGING OUT

Once thought of as happening only in physical spaces, such as shopping malls, suburban parks, downtown streets, or coffeehouses, hanging out now can also occur in electronic spaces like live-tweeting events, Google Hangouts, or Facebook Live. While physical proximity used to be a basic requirement for hanging out, technological advances have radically changed this. We are no longer bound by where we live and those we live around when it comes to hanging out. While during much of the 20th century, hanging out in front of the television and watching a movie with a group of friends meant that one was sharing a room—and often a sofa—with those they were watching with, watching a movie with friends in the second decade of the 21st century might well mean that one friend is in Dubai, another in Denmark, and a third in Detroit, streaming the latest Channing Tatum or Queen Latifah film through their computers at the same time while group chatting with each other to share reactions, laughs, and questions about the plot.

In the past, researchers who studied hanging out talked about the importance of physical places where people could congregate and meet and engage in a shared purpose, goal, or behavior. These had been understood as places that could range from a city, a neighborhood, an amusement park or stadium to a bar, a school, a residence hall, or a church. Increasingly, these include electronic and virtual spaces like social media platforms where one can connect and hang with someone they may never meet face-to-face. Shared spaces no longer must be physically or geographically bounded. Interestingly, as these technologies continue to develop, the virtual and the real worlds converge increasingly. We see this in the July 2016 launch of the runaway hit app Pokémon GO. In this augmented reality game, where gamers use their smartphones and tablets to catch all the Pokémon that appear before them (through the use of their camera) in real-world bushes, parks, and buildings, groups of strangers who are playing in the same physical space have begun to play the game together and participate in more traditional forms of hanging out.

Given the ways that productivity is encouraged and emphasized in American culture, hanging out is often regarded as a luxury, a sign of laziness, or a road that will lead to trouble. Due to these perceptions, merely hanging out without an explicit end-goal or product is seen as something one should at least minimize if not avoid altogether. Hanging out is often seen as more valid and socially acceptable when it is structured rather than unstructured.

STRUCTURED VERSUS UNSTRUCTURED

Since socializing is so voluntary, it is hard to think about it as more than unstructured. Think of all the times you ended up in a friend's TV room, at a movie, in the food court at the mall, or in the closest park with very little planning or even idea of how and why you got there. When we hang out with those we choose to, it is often very spontaneous and unstructured. Contrast this to what happens when we tell someone "We should hang out together soon." Though we mean it and the person we want to hang out with also seems genuine in his or her desire to spend time with us, concretizing plans and actually meeting for coffee or dinner or a walk in the park together happen far less than we want. Without the spontaneity and impulsiveness that often undergird these informal relationships, we find it hard to actualize our best intentions.

Age is quite important to reckon with here. When older children and teens have large blocks of time without adult supervision or academic, artistic, or athletic pursuits to engage in, there is a concern about their unstructured socializing. There is great concern by a host of people and groups, including parents, educators, and community members as well as social service providers, policymakers, law enforcement, and medical professionals, that increases in unstructured socializing will lead to increases in undesirable and troublesome behaviors among children and adolescents. These include substance use and abuse, delinquency, risky sex, and crime and the potential to experience and/or perpetrate violence. After-school programs, camps, churches, sports and arts programs, and park districts offer a host of activities that are intended to offer alternatives to the negative perceptions associated with young people who do not have structured opportunities to be around similarly aged peers.

The focus on planning out any free time to concentrate on taking steps that will yield brighter futures, social mobility, and other forms of success while avoiding a litany of pitfalls along the life course ignores the benefits of unstructured socializing. One benefit is that it is fun. Spending a day, with no definitive plans or purpose, among those you like and who like you can be one of the most rewarding experiences we have. Rather than feeling the stress that comes with planning activities and excursions, hanging out can often be liberating and relaxing. Another benefit is that its spontaneous nature can allow us to meet people and go places we otherwise would not. It can also be in these unscripted moments that we more deeply bond with those in our social circles. Passing the time, hanging out, and chilling often further connectedness, encourage intimacy, and strengthen ties in ways that playing together in a baseball league, writing computer code together, or other more formal activities do not lend themselves to. We can work out the ups and downs of life, discover who we are, and realize what we like (and dislike) with our friends and buddies in these informal, unstructured times. Not only are there benefits to unstructured socializing, there are also pitfalls inherent to overly scheduled free and social time.

For those who are used to having every hour of the day carefully scripted and managed by someone or something, large blocks of free time can be disconcerting and disorienting. Making the transition from a strictly scheduled life to a more unstructured one can be difficult. Children and adolescents whose parents have had them in extracurricular pursuits and athletic endeavors in an effort to give them something productive to do, prepare them for college, and otherwise enrich them for years often face discomfort as they leave home for college, work, and adulthood where they are more in control of their time.

As we move further into adulthood, those we socialize with may change. Work parties, teambuilding activities, study dates, and group projects that blend our social life with work and school are ways that the lines between voluntary and compelled socializing blur. This can also occur as we become parents and find ourselves spending time in our children's scheduled lives. We may then begin to spend time, share meals, and attend parties with our children's friends, teammates, and schoolmates and their families rather than those who are in other parts of our social circle. Their social relationships and structured activities then come to structure our socializing.

CLIQUES/CROWDS

Though cliques can occur among any age group, they are mostly associated with adolescents. Adolescents typically are a part of a broad social system. Two types of social groups that are particularly common during adolescence are cliques and crowds. A clique is made up of approximately four to six individuals who are good friends and tend to be similar in age, sex, race, and interests. The members of a clique spend time together and often dress alike, act alike, and talk in a similar fashion. Cliques, especially female cliques, have a clear-cut status hierarchy. The higher-status members of the clique mock peers who are not part of the clique in addition to low-status members of the clique to keep them in check. High-status members also determine who is permitted to join the clique. Not every adolescent is a member of a clique. According to researchers Susan Ennett and Arnold Bauman, about 30 percent of adolescents are liaisons. Liaisons serve as bridges between cliques and become more common as adolescents get older. There are also some adolescents who have very few friends. These adolescents and adolescents who are considered "loners" are at risk for bullying.

Cliques are often part of a larger group, too—a crowd. A crowd is a larger mixed-sex group of adolescents who have similar values and attitudes and are known by a common label. For example, some common labels are jocks, preppies, burnouts, goths, nerds, brains, druggies, emos, and so forth. Adolescents that are a part of ethnic minority group typically belong to such crowds as well as to ethnically based crowds. In contrast to cliques, which get together all of the time, crowds typically get together on weekends or every once in a while. For example, there may be party at someone's house on a Saturday night. Some crowds have higher status than others. For instance, in many high schools, "jocks" and "preppies" are the most prestigious crowds, whereas the "burnouts," "goths," and "druggies" are among the least prestigious. In addition, self-esteem of members often reflects the status of group. During adolescence, teens from high-status crowds tend to have greater self-esteem than those from low-status crowds. Adolescents from lower-status crowds may experience anxiety and unhappiness as a result of belonging to a lower-status crowd. Some of these adolescents may feel put down and may be picked on or even bullied by some members of higher-status crowds. In general, adolescents are not very tolerant of those who are different from themselves, which would explain why this teasing and bullying occurs.

In 1963, a professor at Harvard University, Dexter Dunphy, researched the structure and functions of groups of young people. Even though his observations took place many years ago, they still hold true today. According to Dunphy, there are five stages of group formation in adolescence. Stage 1 occurs in early adolescence. Young people form cliques, usually small groups of the same sex. Each clique is somewhat isolated from one another. These cliques typically meet often to plan social activities, engage in self-disclosure, and gossip about others. Membership requires conformity (especially in terms of the way they dress), and there is often a group membership (whether it is apparent or not). In order to have continued membership with the clique, it is essential that members form close personal relationships with members of the opposite sex at the same time. In Stage 2, before dating begins, male and female cliques come together and interact with one another to form a crowd. Crowd activities are commonly seen together on weekends, at shopping malls, parties, and other social activities. This allows adolescents to spend time with members of opposite sex without responsibility of one-on-one interaction. The peer group changes in response to changing needs and interests of adolescents, which facilitates the development of relationships with other sex. In Stage 3, there are changes in the structure of the crowd; the process of dating begins. As a result, higher-status members form smaller cliques. These leaders begin to date and form mixed-sex cliques. In Stage 4, there is a fully developed crowd, composed of a number of couples in close association with one another. They come together for social activities, but group membership tends to change over time. Some adolescents who do not keep up with the changes in the group will be left behind. Stage 5 occurs during late adolescence. In this stage, we see a disintegration of the crowd. Couples break off from the larger group, begin to go their separate ways, and become less part of the crowd. During this final stage, couples may still associate with other couples, but the large crowd is no longer needed as a context for socializing. The overall group changes in ways that facilitate growth of close relationships; there is a shift from shared play and sports in childhood to more intimacy in adolescence. For younger adolescents, becoming a couple and dating offers companionship, but for older adolescents, it provides trust and support.

The transition from childhood friendship to adolescent peer group to dating couples prepares adolescents for developing close relationships in adulthood. These changes in the adolescent peer group help adolescents to make the transition from gender-segregated peer groups in childhood to close relationships in adulthood.

Though the emphasis here has been on adolescents, recent attention is being paid to the ways that cliques continue past high school and college, and there is concern about their impact in neighborhood settings, among groups of parents in schools and on teams, within workplaces in political and civic organizations, and beyond.

FRIENDSHIPS

> For without friends no one would choose to live.
>> —Philosopher Aristotle

> The only way to have a friend is to be one.
>> —Poet Ralph Waldo Emerson

> I pick my friends like I pick my fruit.
>> —Singer Erykah Badu

In these words, we see great insight on friendship and the ability to socialize that these provide. These relationships contain a host of behaviors and activities, including greeting someone you pass on a walk in your neighborhood, occasionally calling someone on the phone, grabbing coffee or lunch with someone, or signing up for parasailing classes or a Zumba class with someone you know.

Friendships are different from other social relationships. In contrast to other social relationships that may be limited to certain parts of one's life (e.g., spouse, student), friendships exist throughout the life span (see Chapter 5 for socializing throughout the life span). Friendships are important in the provision of basic needs for contact, communication, and community. A quick perusal of self-help sections of bookstores, letters to advice columnists, and TV talk shows will show that much attention, angst, and anxiety surround our quests to start, maintain, improve, or end friendships. If we watch someone's social media feeds long enough, the chances are high that we will see numerous dramatic demonstrations of the life cycle of friendships that play out in real time. Headlines in our newspapers and news feeds regularly inform us that friendships in the United States are in trouble. Whether this is actually the case is widely debated. What is not debated is why these headlines are attention grabbing in the first place—we need and want to be connected with others. Americans have been concerned about decreasing community and social bonds for quite some time now. We see that community, particularly the personal community—that is, members of one's social network (which is a set of social relations that exists through ties between individuals)—did not disappear with the advent of capitalism, industrialization, technological advances, urbanization, or deindustrialization, despite fears to the contrary that date back to the Industrial Revolution. Though this is nothing new, these concerns take on a different dimension today as the ways that we communicate, connect, and create and continue social relationships have changed due to the pervasive reach of the Internet and the communication technologies that have risen in its wake. Obviously, given the importance of friendship and concerns over its demise, there is something to having friends and socializing with them.

ROMANTIC ENCOUNTERS

As we move from childhood and adolescence into adulthood, the concerns, character, and composition of our networks and socializing change. Around puberty, a shift to romantic relationships occurs, and this intensifies as we begin searching for, forming, and maintaining romantic and sexual relationships. In adolescence and early adulthood, we start to spend less time with our (nonromantic) friends and more time with romantic partners. We still invest our time in socializing and other pleasurable social relationships but switch its focus through late adolescence and emerging adulthood. The activities we engage in also tend to switch as well as they become more planned, formal, and structured as we date and have other romantic encounters—at least at the start of such romantic relationships.

A restaurant on a Friday or Saturday night is likely to be patronized by a number of different parties. A large percentage of these will be couples (seeking to be) in romantic partnerships. Some will be out on a first date, others celebrating an anniversary, and others still enjoying a rare date night as the kids are with the sitter, while some will be staring longingly across the table at each other and some others will be barely talking to each other. These interactions allow couples to get to know each other, remain connected, rekindle a spark that is dying out, or decide that a relationship has run its course.

As we move to and beyond the Industrial Revolution and the massive societal, familial, and geographic changes that occurred in its wake, the importance of friendship and all that accompanied it subsequently caused changes in Western ideas, expectations, and behaviors around partnering, love, and commitment. Rather than an almost singular rationale for relationships based on political and economic motives, compatibility and affection became requirements for partnering, commitment, and dating. An emphasis on companionate love—the desire for a romantic partner with whom we would be best friends, share all aspects of our lives, and be deeply committed to because of a shared set of interests, passions, and values—developed. Magazine articles, TV talk shows, and advice from marriage and other relationship experts that stress the importance of quality time, couple time, date nights, and the like show that this is still a key component of romantic relationships. Similarly, anecdotes, conventional wisdom, and academic research all point to friendship, shared experiences, and common interests as topping any list for beginning and keeping successful romantic relationships. Social psychological theories support this as well. One such theory is Reiss's Wheel Theory of Love, which proposes that a lasting, loving relationship must develop over time as an interdependent cycle (or wheel) that leads to greater, closer commitment as it begins with (1) rapport—occurring as couples spend time with each other in ways that make them feel comfortable and good when they are together; (2) self-revelation—occurring as each member of the couple shares intimate and personal information that they would be disinclined to share with many others; (3) mutual dependency—occurring as couples come to see their happiness, lives, and needs tied to each other; and (4) intimacy—occurring as couples find their personal needs fulfilled within the relationship, build lives together, support each other, and continue to share more. These are like the spokes of a wheel, constantly in motion and constantly being repeated as they take the relationship forward. Another theory is Sternberg's triangular theory of love. In this, he discusses three cornerstones for romantic relationships: intimacy, passion, and commitment. Intimacy here refers to connectedness and closeness; passion refers to romance and attraction, including but not limited necessarily to sexual desire; and commitment refers to the initial decision to partner and the subsequent decision to stay partnered for the long haul. A strong, lasting, fulfilling relationship requires the simultaneous presence of all three. Though particular to romantic pairings, as discussed elsewhere in this chapter, many of these are also important factors in socializing and friendship in general.

An article published in the *New York Times* in 2014 asserted that our social networks can affect the ways that we perceive our romantic relationships. In the article, journalist Hannah Seligson explains that when our family and friends approve of our romantic relationships, we can have more positive and stable relationships. When we think that our friends and families approve of our romantic relationship—whether they actually do or not—we develop stronger, more loving, and longer-lasting relationships with our partner. Conversely, when family and friends disapprove of our romantic relationship and/or partner, this can contribute to more negative interactions, including breakups, with our romantic partners. Couple friends—friendships with other couples that we share with our romantic partners—have also been shown to be important for increasing our feelings of connectedness with our own partner, according to research by others.

ONLINE

With the emergence of new technologies, such as cell phones, the Internet, text messaging, and various social media channels, the ways that we connect with others have changed. This has led to fears about the decline of friendships and other close relationships. While understandable, these fears are overblown. Research suggests that to the contrary, our interactions and networks have increased with the advent of these new methods of communicating. Indeed, they aid in the building and maintaining our personal communities.

Looking at a platform like YouTube can be instructive here. Rather than watching TV together in the living room, people can watch YouTube in the park or sitting side by side at a concert. YouTube users consume content together in a way that crosses time and place in ways never imagined. This also allows for connections never imagined. Another example of connections made because of—not despite—the increased amount of time that we spend online is from the Grammy-Award nominated music group The Foreign Exchange. It is comprised of native North Carolina singer and rapper Phonte Coleman and Dutch producer Nicolay. The duo met on a popular music site's comment boards. It was there that they realized their shared interests and started e-mail exchanges with each other. Through e-mail communication, they shared ideas and music and decided to form a band they appropriately named The Foreign Exchange. The Foreign Exchange released their first album together—aptly called *Connected*—all before Phonte and Nicolay had ever met the other in person.

These are not the only forms of connecting online. Online spaces are particularly helpful in helping those who or whose interests fall outside the mainstream in their community. Someone who is transgender and living in a small, conservative, religious community might not find anyone they can relate to or who understands what they are experiencing in their geographic area, but they can find an extensive community of supportive people encouraging others through their computer or phone. Rather than limiting friendships and socializing, we can look to the ways that online technologies expand and open possibilities for new relationships and forms of relating up in ways unimaginable a generation or two ago.

Despite stories and outcomes like these, there is often concern on the parts of family members and friends when an online social relationship moves from the digital world to the physical world. Though it is increasingly common to move from tweeting each other to meeting each other and from swiping right on Tinder (a dating app that has users "swipe right" to indicate an interest in a potential match and "swipe left" to indicate a lack of interest) to being right next to each other at a café, there remains fear and trepidation at removing the anonymity of the Internet and meeting someone otherwise unknown and unvetted. Part of this fear arises when there are reports of being catfished or falling vulnerable to someone who has created a false online persona with the attempt of reeling in their prey, much as a fisher does a catfish, and taking advantage of them reputationally, emotionally, or financially. Other fears center around being harmed in worse ways, such as sexually or physically assaulted, kidnapped, or killed. Indeed, even in less extreme cases, there remains stigma and an aura of inferiority around digital relationships in comparison to those that exist IRL or "in real life." Nathan Jurgenson, a sociologist who studies social media and is a researcher for Snapchat, discusses this as something he terms "digital dualism." Digital dualism is a fallacy or a bias, according to Jurgenson, that supposes that things and relationships that occur IRL are more real or valuable or authentic than those that occur online and through social media. Instead of falling for this fallacy, Jurgenson asserts the importance and ubiquity of these technologies is that our real lives, real worlds, and real relationships are simultaneously both digital and physical. We also see this in another way that socializing has changed with the advent of social media such as when we are deciding whom to follow, like, or DM (direct message) on Twitter or friend or Inbox on Facebook. This becomes a particular challenge when you are digitally interacting with someone from your physical world whom you might not want to fully see your online or social media self.

In a similar cautioning against the doom and gloom perspective on the impact of social media on socializing, John Cacioppo, a leading researcher on loneliness and its cognitive and physical effects, asserts that online ways of socializing are tools that replicate one's social interactions and networks in the nonvirtual world. In this, social media and other emergent technologies are more neutral, working in ways that neither destroy nor create new friendships. They merely enable one to find alternative and additional ways to be together. Cacioppo sees any potential pitfalls of Facebook, Twitter, and the like with the consumers of such technologies rather than with the technologies themselves.

Going online to cultivate and nurture relationships has always been associated with the youngest cohorts in our society. Since the advent of the Internet, its use has been seen as the province and domain of the young. At the same time, older people have been cast as suspicious of and inept at using the Internet. Recent data show that this conclusion is not an entirely accurate one. In 2014, according to a Pew Research Center study, more than half of seniors in the United States, defined as those who are at least 65 years old, who are online reported using Facebook, an increase of over 11 percent from the previous year. A 2015 Pew Research Center report shows that though American seniors are less likely to use and adopt new communication technologies, when they do, they describe the experience as "liberating." When asked which metaphor—"freedom" or "a leash"—best described their smartphones, 82 percent of seniors described their phone as freeing, compared with 64 percent of those respondents who were between 18 and 29 years old. Indeed, twice as many adult smartphone owners under the age of 30 described their phone as a leash, compared to those over the age of 65. Seniors were more likely to describe their smartphones as offering connection rather than distraction. Additionally, they demonstrated positive feelings and attitudes about the impact of online access and connection in their lives. Seniors were also half as likely to describe their phones as distracting, compared to adults under the age of 30. Their use of smartphones increased by 8 percent compared to the previous years.

Social networking platforms are increasingly popular among all American adults. Results from a 2015 Pew study of social media use indicate that Facebook is the most popular site, used by 71 percent of adults who use the Internet. This is followed by LinkedIn, Pinterest, Instagram, and Twitter, used by 28 percent, 28 percent, 26 percent, and 23 percent, respectively. Of all American adults—not just those who use the Internet—58 percent use Facebook, 23 percent use LinkedIn, 22 percent use Pinterest, 21 percent use Instagram, and 19 percent use Twitter. While the number of Facebook users stayed steady compared with the previous year, the other four platforms each significantly increased their percentage of users during that time frame. Not only are more people using these social media sites, but they are also using social media sites, like Facebook and Instagram, more often. Each saw users increase their daily use of the sites. Twitter, however, saw a decline in daily users. The Pew study also found greater instances of user engagement. There are some differences among users by platform that should be addressed. Pinterest is more likely to be used by women—42 percent of women online use Pinterest compared to 13 percent of men. LinkedIn increased the number of its key demographic—those who are college educated and professionals. The number of people using more than one social media platform is also on the rise, according to these Pew Research Center data.

SOCIAL ISOLATION

In 2011, a documentary captured international attention. Its subject was Joyce Vincent, a beautiful English woman of African descent in her late 30s. In 2006, she was found in her suburban London apartment, in front of an open window and a TV showing programming from the BBC. She was found dead by law enforcement officials carrying out an eviction for nonpayment of rent. An autopsy of her skeletal remains, while failing to conclude a cause of death, established that she had been dead for three years. During that time, though no one she knew had heard from or seen her, no one had stopped by to check on her. She died—and remained dead in her living room—by herself, in isolation. Though perhaps not to this extreme, social isolation—the lack of a sustained connection with others—is not isolated to this case or to the United Kingdom. We find it quite abundant in the United States, across a spectrum of social character-istics and with a wealth of negative outcomes.

We often think about gun violence, cancer, heart attacks, obesity, drunk driving, and alcohol as leading to untimely deaths. Rarely do we think about loneliness as being indicative of a shortened life span. It is important to note that when we are talking about loneliness, we are not just talking about being alone. We are more likely to live alone now than ever before in the United States and other Western countries. Census data show that in 1950, about 10 percent of Americans lived in a single-person household; 60 years later, that number was almost three times higher as 27 percent Americans lived in a single-person household in 2010. We are also more likely to report fewer visits, conversations, and outings with others now, particularly as we age. As we shop from our bed-rooms, work from home, and take online classes in our living rooms with more frequency, this is not just an issue that the elderly face. None of this is necessarily risky in the ways that loneliness is.

Instead, loneliness can be understood as the negative emotional state caused when one yearns for connection yet feels disconnected. One can experience this in the midst of a crowd at a baseball game, in the midst of a high school classroom, or in the midst of a romantic relationship. Unlike being alone, which is a temporary and voluntary choice, loneliness feels inflicted by an external source and as if it may never end. The numbers of those reporting loneliness are high. Using the UCLA Loneliness Scale, a 20-item questionnaire on feelings relating to social isolation and perceptions of connectedness and closeness, almost one-third of Americans report feelings of loneliness or being socially isolated at some time. This becomes even more alarming when we consider the vast array of negative implications associated with isolation and loneliness.

We are learning much more about these through research conducted by those in the health, biological, and social sciences. Experiments have demonstrated that the pain of social rejection is akin to the physical pain. Being rejected literally hurts as was the case in work done by a UCLA social psychologist. After a subject was ignored during the course of an online game, an MRI scan showed that the same region of the brain that lit up when physical pain is felt lit up when this exclusion occurred. Those who report feelings of loneliness are also more likely to have lower levels of healthy eating habits, self-esteem, and physical activity. These are then associated with a host of negative outcomes on mental and physical health. Likewise, social isolation has been shown to weaken the immune system, leading to vulnerability to illnesses, infections, and diseases. Studies indicate that both diminish quality of life and health and lead to higher mortality. Though we all experience stress in our lives, a connected social network that can be counted on to provide comfort, love, and support during those stressful times can be the difference in whether we weather the storms. Indeed, a lack of people to socialize with is not just a social issue but a medical one. Those who are more isolated experience greater levels of stress hormones, anxiety, sleep disorders, and depression. Social isolation has also been linked to high blood pressure, stroke, cardiovascular disease, and heart attacks and cognitive decline, including forms of dementia such as Alzheimer's disease. Recently, a study in England found that social isolation causes more harm than having 15-cigarettes-a-day habit. Other studies have found associations between feelings of loneliness, social isolation, and a number of medical conditions, diseases, and death. One study in the early days of research on those living with AIDS showed that men who lacked social support and felt rejected died quicker than those who did not. Another study found that those who are lonely experience increased levels of the stress hormones, cortisol and epinephrine, both of which are associated with an increased risk for a number of psychological and physical problems. As we learn more about sociogenomics—the complex interplay between genetics and social environments, contexts, behaviors, and interactions—we see that chronic stress induced through social isolation and loneliness can lead to changes in gene expression. Indeed, not having these vital social connections can make those who are well sick and make those who are sick sicker.

Those who are most marginalized and vulnerable in our society— women, people of color, people who are poor, people who are old—are also those who are most likely to be lonely and isolated and those who feel the associated problems most acutely due to their already diminished place in the social hierarchy. Social isolation and loneliness occur across the life span and regardless of our social class, gender, and race. However, some of us are more likely to experience it than others, and these factors do shape our experiences of loneliness and isolation. Teens—who are particularly impacted by and through social relationships, compared to other age groups—tend to place a high amount of importance in their friendships. When there are difficulties making friends and maintaining high-quality friendships, social isolation or being cut off from meaningful social relationships with others can result. In a vicious cycle, feelings of rejection and loneliness are associated with poor self-esteem, anxiety, and victimization, which then amplify those feelings of rejection and loneliness, leading to further isolation. There is also a link between the experience of loneliness and social isolation and depression, poor performance in school, as well as suicidal ideation and suicide attempts. At the other end of the life course, the elderly are more likely to report feelings of loneliness and to be socially isolated than those in any other age bracket. This is a growing concern for people in the middle of this range as well. A 2010 survey done by the American Association of Retired People (AARP) found that just over one-third of American people aged 45 and over reported being chronically lonely. This is striking and worrisome when compared to the same survey given in 2000 that found 20 percent of the same population who reported being chronically lonely.

Concerns about social isolation are hardly limited to age and health. A long line of research on cities since the 1970s, for example, has investigated the perils of social isolation, drawing links between a lack of sustained contact with others and particularly others from different economic and racial and ethnic backgrounds, that is associated with higher rates of poverty, unemployment, health challenges, fear, distrust, and other individual and social ills. More recently, there has been a debate brewing between those who contend that Americans are growing more socially isolated and those who counter by saying that Americans remain connected, even if the forms that these connections take might look different than they had in the past, such as those enabled by Internet and other emergent technologies.

NETWORKING

In addition to limiting the possibilities and harms of social isolation, networks are key to amassing resources, experiences, and opportunities that lead to yet more valued resources, experiences, and opportunities that are known as social capital. How many times have you heard the phrase, "It's not what you know; it's who you know"? This is what social scientists, such as political scientists, economists, sociologists, and psychologists, are referring to when they talk about social capital. Our ability to tap into the relationships leads to a host of benefits, particularly ones that we see as facilitating educational, employment, and financial success. Since the 1980s—and predating the increasingly popular understanding of these as a function of our electronically mediated lives and relationships—social networks and the capital embedded within them have emerged as a major interest in a number of areas, including the corporate world; education, political, social, and civic life; economics; and mental and physical health. When we are told to network, it is so that we can gain access to these positive outcomes.

Thinking about social capital as offering either social support or social leverage is particularly instructive here. Through our networks, we get social support that provides access to resources that people can use to ease stress, meet their daily needs, or that they can call on in emergencies while social leverage provides access to resources that can lead to upward social mobility. Furthermore, social support is typically provided by one's intimates, those individuals with whom we are the most bonded and have the most interaction with and the strongest ties to, such as close friends and family members and romantic partners. Social support is important when it comes to things like a place to stay for a while, getting rides to work, childcare, financial assistance, reminders to go to the doctor or to take our medications, hugs at the end of a hard day, or a text message that shows that someone cares about us. These close and intimate ties, referred to as bonding ties, also tend to be people similar to ourselves when it comes to race and social class.

Social leverage is most often found in ties to less close or weaker relationships. These often include friends of friends, acquaintances, or

someone we meet at a work function. When we are strategically networking, it is these ties that we are cultivating and maintaining. In a pivotal
study, Mark Granovetter in 1974 illustrated what he called "the strength
of weak ties." He contended that it is weak ties—people one is distantly
connected to and has little contact with—that are most important when
it comes to finding new information, opportunities, and employment.
This is in contrast to strong ties, which include those intimates one is
bonded with, as discussed earlier. When it comes to information and
opportunities, if one has only strong ties, these become recycled through
the network among people who already are connected to everyone else
in the network. When weak ties are available and used as they are when
one networks by accessing and exchanging new information, ideas, and
contacts that increase those others, they can reach outside of their strong
ties. This is their strength. Because weak ties are more distant, they are
often more diverse and dissimilar from us in contrast to strong ties. These
are referred to as bridging ties, as they offer links or bridges between us
and people we would otherwise not have a way of connecting with.

There is a great deal of overlap between the two forms of social capital
that should be noted as the social support one receives today may facilitate
employment and education that could lead to upward mobility in the
future, and both have been shown to have positive effects on mental and
physical health and other measures of well-being. Those who do not have
access to the most desirable networks and the most valuable capital that
these hold experience greater levels of inequality. In the United States,
this is a particular risk for those who are socially isolated and who are
members of marginalized social groups, such as women, people of color,
recent and undocumented immigrants, and the poor and working classes.
Those who occupy the intersections of these groups, like a poor, undocumented immigrant from Laos or a working-class African American woman
experience even greater isolation.

SOCIALIZING ACROSS CLASS, GENDER, AND RACIAL LINES

"Some of my best friends are _____." This is a phrase often
employed as a dodge by someone accused of being racist, sexist, homopho-
bic, or the like. When this occurs, it is almost guaranteed to be mocked,
parodied, and scorned from Twitter to late night TV. Such was the case
in 2009 when Louisiana justice of the peace, Keith Bardwell, refused to
officiate the marriage of Beth Humphrey, a White woman, and Terence
McKay, an African American man. Bardwell justified his refusal by saying

that it was due to a concern with the well-being and social acceptance of any children potentially produced through interracial unions such as Humphrey and McKay's. When excoriated for his racist and unconstitutional stance, Bardwell adamantly denied that he was a racist, telling the Associated Press, "I'm not a racist. I just don't believe in mixing the races that way. I have piles and piles of black friends. They come to my home, I marry them, they use my bathroom. I treat them just like everyone else." In the wake of this (and certainly countless other similar examples), jokes and derision are widespread. What is less common, however, is an exploration of what undergirds and comprises the establishment and maintenance of social relationships across categories of difference like class, gender, and race.

Class

Since the Great Recession of the late 2000s, class divisions in the United States have widened to points not seen since the Great Depression of the 1920s. This raises concerns for friendships across class lines, as more class instability and insecurity occur. As more attend college, move from their place of birth, and otherwise relocate and work for large, multinational corporations, cross-class interactions are more likely. What then are the implications for socializing and friendships across social class lines?

There is research that indicates that we are most likely—still—to form friendships with those from a similar class background as ourselves. When we do form these relationships across social class lines, those friends with different class statuses talk and spend less time together, laugh less with each other, are more likely to show nongenuine facial expressions, such as smiles, and have more arguments when compared to friends who share a class background. Furthermore, cross-class friendships tend to have lower levels of engagement and connectedness overall when compared to same-class friendships.

Particularly for children, teens, and young adults, outward markers of social class such as clothes, allowance, toys, and, later, cars can cause tensions that even the strongest friendships can be rocked by. Differences in class status can also affect the ability to share in bonding if that means that friends cannot discuss shared experiences of vacationing if one spends his or her holidays at home or across town with relatives and another spends his or her holidays in a glamorous international destination. Differences in disposable income can also have an effect on how friends spend time together. Tensions and relational stress can arise over different priorities and abilities to spend money on leisure and recreational pursuits if one friend can only afford at home manicures, beer and buffalo wing specials, or free concerts in the park and the other can afford a full-service spa day, the hottest, most expensive new restaurant, or box seats at the stadium. There can be pressure to spend money that one does not have, pressure to pay for more expensive excursions, embarrassment that one friend always voluntarily picks up the tab, and resentment that one friend must always be expected to pick up the tab. One way to mitigate against this is to build relationships that emphasize common interests and values while diminishing differences in bank accounts and wealth and where open and honest receptive conversations can be held when tensions do arise.

Gender

The way that we are socialized or taught how to fit into our society or culture means that men's and women's social relationships and ways of socializing will look different. Those who study gender in friendships have largely found that men tend to spend time engaging in shared activities, like watching a basketball game, playing pool, or going to a bar, while women are more likely to spend their time sharing with each other. As such, women's friendships are often seen as having higher levels of intimacy, support, disclosure, and caring than men's. We also see that women's friendships and other relationships tend to be more expressive, focused on feelings of affection, caring, and supportiveness, and men's friendships and other relationships tend to be more instrumental, focused on achieving specific goals and accomplishing specific actions. It has been said that women spend time with each other to grow closer and that men spend time with each other to feel better about their place in the social order. Researchers like Deborah Tannen say that women's socializing includes rapport talk that creates the impression that they are supportive of, in solidarity with, and listening to the other and that men's socializing includes report talk that creates the impression that they are seeking to establish and maintain independence and status in a hierarchy of dominance over the other. As we all have strong needs for intimacy, support, affirmation, and other positive benefits of social relationships, men in contemporary U.S. society are taught through their families, friends, and media and other sources to reserve these for romantic relationships if they are sought at all. Still, research by Niobe Way and her colleagues confirms that despite the presence and prevalence of gender norms that compel boys and men to repress their emotions and deny their need for connection, there are many more similarities between the genders than distinctions. As they age, boys and men yearn for the carefree and caring relationships they shared within their gender when they were younger. In her study of teen males throughout their high school experience, Way finds evidence of boys and young men who crave intimacy and belongingness through their nonromantic friendships with other boys and young men feel they cannot admit that to others, not even their relatives and those they call their friends. Instead, they claim publicly (and often to themselves) that they neither want nor need the friendship or companionship of other boys and young men. Despite growing inclusion of lesbian, gay, bisexual, transgender, and queer (LGBTQ) people, there remains institutional, interpersonal, and internalized homophobia in society, and the denial of men's desire for close friendships with each other is shaped by this. Sociologist Lisa Wade explains that one place this occurs is when men attend movies together, placing a seat between them as a so-called buffer. She states, "So what you're seeing with the buffer seat is this interesting contradiction—men want intimacy and closeness, so they're going to the movie together, but the movie itself is a buffer against intimacy. It's something they can do together without having to interact; without having each other as the object of each other's attention . . . . It's about homophobia, but it's not just about homophobia. It's about this rule that men don't need or want to be close to other people." Still, men's friendships remain idealized. What, though, about friendships across gender lines?

It is important to note that the discussion that follows is premised on nonromantic and nonsexual relationships between women and men who are assumed to be heterosexual. As there is more visibility and inclusion of LGBTQ-identified women and men through American society, this discussion and our anxieties about crossing the lines between friendships and more sexual and romantic relationships become further complicated.

Think about the common term "platonic friendship," which we use to describe a nonromantic or nonsexual friendship held by a woman and a man. It is named for and derives, however, from Greek philosopher Plato's thoughts and writings on relationships between men and was seen as spiritual and as one of the highest forms of friendship and love attainable. With societal change, though, the term has evolved to focus on friendships that occur across gender lines. We use the term "platonic friendship" to differentiate between those and our assumptions that closeness, self-disclosure, and intimacy between those of the opposite sex will ultimately lead to sex. We are also fairly suspicious of these relationships. We often see that as children approach puberty, cross-gender friendships change. The sleepovers and slumber parties that were commonplace at age 6 or 7 are discouraged if not forbidden by parents at age 13 and 14.

Boys and girls who freely played together in preschool distance themselves from each other in middle school. By high school and through adulthood, it is often assumed that when men and women start as friends, they will become lovers. Heterosexual men and women attempting to be friends have served as the plotline for films, sitcoms, songs, and books too numerous to name. Advice columns, cafeteria whispers, and dinner table discussions abound with questions, rumors, and fears that an innocent friendship is more than that or that a supposed affair has been manufactured out of nothing more than great affection and friendly connection. Though men and women are in much greater contact with each other as gender norms dictating that women belong at home and out of the public sphere have weakened, it is still assumed by many that cross-gender friendships are but a pretext to romantic encounters and sexual interludes.

In 2012, a team of researchers from the University of Wisconsin-Eau Claire studying pairs of women and men in a friendship with each other found that there were gender differences in the ways each member of the opposite sex perceived these relationships. Compared to the women, the men in the study reported that they had much higher levels of attraction to their women friends, that they were confident that their women friends were equally attracted to them, and that they wanted to act on this attraction. The findings also indicated that men overestimated the amount of attraction felt by their female friends, while women at the same time underestimated the amount of attraction felt by their male friends. Indeed, while cross-gender friendships occur, it seems that men and women have different perceptions of the same friendship. Women assume that the friendships are strictly friendships, while men see them as at least a breeding ground for something more.

Race

"Social distance," a term introduced by social psychologist Emory Bogardus, measures the level to which members of social groups (i.e., based on race, gender, religion, sexual orientation) have a preference to interact as close friends, neighbors, relatives through marriage, and within other social relationships with members of other groups. Low social distance scores indicate openness to interacting with others from differing social backgrounds, while high social distance scores indicate resistance to such interactions. In terms of race and ethnicity, how much social distance is there in friendships today? Answers to this question were provided in 2014 when a nonpartisan, nonprofit organization—the Public Religion

Research Institute (PRRI)—released a study that examined the racial composition of Americans' friendships.

In it, they found that if the average White American had 100 friends, 91 would be White, one would be African American, one would be Latino/a, and one would be Asian American. Compared to Whites, African Americans reported more racial and ethnic diversity among their friends—out of 100 friends the average African American had, 8 would be White, 83 would be African American, and 2 would be Latino/a. Latino/as had the most racial and ethnic diversity among their friends. Findings from the PRRI show they would have 19 White friends, two African American friends, 64 Latino/a friends, and one Asian American friend. This same study also found that 75 percent of Whites reported that those they rely on to discuss important topics (a common way researchers define friendships) are also all White. In comparison, 65 percent of African Americans and 46 percent of Latino/as reported all African American or all Latino/a networks, respectively. Interestingly, 9 percent of Latino/as reported networks in which *they* were the only person of color.

Why is this? One explanation is residential segregation. Data on where we live show that Whites are more likely than any other racial-ethnic group to live among people of their own racial-ethnic background. If our neighborhoods remain the place where we first consider as we make and maintain the bulk of our friendships, then living in racially and ethnically homogenous communities will lead to racially and ethnically homogenous networks. Another explanation is found in preferences. We have a tendency to prefer people who share what we see as important social statuses, including race. Indeed, there is some truth to the old saying that "birds of a feather flock together." This preference is known as homophily. Multiple studies show that Whites are more likely than other racial-ethnic groups to state and show a preference for other Whites as romantic partners, friends, schoolmates, colleagues, and neighbors. Through their larger share of the population as well as various social policies that continue to create and maintain racial segregation, Whites have greater ability to choose where they attend school, work, and live and whom they befriend and partner with. As such, their preferences are more easily enacted compared with people of color. The patterns that we see in friendships and other social relationships are a reflection of larger societal patterns of racial and ethnic stratification.

Recent experiments find that when socializing does occur across categories like race, especially among those who are least likely to have friends from other backgrounds, anxieties about such interactions decrease and relationships across groups subsequently increase. When dissimilar people come together, they can act as bridging ties, which are those existing social bonds that can create links between groups of diverse others, as mentioned earlier. These are particularly important because they can mitigate or limit the ill effects of inequality. Indeed, these relationships also tend to decrease propensities to engage in stereotyping and prejudice. Research does suggest that, due to historical and contemporary racism and race relations, socializing across racial and ethnic lines is less likely to occur and more likely to end when it does occur than socializing with similar others. Indeed, there are difficulties in establishing lasting friendships across differences in social identities. For members of marginalized groups, there is a weariness and wariness of having to explain and justify one's identity and experiences to those unfamiliar with him or her. There is also a weariness and wariness around being on the receiving end of comments and behaviors that range from clueless and naïve to discriminatory and abusive. From the perspective of the more privileged, there is often a stated discomfort and unease associated with saying or doing something perceived or felt as prejudiced or discriminatory, despite their intent. If socializing is supposed to be about finding ease, comfort, and relaxation, relationships that bring with them contexts of tension and power differentials become harder to initiate and maintain and easier to avoid and dissolve. In order to successfully socialize across categories of social difference, an acknowledgment of the differences, the contexts that create and maintain said differences, one's own relationship to privilege and marginalization, as well as relational reciprocity and high levels of closeness, marked by rapport and self-disclosure, are necessary.

It is important to realize that in assessing the value of social relationships and all that flows through them, just as with much of the rest of life, the quality of relationships matters more than the quantity of people you know and interact with for positive social, psychological, and physical outcomes. This is more fully addressed in the next chapter.

2

Why: The Importance of Socializing in Our Lives

In 350 BCE, in his *Nicomachean Ethics*, philosopher Aristotle described a close friend as "another self." In 1937, in her *Their Eyes Were Watching God*, anthropologist and novelist Zora Neale Hurston had her character Janie, an African American woman living in a close-knit African American community where she was the subject of gossip as she lived life on her own terms, describe a close friend similarly:

> Ah don't mean to bother wid tellin' 'em nothin', Pheoby. Tain't worth de trouble. You can tell'em what Ah say if you wants to. Dat's just de same as me 'cause mah tongue is in mah friend's mouf.

Both of these well-recognized treatises suggest the power of social relationships for the self and in the way that one interacts with and is seen within his or her community.

Shayna Plaut, a human rights activist, consultant, and social analyst, wrote in May 2017 about the distinction between having a coffee and drinking coffee as a way to tease out the significance of face-to-face interactions, even if they involve doing mundane things. In her activist community, for example, there is concern around overwork, burnout, few rewards, and what seems like ceaseless work. Taking time out to have coffee with others offers chances for connection, renewal, and breaks that then ensure that the work—and the workers and the relationships they have to their missions and to others—can be sustained. She states that it is in the action of taking time out together with others "that ideas flow, relationships strengthen and trust is maintained." This is an issue certainly for activists as well as for others among us, engaged in any manner of endeavors. The rest of this chapter further delves into the necessity, consequences, development and sustenance, and benefits of social relationships with others.

THE NECESSITY OF SOCIALIZING

We humans are social creatures. We need others. We thrive in community. Without these, we cannot fully realize our potential, nor can we fully realize our humanity. We become human through socialization—the ways through which people learn and internalize the values, beliefs, and norms of a culture or society they belong to. We learn how to fit in our peer group and our larger social group, culture, or society through the range of our social relationships—we are socialized as we socialize within these groups. It is through these that we receive affirmation when we do get things right and reprimanded when we do not. We get cues about what is socially acceptable and normative through what we witness and do in interactions with others. This also leads to—and further develops—social cohesion, which is the extent to which a community's or group's members are bonded. Social cohesion is key for establishing social integration—that is, how well incorporated one is to and within his or her social group. When one experiences social disintegration—that is, he or she does not achieve social integration—he or she is often perceived as loner and treated as outcast, both of which can be internalized, leading to a self-fulfilling prophecy and social isolation. Being a newcomer to a community, such as a teen starting a new school, an employee on his or her first day at a tight-knit company, or an immigrant relocating to a new country, can heighten the chances of experiencing a lack of social integration. As one spends more time within the new group, these initial feelings may subside and one can become a full-fledged participant of the new culture. Members of marginalized groups, such as people of color, women in traditionally male spaces, religious minorities, and LGBTQ people in a heteronormative culture, also experience a lack of social integration when they are in communities where members of the dominant group maintain power and privilege. Whether they achieve social integration or remain excluded is complicated and often depends on societal norms around inclusion and exclusion on a macro level and the degree to which the marginalized assimilates or is deemed similar to the dominant on a micro level.

Social integration, cohesion, and interactions are important in other ways as well. Social relationships and the activities that rise from them are particularly important in staving off a host of ills, including social disorganization and social isolation. Social disorganization is understood by social scientists as a social group's lack of solidarity, cohesion, and interaction. Often created and worsened by a lack of positive relations, trust, and shared interests, social disorganizing is associated with an escalating spiral of decline, and once it ensues, informal social control (the ability of a social group to create, maintain, and enforce social norms, order, and regulations from within, without external groups or institutions) can weaken, both further hampering the creation of supportive and positive social bonds. This leads to the fear that social isolation—discussed at length in the preceding and subsequent chapters—and all the ills associated with it could occur. This causes a cycle that ultimately fosters even greater levels of social disorganization and social isolation.

Because social relationships are so vital for us, there has been concern with the impact of social changes, whether caused by urbanization in the late 19th and early 20th centuries; civil, political, and social rights for people of color and women in the middle of the 20th century; or the rise of the Internet and new communication technologies from the mid-1990s through the present. In the late 1800s, social theorists, such as French sociologist Emile Durkheim, issued claims—and warnings—about the lack of social connectedness. Durkheim's research indicated that a lack of connectedness would lead to anomie—a sense of despair and normlessness due to a lack of accountability to others—and increases in one's likelihood to commit suicide shows concern about what would later be called social isolation. Other pioneering scholars, such as W.E.B. Du Bois, Georg Simmel, Robert Park, Ernest Burgess, E. Franklin Frazier, St. Claire Drake, and Horace Cayton, who were analyzing the rise of the modern city in the wake of industrial capitalism, concerned themselves with the impact of urbanization on primary or close, intimate relationships. Simmel and Park described encounters in the city as more transitory and less stable than in smaller communities. As a result, urban residents responded to these new interactions with hesitancy, detachment, and nonchalance in order to inoculate themselves from the rush of various and unfamiliar encounters that are inherent to the city. The nature of the city was believed to discourage the formation of the type of intimate, reciprocal relationships found in more rural areas, fostering social disorganization through the destruction of traditional forms of authority and social control, as exemplified by higher rates of crime and other forms of disorder. Though subsequent research has shown this concern to be largely unfounded, we still realize the importance of social connections and the benefits they provide.

Our connections serve a number of purposes for us, including the provision of emotional support, material resources, information, and camaraderie. In addition to providing a variety of supports, social networks are important in the provision of basic needs for contact, communication, and community. Community, particularly the personal community—that is, members of one's social network—did not disappear with the advent of capitalism, industrialization, technological advances, urbanization, or deindustrialization, despite fears to the contrary. Indeed, social networks can be used to create social capital, which in direct opposition to the effects of social isolation can be accessed to positively affect one's opportunities to accomplish goals, increase earnings, and gain valuable information such as job openings and potential employer expectations. We also see increasing discussion and evidence of the positive correlation between social connectedness, social capital, and well-being.

Social interaction is important for other reasons as well. When we spend time with our family, romantic partners, classmates, colleagues, acquaintances, and friends, we are not just making calculations about how well these relationships can improve our economic status, reputation, or health. We do it for the personal and affective purposes, too. A strong social network, rich with active participants and experiences, allows us for starters to form relationships and memories that can last through the course of our lives. Important not just for educational and employment opportunities that may result, lifelong connections can provide people we can reminisce and stroll down memory lane with. These then become the backbone of what we recall when we reflect on the moments of our lives. These also become the foundation for the establishment of more shared experiences that will lead to more memories.

As referenced elsewhere, there are mental and physical benefits to social interactions such as the reduction of stress. A strong social life can also provide a release valve that staves off stress or prevent it from becoming overly harmful. Going out, letting one's hair down, and having a good time with friends, family, and others is an excellent way to relieve and reduce stress. Building in time to relax and be social with others is looked forward to after a hard exam, a workweek, or difficult period in life for a reason. Whether dancing, eating, talking, or hiking together, being within a fun, supportive social circle has a pronounced impact on stress levels.

We also feel good and affirmed when we can find someone who likes doing what we like. Having a set of common sensibilities and experiences around hobbies, travels, political engagement, intellectual pursuits, or other interests that connects us with others and strengthens these for ourselves is another way that we can think about the necessity of socializing. We also have fun when we socialize. We often feel fulfilled when we share experiences and bonds with others while engaged in an activity that brings us joy and happiness. Not only is a good social life good for our bodies and minds, but it feels good as well.

While much of the focus here and in the scholarly literature on social relationships is on the physical, physiological, and psychological benefits of socializing and friendships, it is important to note that they have another vital function—they are fun. This fun that we have when we spend time doing what we want to do with people we want to be around is known as sociability, the desire to associate with others for the sake of enjoying another's company. An examination of the pleasure—not just the instrumental or even expressive gains—that one can receive from his or her social ties can extend our understanding of social relationships and their value. Imagine that you are returning from a long weekend and someone asks what you did with that time away. It is doubtful that you will discuss how your activity with your best friend increased your levels of hormones like serotonin and dopamine and decreased your blood pressure and risk of stroke. You are much more likely to go on and on about how much fun you had kicking back and spending time with someone you like to be around.

Likewise, examining the emotional or the expressive component of social ties need not be limited to having a shoulder to cry on or receiving advice. In addition to being both instrumental and expressive, and in addition to providing ties that we can tap into for support and for opportunities to climb the social ladder, the people we know and spend time with can also provide us with someone to talk to on the train, someone to share a good meal with, and someone to go to a club with. Before continuing, we must acknowledge the importance of sociability as a critical aspect of social relationships. This is as necessary as recognizing the ways that socializing and those we socialize with may meet our needs and desires for information; financial, material, and emotional support; and social mobility.

Social relationships and the social networks that contain them are often only viewed in terms of what metrics they can provide. This is especially the case with those concerned with social isolation and its inverse, social capital. Analyses tend to focus on who is connected to whom and what access to otherwise unavailable resources these connections may bestow. Additionally, many institutions, associations, and groups promote occasions dedicated to networking where one can meet and greet others who may enhance one's financial, human, cultural, or social capital. Missing from these analyses and opportunities, however, are the less calculated motivations for socializing with others. Pioneering sociologist Georg Simmel postulates that some forms of social interaction—what he terms "sociability"—can and should occur for their own sake. This perspective affords a view of social relationships that are useful not just for the loans, babysitting, job referrals, and letters of recommendation that they can generate but also for the sense of joy and connection that spending time in the presence of someone we like, share common interests with, or pass time with can produce. It is in sociability that we can forget the burdens and travails of our lives and engage in a relationship where our statuses and responsibilities are replaced by a sense of equality and what Simmel calls the "playform of association." Here we turn to other impacts of social relationships as we explore the social impacts of socializing.

THE SOCIAL IMPACTS OF SOCIALIZING

More than money, career success, popularity, and fame, happiness comes from having strong and positive relationships. Despite any economic, environmental, and political instability, countries and states that indicate high levels of social integration also indicate high levels of happiness. When we feel loved and supported and when we have people in our lives whom we can love and support in return, we are most fulfilled, even and perhaps especially if there are other problems we face. When we have strong and supportive networks, the positive impacts they have on our lives are many. This is certainly the case for when this occurs within our families and romantic relationships. We discuss this less, however, when it occurs within our friendships and other social relationships. Many studies have found that the positive impacts of well-functioning and rich networks are independent and separate from our familial networks. When we have strong, vital friendships, our self-esteem, health outcomes, and ability to deal with stress improve while our risks of depression, substance abuse, and suicide decrease. When we perceive our social relationships as good, when we are satisfied with our friendships, and when we have people we are close to, our overall psychological well-being increases compared to people who do not possess these. It is important to highlight that the social impacts of socializing might well be influenced by our perceptions of those in our network. Some scholars suggest that any effects of our networks are mediated by our perception of whether and how they meet our needs for basics like autonomy, competence, and relatedness. If, for example, we feel affection and support from our relational partners, we see their supporting us through running errands or doing chores for us as an expression of how revered we are to them. If, on the other hand, we do not have these positive feelings about and for our relational partners, we see those same actions of doing chores and running errands as them trying to control us. If we are experiencing depression, the former will help provide some relief while the latter will exacerbate it.

Even if we are unfamiliar with the research that supports the importance and necessity of socializing, we seek its benefits in our lives on a regular basis. We see this reflected when we think about the ways that we spend our leisure time in the United States. Leisure is the time that we spend in activities that we freely choose, like relaxing and on recreation, which includes those activities we enjoy, find pleasurable, and that renews us. A 2015 survey of the ways that Americans use their time, conducted by the U.S. Department of Labor's Bureau of Labor Statistics, found that 96 percent of those 15 years old and above engaged in at least one leisure activity each day. While watching TV is the most common leisure activity—we spend 2.8 hours watching TV each day—socializing is the second most common leisure pursuit. In 2015, we spent 41 minutes each day communicating and socializing with others, defined in the American Time Use Survey, as talking with and visiting friends face-to-face, via telephone, or through social media or attending or hosting social events. Indeed, a 2007 MTV/Associated Press poll found that for 13–24-year-olds, spending time with friends ranked as second in importance for causing happiness, preceded only by spending time with family. This is true when we are in adolescence, adulthood, and old age. Across the life course, high-quality friendships are positively associated with high-quality lives.

Surely, we know that friendships are desirable relationships. We also know that we want to spend time with others and have others want to spend time with others. Think back to your childhood days—do you recall arguments over who had the most friends? Arguments over who was most (or least) popular? Arguments over who had the best weekend plans or the coolest summer vacation? Do you remember the sting of losing a friend over one of these arguments or the sting of having no one to play with you or to play what you wanted to play? All indicate the power of friendships and activities with friends from very early on. We typically gain our first friendships as children—with relatives, neighbors, classmates, and our parents' friends' children. We learn through these relationships how to interact with others. We learn how to take turns and how to play nicely (i.e., no hitting or biting). We learn how to give and take comfort in others. We also learn how to compromise to accommodate someone else and how to negotiate to get what we want. We learn through these relationships how to use and develop our vocabularies and nonverbal and oral communication skills. We learn how to make and keep friends. We learn these lessons early on and continue to use and refine them through our lives. Experts believe that lessons learned in childhood have lifelong reach in our ability to make and keep any relationships, let alone ones that are positive. Some of those characteristics are internal to us. Our capacity to listen to others and control our own impulses goes a long way in ensuring smooth interactions with others that support socializing, sociability, and friendship. We also have to be proficient in our engagement with others, such as our facility to act cooperatively and communicate effectively. We begin to gain these abilities in early childhood when we share toys with our siblings and cousins, dress up in costumes during a play date, finish a puzzle with our tablemate in preschool, and exchange jokes and giggles with the person we sit next to in kindergarten. As we continue along the life course, these skills will stead us well to be sure.

While having associates, acquaintances, and friends matters greatly, it is having close friends that matters the most. Research indicates that for adults, those with close and long-lasting friendships have more positive outcomes than those who do not. These friendships led to those who possessed them having improved physical health, emotional health, moods, and functioning compared to those who did not have close, long-term friendships. A list of benefits of friendships issued by the Mayo Clinic notes that friends increase a sense of belonging and purpose; boost happiness and reduce stress; improve self-confidence and self-worth; help one cope with traumas, such as divorce, serious illness, job loss, or the death of a loved one; and encourage one to change or avoid unhealthy lifestyle habits, such as excessive drinking or lack of exercise. Church attendance also boosts well-being along a number of measures but not necessarily because of a belief in a deity or a message from a clergyperson. There is scholarship that indicates it is being in a community with others rather than religiosity that leads to these positive outcomes. This is evident as the researchers found that even among those who attended religious services, those who report the largest number of social ties at those services, were two times more satisfied with life than those who report having no social ties to others at those services.

Increasingly, there is research that supports network effects of and on behavior. One example of this is found when we consider the effect of family on friendships. When we have families that provide high levels of social support to us, we are more likely to have strong friendships and other relationships with our peers and contemporaries. Supportive families— families where we feel that we are loved, valued, accepted, connected, and treated well and that we can come to get our needs met—are positively associated with the ability to provide and receive support in our friendships. Similarly, when we have families that are warm, caring, stable, and trusting, we are more likely and more equipped to bring these traits to other relationships with us. As these are constitutive of good relationships, it becomes easy to see how positive familial interactions translate into positive social interactions outside the family in and after childhood.

A number of recent studies have found that illnesses such as the common cold, weight gain, and depression tend to cluster within networks. Depressive symptoms were found with as many as three degrees of separation—in other words, one's friends' friends' friends would show signs of depression. This was pronounced within women's networks, perhaps because women are socialized to empathize and make deeper emotional and personal connections more than men. Similarly, a sort of contagious cognitive vulnerability or strong risk factor for depression has been found to exist in places where there is dense, shared living space, such as the college dormitory. This is associated with age rather than gender, and researchers claim that this cognitive vulnerability develops during early adolescence, remaining consistent throughout adulthood. Other recent studies have found that both depression and positive mood could be found clustered within networks. Other research asserts that the risk of depression could be significantly reduced, and initial diagnoses of depression could be mediated through network effects if there were enough network members who were not depressed. Indeed, it may be that the power of network connectedness means that if one who has been diagnosed with depression has enough social ties who do not have depression, the depressed person has twice as high a change of recovery. Similarly, these network effects mean that for one who has not been diagnosed with depression, a network with an adequate number of other members who do not have depression is half as likely to subsequently be diagnosed with depression.

Certainly, as our social integration and ties add to our well-being, they also add to our being well. More than money, more than fame, more than education, and more than social status, relationships are most strongly associated with happiness and other indicators of well-being. The positive benefits that flow from positive relationships do not just exist, however— they must be cultivated. Relationships must be cared for and nurtured in order to do us good. Happiness and other positive and desirable affective states occur when we can spend time with those who bring us fulfillment and joy. There is also research that indicates truth in the old adage that it is better to give than to receive. Recent findings show that doing things for others that provide them with benefits—whether joy, affirmation, or basic needs—increases our own well-being. This is especially true when this occurs within a reciprocal relationship where we feel we are not being taken advantage of, overburdened, or unduly obligated.

CREATING AND MAINTAINING RELATIONSHIPS

There is more choice about friendships today than perhaps ever before. In preindustrial societies, whether we are discussing nomadic hunters and gatherers or the more geographically rooted agriculturalists, one often had to interact with kin and neighbors to ensure his or her own livelihood as well as group survival. Banishment from the group would result in not just social death but also in literal death if one had no one to rely on for protection from the elements, hunger, dangerous animals, or other humans. The ways and places where we live have decidedly changed, as we have moved from the countryside to cities and suburbs and from farms to offices. This has caused a host of corresponding changes in all aspects of social life, including all of our relationships. No matter your age, even when compared to your parents and grandparents, there are stark societal differences that have affected the ways you connect and those you connect with. While baby boomers may have had access to nightly neighborhood ball games in the summer; weekly dinners with aunts, uncles, cousins, and grandparents gathered around the table; or community-wide picnics in the park, these are not staples of most people belonging to Generation X, Generation Y, or millennials. Even for members of Generation X, it is easy to recall their times as youth playing with whatever kids were outside, finding a pickup game of basketball to join, or spontaneously grabbing dinner with friends in college even as they schedule playdates for their own children, sign up for a recreational athletic league, or make plans to catch up with a nearby friend weeks in advance. Our contemporary lives are much more complicated and busy than before, and this has definite consequences for our social interactions.

Unlike our familial relationships and unlike professional obligations where there are more pressures for interactions (even if we would rather stay home, watching Netflix or reading a book alone), current forms and motivations behind socializing are distinct due to its more voluntary nature. Indeed, there is much more nebulousness around this relational form as there is a lack of societal agreement on its meaning, definitions, obligations, expectations, norms, and structure. While we often cannot choose our family or colleagues, we can choose with whom we socialize outside of these contexts. When we feel positive about those with whom we are related or with whom we work, we may also choose to socialize with them.

A study conducted in 2007 by researchers from UCLA identified 11 commonly cited characteristics of friendship: similarity, proximity, transcending context (i.e., engaging in a number of different activities), companionship, reciprocity, mutuality, intimacy, support, trust/loyalty, conflict management, and stability. Of these, they found that among study participants, the largest emphasis was focused on companionship, transcending contexts, similarity, proximity, and stability. William Rawlins, a communications professor at Ohio University, has said that whether a teen or a senior citizen, people have three expectations of someone they call their close friend: "Somebody to talk to, someone to depend on, and someone to enjoy." Close friends are also those with whom we have intimate relations. While intimacy is often associated with romantic and sexual relationships, it refers to a broader range of social relationships. When we talk about intimacy, we are really talking about feelings of those we feel close to, those we feel connected to. When we talk about intimate relationships, those are really about the interactions, bonds, and exchanges that we share with those we are closely connected to and with. Those we are intimate with are those who are often most like we are: we share not only experiences but also our ideals, beliefs, and values with our intimates. We also share ourselves—our vulnerabilities, pain, and heartbreak as well as our accomplishment, excitement, and joys with our intimates. We self-disclose to those with whom we feel the bond of intimacy, believing (or at least hoping) that they will continue to support us and hold our secrets close and that they will feel they can come to us when they need to. Intimacy and reciprocity are tied together in this.

How do we find people to be intimate with and to reciprocate gifts, time, and support with in the first place? Even in this age of social media, physical proximity is still prevalent as a first step in making friendships. Indeed, we continue to meet our friends at a neighborhood playground, at school, in the church choir, on the swim team, in the college cafeteria, and in the cubicle next to us. When we meet people whom we might let into our lives, we decide to forge ahead and cultivate relationships with those we encounter in these arenas as we discover and bond over our other commonalities, such as love for pizza, Marvel movies, horticulture, or Prince music. We also bond over shared social statuses, such as race, class, gender, and sexual identity, especially if we find ourselves among the

minority or marginalized in a social setting we perceive as hostile or isolating based on those statuses.

A 2013 study conducted by a team of researchers who looked at 3,000
high school students at almost 80 schools across the United States revealed
that the students' social lives were largely determined on those they shared
classes with, even more so than any athletic or other extracurricular activities they participated in. This is in part about not just spending time
together but about how much time is spent together. As students spend
more time in their classes than they do in any of their chosen extracurricular pursuits, it stands to reason that this is a fertile space for connecting
with others. The research team found that those students in smaller, more
specialized courses like music and foreign languages were more likely to
bond with their classmates as they had more commonalities over which
to form attachments than students in larger, less specialized courses like
math and physical education. Scholars note that this is quite consequential for high school students as it provides relief from the otherwise seem-
ingly relentless push for status and recognition often prevalent and
perceived in social arrangements among this age group. These relationships tend to be more egalitarian, supportive, and healthy as they have
fewer status hierarchies and promote achievement for their members.

These bonds, while deep and impactful as indicated previously, are also
fragile, due to their voluntary status. While voluntary, social relationships
are both social and relational, meaning they cannot exist without interdependence. This is a paradox of sorts: it takes at least two people to enter
a relationship that can be ended unilaterally, by either partner, at any time
despite the other's wishes. This is particularly true as we become adults,
busy with school and work and family duties. Social norms, community
mores, and the legal system can make it extremely difficult to part ways
with one's parents, siblings, spouses, and/or children. Financial obligations
and material desires, especially in uncertain economic climates, can make
it harder than we want to find a new employer or a new set of colleagues.
These do not exist for such relationships, and today's best friends forever
may not survive the rumor mill, a cross-country move, the establishment
of one's family of procreation, or the demands of a serious or chronic illness. It becomes more difficult to maintain the intimacy and reciprocity
mentioned earlier when other relationships and priorities vie for one's
attention and energy. A view of social relationships with those we are
not related to or intimately partnered with and socializing across the life
span can be instructive here.

After enduring the ups and downs of changed minds, hurt feelings,
external instabilities, and other tensions that surround social relationships

like friendships in childhood and adolescence, early adulthood is probably the best time for these relationships to flourish. For many, particularly those from the middle classes, early adulthood encompasses the time of life that one will have the most freedom and fewest encumbrances. As such, meeting and getting to know new people, rekindling previous relationships, and growing existing ones are most possible. It is at this stage that we become surer of ourselves, of what we want, of whom we would like to spend time with, and of what we want to spend time doing. If time and money permit, people in this stage of life tend to have the greatest ability for hanging out, socializing, and recreation. In 2014, the American Time Use Survey found that people between 20 and 24 years old spend more time socializing—defined in the survey as "visiting with friends or attending or hosting social events"—each day than any other age group, younger or older. As we become adults, we often find it hard to develop new friendships, while we also find it hard to maintain our existing friendships. We move to a new place or start a new job and wonder how best to fit in and find people we get along with or have commonalities with. We may also find that we have grown distant from those we used to love being with and around. Even if we still like and share things in common with our friends, it may still be difficult to cultivate and deepen our relationships with them. Indeed, as life grows more complicated, responsibilities become more serious, and time becomes more limited, the efforts spent maintaining and strengthening friendships can come to be seen as burdensome and onerous. The investments that one had placed into these social relationships are often shifted into other areas of life, such as romantic relationships, career progression, and familial duties. When the benefits that flow from socializing and friendships are perhaps most needed is also when these relationships are perhaps most likely to change and become increasingly restricted.

Friendship experts describe changes in relationships in other ways as well. One categorization of social relationships like friendships posits them as active, dormant, or commemorative. Active friendships are those that we most readily and often engage with. We keep in touch with our active friends, and asking them for assistance or advice or a visit is expected and encouraged. Dormant friendships are those that we do not stay in regular touch with. We are excited when they call unexpectedly, and they are excited when they bump into us at the library. We are both happy to catch up on all that we have missed in one another's life when we were not in contact. Indeed, these relationships might endure because they offer hiatus from the other. The phrase "absence makes the heart grow fonder" might well give us insight into why and how that is. A commemorative friendship is one that marks our past and those we knew from another time and place. We may be startled to hear from one of these people, and it may take us a moment or two to recall their face, yet they remain important to identify as a friend, if for no other reason because of that shared past.

When we consider how social relationships are formed, we note that there are myriad—and interrelated—types and mechanisms. As we think about the types of social ties we have, we might want to think about how these are typified, as they are created, developed, and sustained in different ways. When we are connected to close family and close friends, we have what are known as primary social connections. When we are connected to people we know through work, school, religious, political, or professional memberships, clubs, or hobbies, we have what are known as secondary social connections. Both are important, and certainly there are copious examples of secondary connections becoming primary ones and primary connections becoming former ones. Some of the mechanisms for relationship formation, especially among secondary types, include proximity—we link with those we are geographically close to; situational—we link with those we share circumstances or availability with; individual—we link with those who are charismatic, have good personalities, display social skills, and are otherwise attractive to us; and dyadic—we link with those who reciprocate our interest, disclosure, and sharing. If these are not present or are disappearing, our desire to remain in the relationship can also exit.

As we in the United States experience more residential mobility—that is, moving from place to place—psychologists Omri Gillath and Lucas Keefer contend that those who experience greater residential mobility also experience a greater tendency to see some of their social relationships as disposable, particularly when they are the secondary type. This makes them more likely to leave people behind in their old place, just as one might leave behind his or her down coat and wool sweaters as he or she leaves Illinois winters for the year-round warmth of Southern California. Interestingly, the researchers found that there were no significant differences in this disposability between romantic relationships and friendships. In these moves, especially when they involve large geographic distances, we make calculations about which relationships are worth holding on to and which should be abandoned. We decide about which members of our social circles are irreplaceable and who can be replaced with someone else in our new location.

Similarly, as we experience moves, we may come to see some of our social relationships as lacking depth and quality, according to research from University of Virginia psychologist Shigehiro Oishi. If we are already introverted, moving around can cause a decline in the size of our social networks as we find it an insurmountable obstacle to replace the friends we had to leave behind. While some people experiencing loneliness might use those feelings to push them into getting to know others in an attempt to expand their social circle, for others this loneliness is more of a paralytic, causing apprehension about meeting new people and potentially risking vulnerability, rejection, and hurt. This ultimately can further feed feelings of alienation, causing a vicious cycle of unwanted aloneness. For those who have tried unsuccessfully to sustain a friendship or other social relationship, fear of continued failure is a disincentive to make, deepen, or maintain other social relationships lest they get burned again. As such, it may be that we try to hold on to those friends we have moved away from, even as distance separates us. Technological changes, including the advent of social media, may prove instructive here.

Regardless of how they start, our relationships with others must be grown and nurtured in order to survive. At the present time, increased social media access and usage has offered a change in how our social relationships are categorized as well as how they are created and maintained. FaceTime, Google Hangouts, and Skype allow this to happen in new ways. No longer must we be beholden to telephone calls where we do not see the person on the other end or wait for infrequent trips to see our friend—we can look to our computer, tablet, or phone screen to see and converse across places, as countless ads remind us. We can see pictures they post to Snapchat, Twitter, Facebook, and Instagram seconds after they were taken. We can see a livestream of whatever it is that our friend sees. These technologies all offer ways to keep friendships vital and relevant even when life's circumstances make this difficult.

While these technologies are feared to be mere substitutes for real, primary connection or as ways to gain followers and likes rather than true friends and substantive bonds, they do hold within them the ability to become and remain close in ways unimagined a little over a decade or so ago. It is also important to illuminate the point that with all these reservations and fears about virtual interactions, it is not unreasonable or uncommon that a relationship that begins virtually can become a more significant, primary one. It is hard for most of us to think of at least one person we know who has not met a real-world friend or romantic partner online, for example. If one is connected to and communicates with his or her friends across a number of platforms—say he or she attends a basketball game on Monday, exchanges Snapchat videos on Tuesday, confirms plans via text on Wednesday, attends a concert together on Thursday, and @ each other with pictures from the night before on Instagram on

Friday—researchers suggest that their relationship will be better compared to reserving communication for one dedicated medium. While our Facebook friends are likely to be only Facebook friends—if friends at all—if that is the only way we are connected to them, if we see them in person, text with them on a regular basis, and have other social media exchanges with them, not only does that deepen our relationship, but it helps to preserve it as well. However, there can be challenges in using new technologies, such as social media, to stay in touch if those do not satisfy one partner's need for more personal methods of communication, such as a handwritten letter, a phone call, or a visit. This is easy to see when a parent, romantic partner, or older relative complains about only getting text or Facebook messages. Despite the relationship type or the mechanism through which it was born, it takes work to hold on to it.

As indicated in a 2015 article in *The Atlantic* on concerns around the current state of Americans' social ties, there are four main levels of maintaining a relationship. The first is keeping a relationship in existence, which can be done technically by liking a tweet or giving a birthday greeting via Facebook. The second is keeping a relationship stable, which can occur face-to-face or digitally by offering support and closeness. The third is repairing a relationship, which also can occur face-to-face or digitally. The fourth is making a satisfying relationship, which, according to relationship expert Emily Langan, is best done in more intimate ways that online communication does not readily allow for. Perhaps this is what is going on when our mothers would rather hear our voice than read our texts, our boyfriends cannot stop smiling when we surprise them by showing up at their jobs, and our bond with our high school tennis partners turns into a lifelong friendship after we spend a weekend with them every year since graduation.

Regardless of how we meet or stay connected, in order to fully support healthy relationships, we should bear in mind a number of ways to cultivate and deepen these. Having strong, nurturing, healthy relationships means that we will have relationships in which we both can give and receive advice, companionship, and other forms of support. Give-and-take is also important as it relates to compromising to ensure that all parties have their needs met. Communication remains important to the maintenance of healthy social relationships and the networks that encompass these. Even if—and perhaps especially—one does not talk with or see his or her social ties regularly (or as regularly as he or she desires), listening fully, attentively, and nonjudgmentally to one's teammate, colleague, or friend; discussing and resolving any tensions; and expressing affection and appreciation are all keys in fostering and maintaining a bond.

Preserving one's relationship also requires that confidentiality, reciprocity, and intentionality are prioritized. When that does occur and friendships are maintained, studies show that relationships become more likely to continue.

No matter how the relationship is formed, at what stage it is found, or how it is maintained, in order to truly reap the benefits that come with a strong social life, it is a matter of putting the quality of the relationship over the quantity of relationships. Unlike retweets or likes, the social, emotional, psychological, and physical impacts of acquaintanceships, friendships, and socializing are measured by their intensity and strength rather than their number. Though a diverse network is valuable for a multitude of reasons, particularly when it comes to getting ahead in life, good friendships are certainly about depth rather than breadth. Still, investments in social relationships tend to yield positive returns, both in terms of their continuance and in terms of social capital in the forms of information and opportunities that lead to upward social mobility.

OBTAINING INFORMATION AND GETTING AHEAD

The quality and quantity of social capital is a function of social networks and the assets and resources the members of those networks bring to the relationship. Those we spend time with—members of our social networks—are important sources of information for us. Whether rooted in marital and other intimate relationships, close friendships, neighboring, or acquaintanceships, we have all gotten and given information through this channel. It is within these contexts that decisions to share and exchange valuable resources, such as money, time, favors, support, knowledge, and information, are made. These decisions are shaped in large part by the amount of trust that members have in each other. Positive interpersonal relationships and social interactions are then positively correlated with trust. It is through dealings with each other and one's reputation among others in a shared network that enough information can be gathered to ascertain whether a person deserves a social capital investment from another. A 1998 research study from Janine Nahapiet and Sumantra Ghoshal discussed social capital as having three components—structural, or an overarching set of connections between members of a social network; relational, or the interpersonal relationships that members of a social network have established as they interact with each other; and cognitive, or shared ideas or knowledge around meanings, symbols, and interpretations, among members of a social network. These facilitate knowing others well enough to vouch for them, give financial assistance, and provide a referral that can benefit them without causing harm to you or your reputation. These require a level of trust that is facilitated through a series or set of direct, personal social interactions or knowledge gained through one's interactions with others. In addition to trust, social interactions that lead to the activation of social capital also require a sense of obligation and reciprocity—the notion that one who has received will give when called upon and that if one person has given within a relationship, he or she can expect to get when it is his or her turn. Shared identification, be it based on membership in a family, friend group, or another group status such as shared ethnicity or race or sexual identity, also aids in the activation of social capital.

That information gained through our social connections is considered a massive payoff of social capital. The knowledge of job openings, recommendations, and referrals for opportunities we would not otherwise have is one of the major ways that our networks are seen as beneficial. We often are told that we should network when we go to a meetup, alumni events, charity fund-raisers, and the like because the people we meet and the information they possess are seen as valuable. This value may come in the moment—we learn about a cool party or that someone can hook us up with concert tickets to see our favorite band. This value is also seen as a long-term investment that should pay dividends well into the future, such as when we need a letter of recommendation for admittance into a prestigious graduate school, an endorsement for a political campaign we are launching, or inside information on an internship for our children years from now.

The use of Briggs's 1998 formulation of social capital as either social support or social leverage is particularly instructive. Social support provides network-based resources vital in both emergencies and the daily survival while social leverage provides network-based resources that facilitate upward social mobility. Social support can be a shoulder to cry on, a ride to the airport, or a babysitter. Social support can also come in the form of help making a credit card payment, providing weekly dinners to a starving artist, or a parent who lets his or her recently laid-off adult daughter or son return home until she or he can get on her or his feet again. Furthermore, social support is typically provided by one's intimates, those individuals with whom one has the closest and strongest ties. Networks are also key to amassing resources, skills, and opportunities that can provide social leverage or an entrée into upward social mobility. These ties are typically formed through associations with more socially distant others and often cross racial/ethnic and/or class boundaries to provide connections to individuals in other circles who are important for accessing resources that may otherwise be unavailable. It is these ties to heterogeneous others as social leverage is often found in ties to less close or weaker relationships. It is these relationships that are said to be more valuable for upward mobility.

Sociologists and other social scientists, borrowing from the work of Mark Granovetter, discuss this as the concept of the strength of weak ties. Many studies use this concept to explain how relatively weak ties (those we do not know very well or are very intimate with, e.g., our college roommate's best friend from back home or a coworker's partner we once met at a holiday party) are in fact very valuable members of our social network because they are more likely to provide new information and opportunities to us. Rather than a strongly embedded tie—someone we share a number of indirect paths with, such as our sibling whom we are connected to through each of our parents, our siblings, our cousins, our neighbors, and so on—it is the less embedded ones that offer most access to the types of opportunities that can then lead to upward social mobility. Consider this: if a social network is very dense—that is, everyone is embedded and knows everyone else—any information on a job opening or scholarship or any opportunity such as a free movie pass or an exciting new experience will be cycled or circulated only within that group of people. If there is any scarcity whether of material resources, desirable information and knowledge, or better opportunities within the network, then only a few will be able to benefit from the information or opportunity. If a network, however, is less dense, then the possibility for new and otherwise unknown experiences and knowledge will open up.

We can also look to the 2001 work of Michael Woolcock, a noted public policy scholar at Harvard University and the World Bank, who seeks to understand the connections between health, wealth, well-being, and social capital. Woolcock extends this discussion to three types of social capital. These are bonding, bridging, and linking social capital. In the first type, bonding social capital ties are based on close and intimate connections and are with people like family, friends, and a select group of neighbors. These are strong, primary ties. The second, bridging social capital ties are rooted in less close relationships with people who occupy a similar position to one's self like colleagues, classmates, and acquaintances. These are weak, secondary ties. The third, linking social capital are ties to people outside of one's personal network and are with those who occupy an either higher or lower social position and are more likely to be secondary ties. These last two forms of social capital are often considered the most likely to lead to new information and opportunities, particularly for those in less advantaged and marginalized positions in society.

With the growth in number of platforms and use and acceptance of social media and other electronically mediated communication, it may be that there are more opportunities to cement bonding social capital that lies in one's strong ties and importantly and interestingly to develop bridging and linking social capital through one's weak ties. Certainly we can friend or retweet someone from our family and friends' circles as traditional takes on weak ties would suggest. We can also develop our own set of weak ties by establishing friends on Facebook and followers on Instagram and Twitter we never would have come into contact with through any other means. These platforms can expand our weak ties, offering bridging social capital and filling structural holes we may not have realized were even present. These can also increase the size of our networks, creating weak ties as we form these diffuse and wide-reaching networks that extend much further than before possible.

Thus, the composition of social networks matters tremendously. The tendency for networks to be homogeneous, comprised of individuals who share a number of characteristics, such as education, geographic location, race/ethnicity, social class, and gender, may limit the amount of capital one is able to produce. As such, if we look at social class, for poor individuals, networks with high amounts of socioeconomic homogeneity are detrimental. For those who are poor and also living in neighborhoods with high rates of poverty, many analysts say that they have a lack of the kinds of valuable social capital that might give them access to networks that can mean opportunities for resources that can help for daily survival as well as facilitate upward social mobility for themselves and, importantly, for their children.

If, however, one who is poor has a heterogeneous network through his or her ties to individuals from whom he or she is dissimilar, availability of access to new information and opportunities increases, bettering chances of achieving upward social mobility. This heterogeneity provides for the helpful presence of what are termed "structural holes" or a gap between at least two members of a focal person's social network who could benefit if the gap were closed. One example of this would be if you needed a place to stay while you visited another country and your neighbor has a sibling who lives in that country. Your neighbor acts as a bridge in the gap between your need and his or her sibling, thus closing the structural hole that had existed between the two of you. It is not enough, however, to know someone who can get you access—they have to be willing to act on your behalf, to share resources, and to actualize any potential social capital. No matter how the relationship is created or maintained or its closeness, distance, strength, or weakness, it is certainly the case that time typically is necessary in order to build the types of relationships and networks through which the social capital discussed here can flow. It takes time to have social interactions. It also takes time—and typically multiple observations and/or interactions—in order to develop trust. When trust is present, social connectedness, social networks, social support, and social integration, along with all of their attendant benefits, flourish. Shared individual and communal goals, shared cooperation, shared safety, and shared opportunities are all positively associated with individual and social trust. Achieving this, though, is certainly easier said than done, particularly as a number of surveys and scholars point to declines in social trust across and within generations, making socializing and social relationships both more consequential and more precarious.

This chapter discussed the necessity, consequences, development, maintenance, and benefits of social relationships with others. Hopefully, by now you can begin to see the important role socializing plays in our lives. The next chapter focuses on not only the benefits of socializing but also the negative effects of it.

3

❖

How: The Positive and Negative Effects of Socializing

When most people think of the word "health," they think of someone's physical health. Take for instance, the World Health Organization (WHO). The WHO website states, "We strive to combat diseases—infectious diseases like influenza and HIV and noncommunicable ones like cancer and heart disease. We help mothers and children survive and thrive so they can look forward to a healthy old age. We ensure the safety of the air people breathe, the food they eat, the water they drink—and the medicines and vaccines they need." What about other aspects of "health"? Actually, the WHO also sees social relationships as a part of a person's "health." The WHO's definition of "health" is in part "a state of complete physical, mental and *social* well-being and not merely the absence of disease or infirmity." This chapter aims to shed some light on the social aspect of health by examining positive as well as negative effects of socializing. In particular, this chapter discusses the physical and psychological effects of socializing, how socializing impacts our life expectancy, and the darker side of socializing, including social isolation.

PHYSICAL HEALTH EFFECTS OF SOCIALIZING

Socializing can provide a variety of benefits to a person's physical health. Socializing has been shown to lower stress, lower blood pressure, lower inflammation, increase cognitive functioning, as well as strengthen the immune system, which means the individual will be better able to fight off illnesses such as the common cold or flu. Data from four separate longitudinal studies on populations that included adolescents through retirement-aged Americans reveal that those who had more friends and opportunities to socialize when they were adolescents and again in old age had lower rates of high blood pressure, inflammation, obesity, and attendant lower risks of cancer, heart disease, and other diseases as they aged. They also observed that this group had lower rates of death.

What is the alternative? For decades, researchers have tracked the effects of loneliness and isolation on individuals' physical health. When people do not have opportunities to socialize, this isolation can lead to depression and stress. Stress in turn can physically manifest in your body. When a person develops stress from loneliness and lack of social connections, he or she may experience bloating and digestive issues and are at a higher risk of becoming sick. In addition, individuals are at risk factor for a number of adverse conditions, including high blood pressure, heart disease, and diabetes. Stress from this social separation can also cause inflammation throughout the body. When inflammation occurs in the body, it can lead to bloating, increased risk of illnesses, digestive issues, and inability to function normally. Furthermore, a lack of social connections can produce an increased risk for tumors and abnormal growths. One study using mice found that isolation could increase cancerous tumor growth. In another study, researchers had participants estimate room temperatures after recalling a time that they were snubbed or socially excluded. Participants in this condition reported colder room temperatures than participants who were asked to remember times with friends, thus suggesting that we can actually *feel* social chills. The effects of social isolation will be discussed in greater detail at the end of this chapter.

According to psychologist Susan Pinker, face-to-face encounters are the most protective and promotive of health. She asserts that for men who have had strokes or heart attacks, for example, who participate in groups, join teams, and are in romantic relationships, get more benefits from these interactions than they do from prescription medications. Pinker details two kinds of necessary relationships to have and foster: those that are routine and those that are part of your daily life, such as the chat you have with your favorite barista at your favorite café, the small talk you make with your colleagues while waiting for the next meeting to start, and the backyard conversations you have with your neighbor from down the street and maintaining close familial ties, even if your relatives live far away. Developing and keeping healthy bonds is a process that is best done from an early age for the greatest health outcomes.

PSYCHOLOGICAL EFFECTS OF SOCIALIZING

Intimate relationships and social interactions often lead to the development of resilience, coping skills, and higher self-esteem. Psychologist Richard Robins and colleague Kali Trzesniewski reviewed several studies concerning the development of self-esteem and how it changes across the life span. According to Robins and Trzesniewski, recent studies reveal young children tend to have relatively high self-esteem. This is most likely because views of themselves are unrealistically positive. Just ask any three- or four-year-old about his or her ability to do something he or she has never tried before, for instance, climb a rock wall, hula-hoop, or ride a bike or scooter, you will gain firsthand knowledge about his or her elevated sense of self-worth. Children at this age tend to think they will be great at everything they do and that they can beat anyone at anything (e.g., a running race, a board game, arm wrestling).

Self-esteem gradually declines over the course of childhood most likely due to advances in cognitive thinking as well as social interactions with others. As children develop cognitively, they begin to compare themselves to others and start to base their evaluations on the feedback given to them by those they encounter (e.g., parents, peers, teachers). When they make social comparisons to others, they begin to realize others may be better at certain activities than they are (e.g., playing a sport or solving math problems). In addition, the feedback they receive from others may not always be positive. For example, in school, a child may earn a poor grade on a test. As children enter adolescence, their self-esteem continues to decline, especially for females. This is attributed to the onset of puberty and the physical and psychological changes experienced because of it.

Self-esteem gradually increases throughout adulthood peaking around the late 60s but then begins to decline again in old age. Some studies suggest that self-esteem begins to decline around age 70. This drop in self-esteem may be due to a decline in physical health as well as changes in older adults' social roles (e.g., retirement) and social relationships (e.g., loss of a spouse). As mentioned earlier, social relations often lead to the development of resilience, coping skills, and higher self-esteem. When these essential social connections do not exist, it is much easier for isolation to form, which can lead to loneliness. Registered dietitian and certified lifestyle eating and performance therapist Elizabeth Ann Shaw, in an e-mail exchange to *Bustle* magazine, commented that she has seen this through her work with clients "who were continuously isolated day in and day out . . . [they] developed a poor body image and self-esteem over time." Thus, it is important for older adults to stay both physically and socially active.

Social experiences are crucial to a person's mental health. According to the American Psychiatric Association, depression is a common and serious medical illness that negatively affects how a person feels, the way a person thinks, and how a person acts. Depression causes feelings of sadness and/or a loss of interest in activities the person once enjoyed. It can lead to a variety of emotional and physical problems and can decrease a person's ability to function at work and at home. According to an article written by certified health coach Isadora Baum about the negative effects of lack of socializing, isolation and lack of socialization are commonly linked to depression, especially for people who do not socialize for multiple days in a row. A person does not need to engage in scheduled activities every day; however, it is beneficial to go to a fitness class, call a family member or friend, or talk to colleagues on a regular basis. In addition, in an interview with the *Huffington Post*, Emily Moyer-Gusé, an assistant professor of communication at Ohio State University in Columbus, commented, "If a person stays in too often to binge watch TV shows, games, or movies, and they come to an end, it can produce depression due to the perceived loss of reality." For example, in 2009, some *Avatar* fans reported feeling depressed and even suicidal because the movie's fictional world was not real. There was a similar reaction to the final installments of the Harry Potter movies. "People experience distress when they're watching primarily for companionship." With *Avatar*, Moyer-Gusé thinks people were "swept up in a narrative forgetting about real life and [their] own problems."

How about social networking sites? How much time do you spend on them? A number of studies now suggest that spending too much time on social networking sites can be associated with depression, particularly for teens and preteens. Internet devotees may struggle with real-life human interaction and a lack of companionship, and they may develop an unrealistic view of the world. Deciphering between fantasy and reality is important, and alienating yourself to watch media or spend time on social networking sites too often can interfere with your brain's ability to function properly. Social neuroscientist John Cacioppo at the University of Chicago found through his research that people who are lonely are less empathetic than happier, socializing people, when shown images of pleasant and unpleasant scenarios. This loneliness can cause changes in the brain decreasing a person's ability to learn as well as to empathize with others. By not interacting with people, you are changing your brain's neurological pathways, and as a result, you may have a harder time processing your feelings, which may hinder your ability to love as well as other people, who socialize with others on a regular basis. Think about how much time you spend at home watching some type of media or on social networking sites. If you notice any of these aforementioned conditions from staying home too often, try to get out more and make plans with your friends, family, or coworkers. Being around people and having close social connections does a world of good for your overall psychological health. Therefore, try and find a better balance between nights you spent by yourself and nights spent with others—you might just find that you are happier and healthier.

Several research studies have shown that one sure way of improving your mood is to work on building your social connections. Socializing will allow you to enjoy better mental health. Interacting with others boosts feelings of well-being and decreases feelings of depression. Many scientists believe that social interaction is necessary for maintaining good mental health and may even help prevent or delay certain mental disorders, including dementia and Alzheimer's. For example, studies show that older women who have large social networks are at less risk of developing dementia and cognitive impairment than women who do not have large social networks. The topic of socialization and Alzheimer's disease will be further discussed in the next section.

HOW YOUR BRAIN RESPONDS TO SOCIALIZING

A study conducted by researchers Karen Ertel, Maria Glymour, and Lisa Berkman, published in the *American Journal of Public Health*, suggests that strong social ties, through friends, family, and community groups, can preserve our brain health as we age. These researchers used data gathered from the Health and Retirement Study, a large, nationally representative population of over 16,000 American adults ages 50 and older who were followed prospectively for six years. They examined whether social integration (i.e., how well incorporated people are to and within their social group) predicted memory change. The researchers measured social integration based on marital status, volunteer activities, and frequency of contact with children, parents, and neighbors. Participants took memory tests at two-year intervals during the course of the six years. Researchers read a list of 10 common nouns to survey respondents, who were then asked to recall as many words as possible immediately and again after a five-minute delay. It was found that individuals in their 50s and 60s who had high levels of social integration also had the slowest rate of memory decline. In fact, compared to those who were the least socially active, participants who had the highest social integration scores had less than half the rate of memory loss. The researchers controlled for variables like age, gender, race, and health status. Those who had the fewest years of formal education appeared to have the most to gain from an active social life as they aged. The study also revealed that the protective effect of social integration was greatest among individuals with fewer than 12 years of formal education. Being in the highest level of social integration contributed to more than half of the age-related decline in memory. Social engagement is what makes a person mentally engaged.

Furthermore, in the *New York Times Well Blog* by Tara Parker-Pope, Berkman says, "You can't sit and withdraw if you're constantly talking and working on things and figuring out problems in your daily life. It's not just completing a crossword puzzle, it's living your life." The data from this study are particularly important for those caring for aging family members. Simply visiting and giving support to an older family member does not make him or her socially engaged. "A lot of people when they think about the elderly focus on social support—things like what can I do for an older mother," Berkman said. "But having someone to count on is not what we're measuring. It's not about support, it's about being completely engaged and participating in our society." Overall, the results from this study suggest that increasing social integration may be an important component of efforts to protect older Americans from memory decline.

Some people long for alone time, but more often than most people would like to admit, they get lonely. According to John Cacioppo, at any given moment, 20 percent of all people are unhappy because of social isolation. As mentioned earlier, he has studied the minds of the socially isolated, and he and his research team have found that the brains of lonely people react differently than those with strong social networks. Cacioppo and his team of researchers showed lonely and nonlonely people photographs of individuals in both pleasant and unpleasant settings. When viewing the pleasant pictures, nonlonely people showed much more activity in a section of the brain known as the ventral striatum than the lonely people. The ventral striatum plays an important role in learning. According to the website Neuroscientifically Challenged, the striatum (Latin for striped) is one of the principal components of the basal ganglia, a group of nuclei that have a variety of functions but are best known for their role in facilitating voluntary movement. The striatum is sometimes conceptualized as being divided into dorsal and ventral sections. The ventral striatum contains the nucleus accumbens, a nucleus that has been extensively studied for its role in rewarding experiences. The nucleus accumbens along with the ventral striatum as a whole is associated with reward, reinforcement, and the progression from just experiencing something rewarding to compulsively seeking it out as part of an addiction. Thus, the ventral striatum is activated when we do, or even just anticipate doing something we know will be pleasurable. The lonely people displayed far less activity in this region while viewing pleasant pictures, and they also had less brain activity when shown the unpleasant pictures. When non-lonely people viewed the unpleasant pictures, they demonstrated activity in the temporoparietal junction, an area of the brain associated with empathy; the nonlonely people had a lesser response. So what does all of this mean?

HowStuffWorks contributor Molly Edmonds writes that what is still unclear is whether loneliness rewires the brain to function differently, or whether the brain predisposes certain people to feel isolated. Is loneliness a result of not being able to see the rewards right in front of you? Edmonds goes on to say that while researchers try to answer such questions, Cacioppo's study and others similar to it offer some mental health implications. In 2008, a team of researchers at the University of Michigan evaluated the relationship between social isolation and mental functioning. They conducted a study that measured memory and intellectual performance in groups that had just spent 10 minutes socializing as well as groups that spent 10 minutes reading and completing crossword puzzles. They found that groups that spent their time interacting with others performed just as well as groups that were engaged in cognitive tasks (e.g., reading or completing crossword puzzles). Since we know through Cacioppo's research that the ventral striatum is associated with learning, this may help to explain this finding. Therefore, if you are looking for ways to keep your brain sharp, think about hanging out with a friend.

As mentioned earlier in this chapter, connecting with friends may improve the health of your brain as well as lower your risk of developing dementia. According to the Alzheimer's Association, dementia is not a specific disease. It is a general term that describes a wide range of symptoms associated with a decline in memory or other thinking skills severe enough to reduce a person's ability to perform everyday activities. It is caused by physical changes in the brain. The most common type of dementia is Alzheimer's disease. The disease accounts for 60–80 percent of dementia cases. Alzheimer's disease causes problems with memory, thinking, and behavior. Symptoms usually develop slowly and get worse over time, becoming severe enough to interfere with daily tasks.

Several studies conducted by Laura Fratiglioni, the director of the Aging Research Center (ARC), and her colleagues have found that engaging in mental and social activities with others is associated with lower rates of dementia. This suggests that both intellectual stimulation and social interaction may be important to maintaining mental functioning as we age. In other words, people with active social lives are less likely to experience a decline in their mental abilities than those who are not as socially active or, at the extreme, socially isolated from others. From time to time, everyone needs some time by themselves, and some people tend to be more shy or introverted than others; however, too much time by oneself can be harmful.

In an interview with the Population Reference Bureau, researchers explain that it is our social connections to others that help to manage and even buffer stress hormones like cortisol and epinephrine that when experienced chronically can cause physiological reactions, including decreased immune system, cardiovascular and metabolic functioning and increased heart rate, inflammation, and blood pressure that are harmful to our health. In this way, connectedness is important for us all and of utmost importance for those of us who experience chronic stress in our daily lives, such as that caused by poverty, racism, and violence in general. Even when these stressors are present, friends, families, and others who offer strength, understanding, and other resources can mitigate these social, mental, and biological harms.

THE EFFECTS OF SOCIALIZING ON LIFE EXPECTANCY

Want to live longer? The answer is likely yes. Do you know how? The answer to that is also likely yes. If asked to detail what living a longer life would take, the answer would be something along the lines of these well-known keys to longevity: establish a healthy sleep routine; get some form of exercise most days of the week; eat a well-balanced, nutritious diet filled with lean proteins, leafy greens, and plenty of fruits; do not smoke; avoid excessive drinking; wear a seatbelt every time you are in a car; and make lots of friends. Yes, though good friends may indeed be hard to find, having them or at least people to spend time with is known to have a positive correlation to life expectancy. Social isolation, no matter one's age, gender, or diet and exercise patterns, increases one's likelihood of disease and death in ways that are independent of these factors. One 2015 study conducted by researchers from Brigham Young University found that people reported as living alone, lonely, or isolated saw a 6 percent increase in their risk of premature death.

In 2009, National Geographic fellow and *New York Times* bestselling author Dan Buettner gave a TED talk about how to live to be 100 years old. In his talk, he discussed Blue Zones, which are places in the world where people live longer and healthier than anywhere else. The approach taken to find factors that contribute to longevity was to team up with National Geographic and the National Institute on Aging (NIA) to find the demographic areas where people live the longest and then bring in a team of experts to study the people in those geographic locations. The four places in the world where people live longer than anywhere else are Sardinia, Italy; Okinawa, Japan; Loma Linda, California; and Nicoya Peninsula, Costa Rica.

They found some common elements that contribute to longevity in each of these four locations. People in these places have the right outlook on life. For example, they take time to slow down and pray and wake up each day with a purpose. They do not exercise in the way we typically define it; however, they move naturally all day long. For instance, in Okinawa women get up and down off the floor multiple times a day. They also tend not to rely on or use modern conveniences, rather they do things by hand (e.g., yardwork, cooking). Instead of using an electric hand mixer, they use a manual one (i.e., their arm). All of these constant physical movements burn calories. People in these places also eat wisely. They drink a small amount of wine each day; they eat a plant-based diet and have strategies for not overeating (e.g., use small plates or stop eating when their stomach is 80% full). However, the biggest contributor to longevity in these places is their social interaction. They put their loved ones first by taking care of their children and aging parents. They belong to a faith-based community, which research shows can add 4–14 years to your life expectancy if you take part in it at least four times a month. They also surround themselves with the right people. Think about it: if your friends are active, you will be too; if they are not, you won't be either.

In Sardinia, Italy, there are 10 times more centenarians (i.e., people who are 100 or more years old) than we have in the United States. At this age, these individuals still ride their bikes to work, chop wood, and engage in a variety of other physical activities. However, according to Buettner, the secret to their longevity is in the way they organize their society. They value older people and treat them with respect. The older you get, the more celebrated you are. This is beneficial for both the older adults as well as the children. As an older adult, being around your children and grandchildren typically adds about four to six years to your life expectancy. For the grandchildren, being around their elderly grandparents is associated with lower rates of mortality and disease. They call this the "grandmother effect."

Buettner goes on to say that Okinawa has the oldest living female population. It is a place where people have the longest disability-free life expectancy in the world. They tend to live on average seven good years longer than the average person in the United States. There are also five times as many centenarians in Okinawa as compared to the United States. They have significantly lower rates of breast and colon cancer as well as cardiovascular disease. Why? What is happening in this part of the world contributing to all of these differences? They engage in many of the key elements mentioned earlier. For example, they eat a plant-based diet; they eat about eight times as much tofu as Americans do. They have a variety of strategies to keep them from overeating. For instance, they eat their food off smaller plates and eat fewer calories at each meal. However, like Sardinia, Okinawa has a few social customs associated with longevity. In the 1990s, the average American had three good friends; nowadays we only have one and a half good friends. The Okinawa social system called *Moai* is structured in such a way that when you are born, you automatically have about six friends with whom you travel through life with. If you are in a *Moai*, you always have someone who is there for you in good times and bad. Buettner gave an example of a *Moai* that consisted of five females who were together for 97 years; their average age was 102. When it comes to longevity, there is no short-term fix, no pill to take or drink to consume; rather the most vital thing you can do to add more years to your life is to have friends.

As the U.S. population of those over 55 increases, there is growing attention to their needs. There are planned communities with housing open to only those in this age group, for example. At some residential communities for those 55 and older, there are efforts underway to ensure that they have plenty of opportunities to socialize with others in ways both familiar and new. This is especially important as many in this age group are moving from established communities and social groups into new places and around new people as they relocate and retire. These planned communities offer lots of social gatherings and encourage the development of new hobbies for their residents. Why? In part, because they know that there are sustained links between socializing and positive outcomes along a number of measures. As mentioned earlier in this chapter, not only is socializing shown to lower stress, lower blood pressure, lower inflammation, increase cognitive functioning, strengthen the immune system, and lead to greater happiness, but it also adds years to our lives.

Socializing, whether with family, friends, acquaintances, neighbors, members of your mosque, the people in your yoga class, or fellow volunteers, leads to longer life spans, regardless of the activities in which you find yourself engaged. Research from a 2016 study published in the Proceedings of the National Academy of Sciences revealed that socializing at an early age can have lifelong impacts of health and life expectancy. Being a part of a community, having friends, and hanging out as a teen can have as much consequence for how long one lives as how much one exercises, according to the conclusions the study authors draw. Indeed, there was a positive relationship between number of social ties and health along the life course. In other words, those with more connections to others when they were young were more likely to be in better health as they aged. Recall from the beginning of this chapter: data from four separate longitudinal studies revealed that those who had more friends and opportunities to socialize when they were adolescents, in old age they had lower rates of high blood pressure, inflammation, and obesity and lower risks of cancer and heart disease as well as lower rates of death. Interestingly, the research team found that during middle age, it was the quality of relationship rather than the quantity of social ties that was more important. For all of us, no matter our ages, social relationships with others are all linked to better qualities of life, longer life expectancies, as well as lower death rates. This is not only a social and psychological story but a biological one as well. Still, it is important to explore other consequences that flow from our socializing with others.

THE DARK SIDE OF SOCIALIZING

As noted previously in this chapter and earlier in this book, there is an abundant body of research on the importance of socializing for fun as well as obtaining information and resources for getting ahead. However, there can also be a cost—a dark side—to socializing. While connectedness is important, it can also be a double-edged sword. There are also negative aspects of socializing that merit discussion. While the people we know and spend time with may certainly give us support, meet our material and financial needs, and show us a good time, they can also cause distress, plunge us into crises, and bring with them other negativity. Indeed, socializing has both its benefits and its costs. This, however, has largely been ignored as there is a definitive emphasis on the positive sides of social relationships. When there is a discussion of the costs, it is often on the disadvantages of having the "wrong kind of people" around or on having too limited a social network or a network that contains too little of the most valuable forms of social capital.

When one in deeply embedded in a relationship with someone else, there can be material prices one bears. A man may spend more than she can afford on an engagement ring for her fiancée. A sister may put herself into debt to ensure that her brother does not lose his house when he can no longer pay his mortgage after losing his job. An adult son may use some of his retirement savings to ensure that his father can live in a decent assisted-living facility. Additionally, there is an emotional price to this, which can produce greater vulnerability and greater chances of being hurt emotionally, stressed out, angry, and depressed when those one is close to suffer or cause suffering. This may lead to "negative interactions," the term used when a negative aspect of socializing arises.

These negative interactions have damaging impacts on multiple measures of well-being, cause additional stress, and include social exchanges full of tension, demands, and criticism. These kinds of interactions are further associated with a number of psychological costs. Negative interactions might lead a person to have lowered expectations that they could handle difficult situations and to greater difficulty in coping abilities, which then would lead to a number of other corresponding negative outcomes. Where and how do negative interactions occur? They could develop or worsen when there is jealousy and envy at one person's good fortune. They could also happen or become exacerbated if one is repeatedly asked for financial assistance from the same person. They could also start or deepen when expectations of reciprocity are unmet, such as when a person one has helped in the past fails to help that person when he or she is in need. Any social network and any social relationship have the potential —and often manifest—for both coexisting supportive and negative relationships. Research shows that when there is the presence of negative interactions, they are given more weight than positive ones. This is what is behind this oft-heard phrase within romantic or child-parent relationships: "All you ever focus on is the negative." Indeed, we often recall those interactions where we did not feel heard, validated, loved, or important, while we simultaneously fail to remember the times when we did feel these ways. It becomes easier to downplay the prevalence and importance of our positive interactions and to overemphasize the negative ones. These factors can diminish our perceptions of how much and how valuable the actual support we receive is. This in turn can be painful for our interaction partners, leading to a further negative spiral.

Another way that negative interactions work can be found when one determines that the cost of maintaining a relationship is too high to pay.

Being in relationships and having social interactions rely on exchange, reciprocity, and often sacrifice, whether of time, energy, emotional bonds, money, or all of these. These are the costs of doing (relational) business. Just as a shopper or an entrepreneur may decide that he or she is willing to walk away when he or she feels that a price is not fair, the same is true within socializing relationships. Indeed, sometimes the costs are too high for one to justify maintaining his or her relationships. In this case, the person decides it is better that he or she terminates his or her relationship, perhaps with extended family members, a study partner, a date, or in other cases, a boyfriend, wife, sibling, or parent. When there is negative interaction within a relationship, even when relationships continue, those who are on the receiving end of support might have feelings of guilt and pressure to reciprocate and those on the providing end might have feelings of being exploited or financial strain. There can be real costs associated with this as the giving of financial and other material forms of aid might compromise a person who offers this chances for social mobility and economic independence, making it impossible to disengage from the exchange system, as research by people like anthropologist Carol Stack and sociologists Silvia Dominguez and Celeste Watkins shows. When one is deeply embedded into a social network, he or she is expected to help those who need it. While this assuredly is beneficial for the recipient of assistance, the provider will suffer in any attempts to amass greater financial security and upward mobility. Dense social networks, where there are layers of connections, deep senses of obligation, high expectations for provision of support, and certain admonition and scorn when this does not happen, can become fraught with tension if individual people participated in activities or with others that draw their attention and resources away from the network. In these cases, when members' expectations about responsibilities, obligations, and availability come into conflict with an individual's upwardly mobile behaviors such as attending school, moving to a different locale, or seeking other employment, negative interaction and often unspoken dimensions of social relationships arise.

Another dark side of socializing is found through whom one does not socialize with. The same processes that bond some people exclude others. Social scientists warn of the dangers of social closure—the ways that social groups keep resources and opportunities for themselves by closing off acceptance and access by keeping others out. This diminishes opportunities for upward social mobility, information sharing, and inclusion for those on the outside of the favored group. In places like the United States, social closure has been seen as limiting possibilities and full access for people of color, women, those from the lower ends of the socioeconomic ladder, LGBTQ people, religious minorities, and members of other marginalized communities while benefiting those who enjoy the social advantages of the privileged. Social closure is also associated with social isolation, a concept introduced in the first chapter and discussed at length in the following section.

THE IMPACTS OF SOCIAL ISOLATION

An article in the April 2017 issue of the magazine the *Atlantic* cites data from studies that claim between one quarter and one half of respondents report feelings of loneliness. Even at low end, longitudinal studies of adults in the United States show that when we look across time, loneliness has increased up to 7 percent over the past two decades. In a 2016 TEDMED blog post, U.S. Surgeon General Dr. Vivek Murthy declared that Americans are currently undergoing what he called "an epidemic of loneliness and social isolation." When we refer to social isolation, we are not just talking about being a loner at school or the office. Social isolation is also not about those who are shy, prefer their own company, or need some downtime to recharge their battery at the end of the day. Social isolation is when one is cut off from others, or disintegrated, in several common arenas of life. A person who is socially isolated does not have meaningful or sustained interactions with family, friends, neighbors, schoolmates, colleagues, or others. As with all epidemics, there are widespread social roots of this condition. According to Dr. Murthy, these roots expand beyond an individual's circumstance and spread into other factors like poverty, access to health care, and exposure to violence. There is a strong relationship between where one lives, whom one is connected, and how one feels physically, mentally, and emotionally. Because of these relationships, they cannot be looked at in, well, isolation. Dr. Murthy points to the creation of community in promoting increased social connectedness in the midst of violence and poverty. In areas where this has happened, there have been some promising results, including improved school performance and decreased school suspensions for children and increased commitment of teachers as well as lower rates of anxiety and sleep disturbances. The health impacts of social isolation are serious indeed—it is more deadly than obesity, diabetes, and a lack of exercise and is at least as deadly as smoking.

A prescription for social connectedness might well be in order as an antidote, leading to reduced risks of obesity, stroke, diabetes, heart attack, and high blood pressure and increased resiliency and life expectancy. Dr. Murthy also noted that social isolation—and its opposite, social connectedness—is not just experienced on an individual level, but its impacts can ripple across generations. Those who are socially isolated are more likely to have children who engage in crime and drug use. Likewise, those who have higher rates of connection with others have children who demonstrate lower rates of involvement with crime and drugs. This is due to the negative relationship of social isolation with emotional well-being. In other words, the more disconnected you are from others, the less emotional well-being you will experience.

Even as the ability to keep in touch and stay abreast of what is going on with others has increased due to social media platforms like Twitter, Instagram, and Facebook, connectedness has not necessarily been abated. As a matter of fact, there is some evidence that checking in on the lives of others decreases our own happiness and makes us envious and feel less close to those whose lives we are seeing from the outside. Some scholars, such as John Cacioppo, a University of Chicago psychologist, contend that it is how one uses Facebook and other social media platforms rather than their use alone that is associated with feelings of (dis)connectedness. If social media are used to facilitate face-to-face gatherings, users report fewer feelings of loneliness. If, however, social media are used as a substitute for face-to-face gatherings, users retreat even more and subsequently but perhaps not surprisingly report more feelings of loneliness. Dr. Cacioppo furthers explains that for those struggling with connection and relationships, these virtual interactions might lead to the creation of a nonauthentic self, which amplifies loneliness, social disintegration, and social isolation.

A 2017 study from a group of researchers based out of the University of Pittsburgh indicates that the more participants used social media, the more they saw themselves as disconnected from others. This study of nearly 2,000 people between 19 and 32 years old asked research participants to indicate how much they agreed with statements like "I feel that people barely know me" or "I feel that people are around me but not with me," and those with the highest uses of platforms like Facebook, Twitter, Instagram, and Reddit perceived themselves to be more socially isolated than those who reported lower usage rates of such social media platforms. In this study, the researchers note that just feeling like one is socially isolated, whether this is matched by one's actual reality, can lead to the negative impacts of isolation like higher weight, a compromised immune system, and poorer sleep. As this study focused on younger people assumed to be the major beneficiaries of social media use, the findings came as a real surprise to the research team. As one of the researchers, Brian Primack, the director of the Center for Research on Media, Technology and Health at the University of Pittsburgh, told National Public Radio, the findings were counterintuitive as the team had presumed that since they were looking at social media, people would be connected. Their findings, however, belied these expectations. Instead, their research suggested that those who spent more than two hours a day on social media reported that they felt socially isolated more than two times as much as those who spent a half hour or less a day on those social media. Feelings of social isolation also increased as visits to social media platforms increased: those with 58 visits or more per week experienced more than three times as much perceived social isolation than those who visited fewer than nine times per week. While it is unclear, according to Dr. Primack and his team, whether people who are socially isolated are more likely to use social media to escape their feelings of loneliness or if those who spend much of their time on social media are neglecting those in their day-to-day life and feeling increasingly lonely as a result, there is a correlation between social media usage and isolation. In 2017, another nationally representative study of over 5,200 participants looked at correlations between well-being and Facebook use and had similar findings. In this study, researchers discovered that the more one used Facebook, the less positive association there was with physical health, mental health, and life satisfaction. The findings were reversed for offline, face-to-face interactions.

According to Dr. Primack, this study and its results should not be seen as indicative of the influence of social media on all age groups. He reminds us that since this research was on a specific age group, it should not be generalized to those older or younger than this particular group since both social media usage and social isolation look different as we look at younger people and older adults. While those between 19 and 32 years old might use social media as an escape from the varied types of face-to-face interactions they have offline, older people with fewer opportunities to spend time with others in real life could engage with social media in order to foster deeper connectedness. There is also a gendered connection with age when it comes to social isolation. As they age, men are at particular risk for social isolation and its social, physical, emotional, and mental ills. For example, Rutgers University sociologist Julie Phillips has called attention to the risks of social isolation for middle-class men in the United States. She has noticed an increase in men's suicide rates starting in the late 1990s. Since then, for men between 50 and 54 years old, suicide rates have increased by nearly 50 percent. As it currently stands, middle-aged men are more likely to commit suicide than those from older generations. This trend is particularly pronounced for those middle-aged men who were less educated, though suicide rates for college-educated middle-class men are also on the rise. Dr. Phillips attributes these changes, at least in part, to the increased social isolation of men. As an explanation, she offers that a decline in face-to-face interactions, a growing tendency to live alone, an increase in spending leisure time at home rather than at public spaces such as theaters, bars, or sporting arenas, and the spread of social media are contributing factors in social isolation that hit men particularly hard. As this generation ages, Dr. Phillips anticipates that their suicide rates will continue to increase, just as she anticipates the same trend for younger cohorts of men as they enter middle and then old age.

A March 2017 story in the *Boston Herald* also noted this difficulty for middle-aged men in particular. The reporter, Billy Baker, using personal anecdotes and social science research highlighted the difficulty that men in midlife have in maintaining and creating social relationships. He discussed the hard time they have in establishing and holding on to deep and meaningful social relationships with others as they balance work, household responsibilities, intimate relationships (and their dissolution), and children's activities, all while yearning for these interactions. As we know, social isolation is amplified when one wants social connectedness that he or she fails to obtain. No matter age, race, class, or gender, it may be that feelings of isolation are more important than how many actual social ties one possesses. For middle-aged men, they may meet others they want to hang out with, but the desire rarely gets out of that initial stage, and when it does, it is rare that they get together and hang out more than once and rarer still that this is converted into a meaningful relationship that can stave off the feelings of isolation and the harms that accompany these. Increasing suburbanization over the last half century or so may exacerbate this.

With their lower concentration of people, dependency of private automobiles, and distance between residences, there is also concern that suburban life leads to social isolation. When we live in suburbs that are increasingly distant from urban centers, we tend to spend more time alone in our cars. Indeed, the average full-time American worker is now commuting an average of 50 minutes each day, according to a 2015 report by the Office of the New York City Comptroller. This is an increase of almost 30 minutes since 1990. Other societal changes have led to increasing lacks of social connectedness.

In their book *The Lonely American*, psychiatrists Jacqueline Olds and Richard Schwartz determine that a growing sense of individualism that centers choice at the expense of satisfaction and changing economic conditions and cultural expectations that necessitate our always being busy, at work, at home, and at play leads to a diminishing capacity to cultivate and nourish friendships and other personal relationships that ward against disconnection. They also tell us that as kids lead increasingly complicated and busy lives, their parents' friendships with other adults may pay a price and cite the rise of new and emerging technologies that change the way that we communicate as altering the ways that we connect—and offering more room for isolation as we have more interaction but perhaps less intimacy. Dr. Olds and Dr. Schwartz offer a cautionary tale of a couple who seek relief from the strains of their work life and social pressures from friends and acquaintances so they move to their version of paradise in a more rural setting. Once there, they find it difficult to form relationships in their new home, and they find that they are largely divested of their old social relationships. Dr. Olds and Dr. Schwartz further note that there is a real stigma around admitting one is lonely or isolated, more so than acknowledging mental health issues like depression. In a 2017 *Boston Herald* interview, Dr. Schwartz said that "admitting you're lonely feels very much like admitting you're a loser. Psychiatry has worked hard to destigmatize things like depression, and to a large part it has been successful. People are comfortable saying they're depressed. But they're not comfortable saying they're lonely, because you're the kid sitting alone in the cafeteria." The stigma is not just from outsiders but is internal, making it hard to admit to oneself as well as others that one is lonely or seeks the companionship, care, and comfort of another.

Once one is isolated, it is easy to become trapped in this—socially isolated people become more fearful and more unlikely to approach others. They also become more unapproachable by others—seeing others as a social threat and being seen by others as the same. This does not mean that all hope of spending enjoyable time with others should be abandoned, however. Psychologist John Cacioppo offers an acronym—EASE—to, well, ease the process of establishing social relationships and avoiding social isolation. Designed for those who express feelings of loneliness, Dr. Cacioppo suggests that one step is to be proactive in shaping a personal community through activities like community involvement, joining an athletic club, or volunteering. Then implement an EASE plan, where E means "extend yourself," A means "have an action plan," S means "seek collectives," and the last E means "expect the best." Practicing EASE might look like attending a meeting for doll collectors where one makes it a point to introduce himself or herself to at least three other attendees (this is extending yourself); map out strategies to get to know others there and to accept when one's efforts are rebuffed (this is your action plan); if you collect African American rag dolls, focus on others who do the same (this is how you seek collectives); and employ a positive attitude about it all (this is expecting the best).

As this chapter illustrates, positive social connections with others increase our longevity, while negative and a lack of social connections decrease our longevity. Even though everyone needs some time by themselves and some people tend to be more outgoing than others, too much time by oneself can be harmful. The next chapter discusses various theoretical perspectives about socializing.

4

Who: Psychologists' Theories about Socializing

A theory is a set of ideas used to explain something. Theories are important because they help us organize information, understand things, and predict behavior. We know that individuals develop socially. But we may want to know how do social relationships develop? What factors drive social development? Theories help us answer these questions. From various psychological theories, we know that culture, biology, and cognition are some of the factors that influence the development of social relationships and drive social development. For example, Charles Darwin developed a theory of biological evolution called Darwinism—one in which all species develop through a process called natural selection. Species that adapt to their environment survive and reproduce; ones that do not, eventually die off and become extinct. Applying Darwinism to socialization, humans have innate or inborn drives to develop social relationships, and certain relationships will promote survival while others will not. This chapter focuses on how specific theories help us understand socialization.

LEV VYGOTSKY'S SOCIOCULTURAL THEORY

Sociocultural Theory seeks to explain human development in terms of the guidance, support, and structure provided by culture and society. Rather than viewing a person as separate, sociocultural theorists focus on the interaction between developing persons and their surrounding social and cultural contexts.

Russian psychologist Lev Vygotsky, a major proponent of the sociocultural perspective, believed that the interaction between a child and his or her social and cultural contexts influences development. His ideas are influential, because he was one of the first theorists to emphasize the role of culture in development. According to this sociocultural perspective, children are products of their culture, and therefore, development is inseparable from social and cultural contexts. Development occurs not alone but in the presence of others—so much so that Vygotsky felt social learning precedes development. According to Vygotsky, every function in a child's cultural development appears twice: first, on the social level and then second, on the individual level, meaning, development happens first outside the individual in his or her interactions with others and then inside the individual. More specifically, people acquire knowledge and new ways of thinking through social interactions with others, in particular, with more mature or skilled members of society (e.g., parents, teachers). Vygotsky called this apprenticeship in thinking. The basis of this apprenticeship is guided participation (i.e., when a skilled tutor or mentor engages the learner in a joint activity). According to Vygotsky, for learning to occur, the mentor draws the child into the zone of proximal development. The mentor should avoid what the child already knows (otherwise the child will be bored) and what the child is not ready or able to learn (otherwise the child will fail). Learning happens best and quickest in a "zone" in which the task is just beyond the child's grasp but not so difficult that the child is overwhelmed. Once the child is capable of completing the task on his or her own, assistance from the mentor is removed. Like other theorists (e.g., Jean Piaget), Vygotsky believed children actively seek knowledge; however, unlike many of his predecessors, he did not view children as solitary agents (i.e., trying to understand the world on their own). Instead, Vygotsky believed children learn best when they are paired with a more skilled partner and that the child and his or her partner work together to solve a problem. In other words, the social interactions children have with more mature members of society profoundly affect their development. These rich social and cultural contexts are the key to a person's development.

PRIMARY SOCIALIZATION THEORY

Primary Socialization Theory (PST) emphasizes that our social behaviors are learned through interactions with primary socialization sources.

Primary socialization sources change throughout the life span. For example, in many cultures, during early childhood, the only primary socialization source is the family. However, as children get older and enter adolescence, besides the family, primary socialization sources include school and peers. After adolescence, primary socialization tends to become more complex with young adults becoming married and forming a new family and/or developing new associations through work. Sources of primary socialization at each developmental stage are determined by culture. For example, during early childhood in most Western cultures, family is the only primary socialization source, the biological parents in particular; however, in another culture, adults other than the parent may share this role. Individuals interact with and learn from these primary socialization sources as well as other secondary socialization sources (e.g., the media, religious institutions). Primary socialization sources influence people to engage in either positive or negative behaviors. For instance, in adolescence, the primary socialization source of family typically serves as a basis for learning positive behaviors. In contrast, peers can serve as a source for learning either positive or negative behaviors.

According to researchers Eugene Oetting and Fred Beauvais during adolescence, the learning of social behaviors frequently happens through interactions with peer clusters (i.e., small groups of friends or couples). The strength of the bond between the adolescent and the primary socialization source plays a role in determining how effectively the behaviors are transmitted. A socialization source can influence any type of behavior, but typically the family and school sources are more likely to convey prosocial or positive behaviors. Peer clusters can transmit either prosocial or antisocial or negative behaviors, but the major source of antisocial behaviors is usually peer clusters. In addition, if the adolescent does not have a strong or close family relationship, this can increase the likelihood that he or she will get involved with a deviant peer cluster and may engage in antisocial behaviors.

DYNAMIC SYSTEMS

Human development is an ongoing, ever-changing interaction between the physical, cognitive, and psychosocial influences. Development is never static but is always affected by, and affects, many systems. Every aspect of development is connected to every other, and the result might change at any moment. A dynamic systems approach highlights the ever-changing impact that each part of a system has on all the other parts. One such system is Urie Bronfenbrenner's Bioecological Systems Theory. Bronfenbrenner, who taught at Cornell University for over 50 years, was well known for his cross-cultural studies on families and their support systems and on human development. Throughout much of his career, Bronfenbrenner was interested in the social forces that "make human beings human." According to Bronfenbrenner, each person is affected by many social contexts and interpersonal interactions. Individuals grow and develop within a set of influences: microsystems, exosystems, macrosystems, mesosystems, and chronosystems. Microsystems are made up of a person's immediate surroundings, such as family, friends, and the peer group. Surrounding and supporting the microsystems are the exosystems. Exosystems are external networks that influence the microsystems. These are environments in which the person does not play an active role but still influence him or her. For example, what happens at parents' workplace may impact a child and his or her development. Even though the child is not directly involved with the parent's workplace, it does influence the child's environment (e.g., money for clothing, music concerts, sporting events, vacations). Influencing both systems is the macrosystem. The macrosystem is the larger social setting, including cultural values, economic policies, and political philosophies. Mesosystems consist of the connections among the other systems. Each person is affected by interactions among overlapping systems. For example, a parent may have had a long day at work and not been able to come home early enough to make/eat dinner with or even see the child before bed. Similarly, a child may have a bad day at school and it spills over when he or she gets home getting into a fight with a sibling. Chronosystem, literally, means "time system." This system that affects the other three systems emphasizes the importance of historical time. People born within the same historical period move through life together and tend to experience the same events, new technologies, and cultural changes at the same ages. This is called a cohort. A change in any one part of a system affects all the other systems over time. For example, machines that made farming more efficient beginning in the 18th century improved the nutrition of pregnant women and added height, health, and decades of life to the average adult. Overall, Bronfenbrenner believed that human development is impacted by social forces, in particular, family. For instance, most people would agree that we learn in school; however, what most people fail to see is that what happens in a family enables us to learn in school. One way we are socialized is in the home, and the socialization that occurs in the home in turn impacts other aspects of our lives—school being one of them.

ASSOCIATIVE LEARNING

Associative learning is understanding how two or more pieces of information are related. An example of associative learning is classical conditioning (i.e., learning that two stimuli or cues go together). For example, when most people go to a scary movie, they tend to experience anxiousness when they hear the music from that movie. Classical conditioning was discovered by Ivan Pavlov, a Russian physiologist who was researching dogs' digestive processes when he made an accidental finding. He noticed that when food was placed on the dog's tongue, the dog salivated as an innate reflex response to the food. In addition, Pavlov noticed that the dogs would also salivate before they tasted any food; they would salivate when they saw the trainer who usually fed them. Why did the dogs do this? The dogs learned to associate a certain cue or stimulus (e.g., footsteps of the trainer) with the presentation of food. For this to happen, the dogs must have learned over time to associate a neutral stimulus (the human trainer) with another stimulus (food) that produced a reflexive response (salivation). Over time, the dogs had become conditioned to respond to these stimuli in the same way they responded to food—by salivating. We often see these types of associations (i.e., conditioning) with our pets. For example, a cat might run to its food bowl when the can opener is being used in anticipation of being fed or a dog may run to the door when its leash is retrieved from the closet in anticipation of going for a walk. Over time, these animals become conditioned to respond to these stimuli (i.e., the can opener or the leash) in the same way they responded to being fed or going for a walk.

We see this type of associative learning in animals all of the time. What about humans? Can humans be classically conditioned? The answer is "yes." The principles of classical conditioning were first applied to humans by psychologist John Watson. He famously said, "Give me a dozen healthy infants, well-formed, and my own specified world to bring them up in and I'll guarantee to take any one at random and train him to become any type of specialist I might select—doctor, lawyer, artist, merchant-chief and, yes, even beggar-man and thief, regardless of his talents, penchants, tendencies, abilities, vocations and the race of his ancestors." Watson believed humans are solely shaped by their environment; all differences in people's behavior are due to the different experiences in which they learn.

Over the years, Watson studied the behaviors of hundreds of babies. According to Watson, humans arrive in this world with a blank slate, called "tabula rasa," and then almost everything is learned. Even things people think are innate, such as fear, can be learned. In order to illustrate that the environment individuals grow up in is more important to development than genetics, Watson conducted an experiment with a one-year-old boy referred to as "Little Albert." Watson classically conditioned "Little Albert" to fear a white rat. When "Little Albert" was first shown the white rat, he was not afraid of it; however, he was afraid of a loud clanging sound, which caused him to cry. Therefore, each time Watson showed "Little Albert" the white rat, he accompanied it with the loud clanging sound. After many pairings of the white rat with the loud clanging sound, "Little Albert" feared the white rat, even without the loud clanging sound. For this to happen, "Little Albert" must have learned over time to associate a neutral stimulus (the white rat) with another stimulus (loud clanging sound) that produced a reflexive response (fear, in the form of crying). Watson believed his experiment was successful because it showed that fears were learned, not inherited, thus supporting the notion that one's social environment matters most. What other associations do we learn from our social environment? A common example is conditioned nausea, meaning the sight or smell of a particular food causes nausea in a person because it had caused his or her stomach to be upset in the past. Some other instances are students who are bullied at school associating school or a particular school subject with fear or anxiety or children associating going to the doctor office with pain because of experiencing a shot in the past. Conditioning can even be seen in TV advertisements that use celebrities or attractive models to sell their products.

Classical conditioning has also been shown to be effective in a number of therapeutic treatments in humans. It has been used as a form of treatment in changing or modifying behaviors, such as substance abuse and smoking. Some therapies associated with classical conditioning include aversion therapy, systematic desensitization, and flooding. Aversion therapy is a type of behavior therapy designed to encourage individuals to give up undesirable behaviors by causing them to associate the behavior with an unpleasant effect. For example, for individuals who suffer from alcoholism, aversion therapy may involve the individual drinking while at the same time having a negative stimulus administered. Nausea is an unpleasant sensation that most humans prefer to avoid. Therefore, the negative stimulus could be an emetic drug (i.e., one that makes the person vomit when drinking alcohol). The idea is that the person would learn to associate drinking alcohol with an unpleasant experience like nausea or vomiting. Systematic desensitization is a treatment for phobias and other anxiety disorders in which the individual is trained to relax while being exposed to progressively more anxiety-provoking stimuli (e.g., an individual who has a fear of spiders would be first asked to think about a spider, then look at a photograph of a spider, then look at a real spider in a closed container, and then along with other behaviors building up to the last behavior, which might be having a real spider crawl on his or her skin). Flooding is a form of desensitization that uses repeated exposure to highly distressing stimuli until the lack of reinforcement of the anxiety response causes its disappearance. In other words, exposing a person to the thing he or she fears until he or she is no longer afraid of it. To apply this to the example of the fear of spiders mentioned previously, the person would repeatedly be exposed to the behavior associated with the highest fear response (e.g., having real spiders crawling on his or her skin) for a designated period of time until the fear response is minimized.

SOCIAL LEARNING THEORY/SOCIAL COGNITIVE THEORY

According to Social Learning Theory, people learn through observing the behavior of others. Psychologist Albert Bandura is a major proponent of this theory. In contrast to associative learning that was just discussed previously, Bandura believed that learning occurs by simply observing someone or receiving instructions without firsthand experience. Social Learning Theory emphasizes the ways in which people learn new behaviors by observing and imitating, or modeling, the behavior of other people they consider admirable, powerful, warm, and nurturing, or those who possess desirable characteristics and skills (e.g., people who are popular or intelligent). By behaving like these models, individuals hope to obtain those valued resources for themselves in the future. Modeling is most likely to occur when we are inexperienced or uncertain about a situation. Early in childhood, many aspects of behavior may be modeled from parents. Some of these behaviors may be positive and others negative. For example, a child may watch a parent allow a car to merge ahead of him or her in a construction zone or listen to a parent use curse words when a car tries to merge ahead of him or her. Social Learning Theory is concerned with how the individuals around us shape our tendency to perform or not to perform various behaviors. To illustrate this, in a now famous experiment conducted in the 1960s at Stanford University, Bandura had children watch a model engage in various behaviors with a Bobo doll. A Bobo doll is an inflatable toy that is weighted down at the bottom, and when hit or struck, it falls down and then comes back up to its standing position on its own. In the study, the children were placed in one of three groups: children who were in condition 1 watched a video of an adult playing aggressively with the Bobo doll by kicking it, hitting it with a mallet, getting on top of it and punching it, and flinging it in the air; children in condition 2 watched a video of an adult playing in a nonaggressive manner with a tinker toy set; and children in condition 3 were the control group, meaning they were not exposed to a video of an adult model. Then, each child was taken separately to a room with a variety of aggressive (the Bobo doll being one of them) and nonaggressive toys. Each child was in the room for about 20 minutes while his or her behavior was observed by researchers through a one-way mirror. It was found that children who watched the model act aggressively toward the Bobo doll were more likely to imitate aggressive behaviors than children in the nonaggressive or control conditions. What was surprising though was that children in the aggressive condition were also more attracted to and more likely to play with other aggressive toys such as guns even though they did not witness those toys being used by the adult in the video. In one instance, a girl who was in the aggressive condition used a doll as weapon; she proceeded to hit the Bobo doll repeatedly with the weapon doll. Bandura's research illustrates that children learn how to act through the process of observation learning, as a result of watching the behavior of another person. When children see adults behaving in a certain way, they believe that their actions are acceptable and therefore imitate them. Young children navigating their way in the world look to adults for guidance and support. Primary caregivers have the important role of teaching children how to regulate their emotions and behave accordingly. If the caregiver is aggressive, the child will learn that the only way to deal with frustration and anger is to act aggressively. Bandura's research has had widespread implications regarding the effects of social media. If celebrities are seen as role models, this could lead to dangerous behaviors being imitated (e.g., extreme diets or plastic surgery, excessive partying and drugs, violence). Since magazines, television, and other various social media outlets continually report negative content, this could impact the behavior of both children and adults. You may have heard the phrase, "Do as I say, not as I do"; however, it seems through Bandura's research that we as humans have a tendency to do as others do, not as they say. Therefore, in the television shows that illustrate individuals engaging in dangerous behaviors, the verbal warning "please do not try this at home" at the beginning of the shows is not much of a deterrent.

People can also be motivated to act like someone based on the consequences that person receives from his or her behavior (i.e., rewards or punishments); this is called vicarious reinforcement/vicarious punishment—in other words, learning the consequences of an action by watching others being rewarded or punished for performing that action. If a person is rewarded for behaving in a particular way, the observer is likely to imitate that behavior. However, if a person is punished for acting in a particular way, the observer is less likely to imitate that behavior. In follow-up study to the initial Bobo doll experiment, Bandura found that children were much more likely to imitate an adult if they saw the adult being rewarded for his or her behavior but were unlikely to imitate the behavior if the adult was punished for it. We often see vicarious reinforcement and punishment illustrated with siblings. If a younger sibling watches his or her older sister or brother get punished for a particular behavior (e.g., staying out too late), as a result, the younger sibling is less likely to make that same mistake.

Social learning is connected to perceptions and interpretations of experience, including self-efficacy (i.e., a notion that one's own effort will be successful). So much so that Bandura expanded his Social Learning Theory to include the role of cognition. This Social Cognitive Theory emphasizes that individuals can actively control the events that affect their lives, rather than having to passively accept whatever the environment provides; they partially control the environment by the way they react to it. Bandura argued that three factors influence how a person acts: (1) environment (e.g., resources, consequences, physical setting); 2) person factors, which include the individual's characteristics, beliefs, self-confidence, attitudes, and expectations; and 3) behavior itself (e.g., actions, verbal statements, choices). Bandura called it reciprocal determinism because it is explained by the interaction of all of these three factors.

THEORY OF PLANNED BEHAVIOR

Theory of Planned Behavior (TPB) is a social-cognitive theory that emphasizes the prediction of a person's intentions. It explains why we do the things we do and predicts the circumstances in which we engage in those behaviors. According to the TPB, behavioral intention, which is one's conscious decision to engage in a particular behavior, is a function of three factors: attitude, subjective norm, and perceived behavioral control (PBC). A key aspect of the TPB is PBC, which is one's perception of how likely he or she can perform a particular behavior. In addition, PBC includes whether the person has control over his or her own behavior.

ERIK ERIKSON'S PSYCHOSOCIAL THEORY

Erik Erikson developed a comprehensive theory of human development across the life span. Erikson was trained by Sigmund Freud and his daughter, Anna Freud. He accepted the basic concepts of the psychoanalytic approach but expanded the theory to stages of development across the life span (from birth to death) and emphasized the development of identity. He modified Freud's theory of psychosexual development. While Freud concentrated on sexual impulses, Erikson focused on social factors. His theory emphasized the importance of the life cycle approach (i.e., older people influence younger people) to personality and placed more emphasis on social and historical influences. According to Freud, there are three parts that make up a person's personality: the id, ego, and superego. The id is present at birth; its function is to express unconscious sexual and aggressive instincts. It wants immediate gratification without regard for anything else. In other words, it wants what it wants and when it wants it. The ego emerges shortly after birth; it is the go-between or the "referee" for the id and superego. It seeks to satisfy the person's instincts safely and effectively in the real world. The superego is the last part to develop; it is the "moral guardian" of the personality. It contains the standards of what the person would like to be and the values of the society in which the person grows up. While Freud believed that ego's main function is to keep the id in check, Erikson believed that the ego is a positive force that creates a self-concept or identity. According to Erikson, the ego is the center of personality and is responsible for a unified sense of self. Erikson defined the "ego" as a person's ability to combine experiences and actions in an adaptive way. He identified three interrelated aspects of the ego: (1) body ego —seeing our physical self as different from others; (2) ego ideal—the image of our self compared to our ideal self; (3) ego identity—the image of our self in our various social roles. Therefore, Erikson placed less emphasis on the id's basic biological urges, believing the ego to be the driving force behind much of behavior. According to Erikson, the ego emerges from and is largely shaped by society and culture. The ego develops within a given society and is influenced by child-rearing practices and other cultural customs. Therefore, he believed society has a profound impact on the development of the child and the ego. Erikson believed the ego develops through various stages according to the epigenetic principle—that is, it grows step by step at a genetically established pace.

Freud's theory contained five psychosexual stages that ended in childhood. Erikson extended Freud's stages to adolescence, adulthood, and old age. He divided the life span into eight psychosocial stages of human development: (1) basic trust versus mistrust (birth to one year); (2) autonomy versus shame and doubt (two to three years); (3) initiative versus guilt (four to five years); (4) industry versus inferiority (six years to adolescence); (5) identity versus identity diffusion (adolescence); (6) intimacy versus isolation (young adulthood); (7) generativity versus stagnation (middle adulthood); and (8) integrity versus despair (late life). Although social factors are key, stages are also biological in nature. Each stage is associated with a different drive and a specific psychosocial problem or "crisis" to resolve. According to Erikson, "crisis" means turning point, rather than period of distress. In every stage of life, there is an inter-action of opposites. Conflict between these opposites produces ego strength. The outcome of each stage is either positive or negative. The overall task is to acquire a positive ego identity. This sense of identity begins during infancy when baby first recognizes mother and feels recog-nized by her and continues to change throughout the life span. Development brings about new abilities that open up new possibilities for behavior, but as a child moves into new social relationships and social contexts, he or she is faced with new expectations from society. Parents, schooling, and other social institutions help the child develop in an appro-priate way at each age, but the child also must adapt to new expectations at each stage of development.

Stage 1, basic trust versus mistrust, occurs from birth to one year of age. During the first year, the goal is to develop sense of trust in others and trust in oneself. An infant must rely on others for care. In this stage, the infant is developing a sense about the world based on the quality of care he or she is receiving. The infant has a special need for loving, physical contact and will develop feelings of trust or mistrust depending on the quality of care associated with things such as feeding, bathing, and dressing. According to Erikson, consistent and dependable caregiving and meeting the infant's needs lead to a sense of trust. If the infant develops trust in his or her mother, the infant will be confident that he or she will get fed when hun-gry, comforted when distressed, and that his or her mother with return when out of sight. A mother must have trust in herself as a parent. Sensitive care fosters sense of trust. Infants develop trust in themselves from a sense that others accept them. Infants who are not well cared for will develop a sense of mistrust. Also, there must be some mistrust at all ages to notice danger. Therefore, there must be some element of trust and mistrust; however, it is better to have more trust than mistrust. If mis-trust dominates, the child or adult may be withdrawn, suspicious, and lack-ing in self-confidence.

Stage 2, autonomy versus shame and doubt occurs from two to three years of age. During this second stage, the child moves away from total dependency on the parent and begins to discover his or her own indepen-dence. The goal is to realize you are an independent person who can make decisions. This is a period of exploration; however, with exploration and independence, the child will also begin to have conflicts with parents. According to Richard Sprinthall and Norman Sprinthall, "Parents who provide an interesting, stimulating environment, talk frequently to their children, give them some initiative, and do a great deal of indirect teaching by asking questions and drawing out their perceptions and ideas, have the most positive effect on their children's developing sense of competency." Therefore, during this stage, it is important to allow children to freely explore their surroundings, without awakening feelings of shame or guilt. Children who are given the opportunity to experience independence will gain a sense of autonomy. Children who are overly restrained, controlled, or punished harshly will develop a sense of shame and doubt. The child not only becomes more physically independent and develops new potential for social interaction but also may face anxiety over a separation from parents. Increased independence requires self-control and brings about the possibility of failure, which can result in shame or doubt about the self. Like Freud, Erikson emphasized toilet training as an area of self-control that is related to sense of self-control versus shame. But there are other areas of achievement that seem to be important at this age as well (e.g., language, peer interactions).

Stage 3, initiative versus guilt occurs from four to five years of age. During this stage, children are exposed to the wider social world and given greater responsibility. The goal is to develop the ability to try new things and handle failure. Child identifies with parents who are perceived as powerful. Child has the increased ability to take initiative, form goals, and carry out his or her own actions and also may have guilt over bad behavior. A sense of accomplishment leads to initiative, whereas feelings of guilt can emerge if the child is made to feel too anxious or irresponsible.

Stage 4, industry versus inferiority occurs from six years to adolescence. Children enter school and become involved in peer relationships to a greater degree. The goal during this stage is to gain knowledge, learn basic skills, and work with others. Children have a desire to master new challenges, and classmates and other peers have an important influence on their lives. A sense of success and achievement leads to a feeling of competence or industry, whereas a sense of being incompetent and unproductive leads to a feeling of inadequacy or inferiority.

Stage 5, identity versus identity diffusion occurs during adolescence. According to Erikson, the primary focus of ego development is adolescence, the time of greatest influence on identity development. The goal of this stage is to develop a lasting and integrated sense of self (i.e., identity). Achieving identity involves exploration, examining life choices, trying out possibilities, and ultimately making a commitment. As adolescents experience rapid physical changes, they must also begin to make choices about the future of who they are and who they want to be (e.g., education, occupation). They try and determine what is unique and distinctive about themselves. They may attempt to try on different roles or styles, make various choices, or belong to certain groups to see if they fit the skills they possess and the views they have about themselves. For young people in Western cultures, identity formation usually involves a psychosocial moratorium (a period of experimentation when adult responsibilities are postponed as young people explore various aspects of themselves). Adolescents have the opportunity to analyze and try out various roles without the responsibility of assuming any particular one. If the challenges of this crisis are met successfully, individuals will form a secure sense of identity. However, if the challenges are not dealt with successfully, they may develop an incomplete sense of self or inability to identify appropriate roles in life. Identity is transformed as individuals pass through each subsequent stage.

Stage 6, intimacy versus isolation occurs during young adulthood. The goal of this stage is the development of relationships with others. Having established a stable self-identity in adolescence, healthy young adults are able to enter intimate relationships with others. The self-definition is "I am what I love." In Erikson's theory, forming close, intimate relationships is the major task of early adulthood. The young adult moves away from home and makes the gradual transition from living in world of parents to establishing own life, new relationships, and eventually his or her own family. It is more than physical intimacy; it is intimate relationships such as friendship, love, and even intimacy with oneself. Intimacy consists of several aspects: a degree of selflessness, sexuality, and deep devotion. Selflessness is the sacrifice of your own needs to those of another. Sexuality is the experience of joint pleasure from focusing not just on your own gratification but also on that of a partner. Deep devotion is an effort to fuse your identity with the identity of a partner without the fear that you are going to lose something of yourself. Intimacy brings the strength of love. Erikson believed the adolescent must develop a strong sense of identity in order for intimacy with others to be possible in this stage. The initial feelings of independence that appeared in the previous stages are tested and extended to social relationships outside of the family. The capacity to develop and maintain commitments with others leads to intimacy, whereas failure to establish and keep commitments leads to feelings of isolation. If attempts at intimacy are successful, the adult will be able to develop loving relationships and close friendships. He or she can form intimate relationships with others on a physical, intellectual, and emotional level. However, if attempts at intimacy fail, the person will feel lonely, social relationships will be more distant and empty, and he or she may even retreat into isolation, eventually becoming fearful of relationships with others. Such individuals are self-absorbed and engage in interpersonal relationships on a superficial level.

Stage 7, generativity versus stagnation occurs during middle adulthood. The goal of this stage is to contribute to the next generation. The adult finds a way to satisfy the need to be generative, to support the next generation, or to turn outward from the self toward others. The self-definition is "I am what I create." Generativity is the process of taking an interest in establishing and guiding the next generation through child-rearing or creative activities. The person develops a concern with helping others, leaving children and ideas to future generations. Caring for others in family, friends, and work leads to sense of contribution to later generations. However, having children does not ensure a sense of generativity. Generativity may develop in other ways such as doing work that provides for the future generation in some way (e.g., teaching, writing, invention). Lack of generativity leads to stagnation or lack of productivity. The person is self-absorbed, concerned with his or her self, not with future generations. Stagnation comes from a sense of boredom and meaninglessness. Generativity allows for the capacity to care, whereas stagnation leads to being an unproductive member of society.

Stage 8, integrity versus despair occurs during late adulthood. The goal of this stage is to achieve a sense of integrity (i.e., a sense of consistency and wholeness of life). If all of the previous stages have been dealt with reasonably well, then you accept yourself as you are. You understand and accept the meaning of a momentary life. The self-definition is "I am what survives me." You need to accept the way you have lived in order to accept your approaching death; otherwise, you give way to despair over never being able to find meaning in life (i.e., you focus on the impossibility of going back and doing things differently). Achieving a sense of integrity allows for the strength of wisdom (a detached yet active concern for a life bound by death). During this stage, people engage in a life review. A life review refers to the tendency for older adults to look back and reflect on the events and experiences they have had throughout their life (i.e., reminiscence) and analyze the meaning of their life. When people engage in a life review, about what do they reminisce? To answer this question, in 1991, researchers Patrick Wong and Lisa Watt studied the types of reminiscence associated with successful aging. Older adults were interviewed about their past, and from these interviews, they categorized their reflections into six types of reminiscences: integrative, instrumental, transmissive, narrative, obsessive, and escapist. The main function of integrative reminiscence is to accept one's past as worthwhile and accept negative life events and resolve past conflicts. Instrumental reminiscence allows people to draw on coping strategies that have worked in the past to deal with current problems. Transmissive reminiscence is indicated by references to the culture and practices of the past, traditional values and wisdom, and the lessons learned through one's past. Narrative reminiscence is mainly a descriptive recollection of the past. The two main functions of this type of reminiscence are (1) to provide routine biographical information, such as date and place of birth and (2) to recount past anecdotes that may be of interest to the listener. Narrative recollections are characterized by statements of autobiographical facts, accounts of past events without interpretation or evaluation, and statements that do not belong to the other five categories. Obsessive reminiscence is demonstrated by statements colored by guilt, bitterness, or despair over one's past. Escapist reminiscence glorifies the past over the present—statements that brag of past achievements, exaggerate past events, or tell of a desire to return to the "good old days." Wong and Watt found that people who are "aging successfully" have more integrative or instrumental reminiscences and fewer obsessive reminiscences.

People must accept and evaluate what they have done with their lives. They need to accept the way they have lived in order to accept their approaching death. Integrity involves a sense of meaning to one's own life, being part of larger picture and continued generativity. Despair involves regret for what one has not done—a fear of death. People who succeed in this final stage gain a sense of order and meaning in life. They reminisce and view their own life as being satisfactory and worth living. People who do not achieve integrity are overwhelmed by despair from feelings of helplessness and the cynical sense that life has been incomplete; they realize that time is too short to follow other paths.

SOCIAL INFLUENCE

Social influence is the affect people have on others' behaviors. There are many forms of social influence (e.g., social facilitation and social loafing, conformity, compliance, and obedience).

Social facilitation has to do with the ways in which groups influence us—for example, one person affecting another and multiple people affecting an individual or individuals or specific groups such as families, coworkers, teams, or committees. Groups can influence us and affect our behavior either positively or negatively. Social facilitation is when the mere presence of others improves a person's performance. For example, we tend to run faster when competing against others than when we are by ourselves just racing against the clock. This does tend to depend on the difficulty of the task. We tend to perform better on a simple or well-learned task (such as running in the example earlier) but perform poorly on a difficult or not-yet-mastered task when people are around. The opposite of social facilitation is social loafing. Social loafing is when the presence of others worsens a person's performance. People tend to expend less individual effort toward attaining a common goal when working in a group than when working alone. This is most likely to happen when the behavior of individuals is not monitored. For example, while working on a group project, depending on the group size, you may find that one or two people are not doing their share of the work.

Conformity is adjusting your own behavior or way of thinking to match those of others or the expectations of others. We follow the behaviors or expectations of others to conform because of pressure to do so; the pressure can be real or imagined. When we conform to the expectations of others, it typically happens in one of two ways: normative social influence or informational social influence. Normative social influence occurs when we want to be accepted or get approval or when we want to avoid being rejected or get disapproval and thus we go along with the group. A person may respect normative behavior because there may be a severe price to pay if it is not respected. Informational social influence occurs when we assume that the behavior of a group provides valuable information about the correct way to act or what should be done. Early research on conformity found that people conform to others' judgments more often when the information is unclear or ambiguous. However, social psychologist Solomon Asch wanted to know if people will conform when information is clear-cut or unambiguous. In other words, will people still conform when the group is clearly wrong? Participants in his study had to decide which of three comparison lines matched the reference line and say their answers out loud. Everyone in the group, but one, was a confederate, who is a person who pretends to be a participant but is actually part of the experiment. Each member of the group was asked to rate which line matched a "standard" line. The confederates were instructed to pick the wrong line 12 out of 18 times. Asch found that 75 percent of the participants conformed to at least one wrong choice. People were inclined to conform to social norms by giving the wrong answer, even when those norms were obviously wrong. Why did they conform to choices that were clearly wrong? It's because of normative and informational social influences. The participants reported having doubted their own perceptual abilities, which led to their conformance. Groups tend to enforce social norms, so in a group situation, most people are willing to accept others' opinions about reality.

There are certain conditions that strengthen the likelihood that someone will conform—for example, if the person is made to feel incompetent or insecure, group size (three or more people), if the group is unanimous (even if one person goes against the group, the likelihood of conformity drops significantly), if the person respects the group's status, if the group witnesses the person's behavior, and if the person has no prior opinion or commitment to a response or behavior.

Compliance is to agree to a direct request from someone. There are three common techniques to get someone to comply with a request: foot-in-the-door, door-in-the-face, and lowballing. The foot-in-the door technique is if you agree to a small request first, you are then more likely to comply with a large request. For example, if you agree to help your friend move his television into his dorm room, you will be more likely to say, "Yes," when he asks you to help him move the rest of his belongings into his dorm. The door-in-the-face technique is if you first refuse large request, you are more likely to comply with a smaller request. For example, if someone asks you to borrow $100 and you say, "No," you will be more likely to agree to lend them $20. Lowballing is when you agree to buy a product for a certain price, you are likely to comply with a request to pay more for the product. For instance, if you agree to buy a used car for $6,000, when the salesperson says she forgot to add in charges totaling $500, you will be likely to pay the higher price of $6,500. There are certain factors that influence compliance (e.g., authority, diffusion of responsibility).

Another social psychologist, Stanley Milgram, conducted a famous study on the effects of authority on obedience. He wondered about how average everyday people could engage in horrific acts such as the massive killings of the Jewish people in World War II. He placed an advertisement in newspapers in communities near Yale University (where he worked) that read: "Wanted: Volunteers to serve as subjects in a study of memory and learning at Yale University." It was not a study on memory, rather a study of obedience. He wanted to know how far a person would go in obeying orders to administer what he believed to be increasingly painful electric shocks to a "learner" who misses questions on a test. He used deception in order to get a true sense of what people would do in this given situation. In this study, there was the experimenter who was dressed in a gray lab coat, the "learner" who was a confederate (a person who pretends to be a participant but is actually part of the experiment), and the "teacher" who was a participant. The "teacher" was unaware that the "learner" was not really another participant. The experimenter led the "teacher" (i.e., participant) and "learner" (i.e., confederate) into a room where the "learner" was strapped into an electric shock machine. The "teacher" was delivered a sample shock of 45 volts supposedly to test the equipment and to show what the "learner" will feel. The "learner" complained of a heart condition and said he hoped the electric shocks would not be too painful. The experimenter admitted the stronger shocks will hurt but added that although the shocks can be extremely painful, they cause no permanent tissue damage. Then the "teacher" went in an adjoining room out of sight of "learner" and was seated in front of an instrument panel with lever switches that ranged from 15 to 450 volts; the switches were labeled ranging from slight shock to XXX. In the meantime, the "learner" unhooked himself from the electric shock machine, so no actual electric shocks could be administered. The "teacher" was to read a list of word pairs to test the learner's memory. If the "learner" got the answer correct, the "teacher" moved on; if the "learner" got it wrong, the "teacher" administered an electric shock (or so he thought). The "learner" had a script to read after certain voltage levels. For example, if the "teacher" got up to 270 volts, the "learner" protested and screamed in agony, and at 300 volts the "learner" yelled, "Let me out, my heart is bothering me." Any shocks after 330 volts, there was no sound from the "learner." If the "teacher" became concerned or hesitated, the "experimenter" urged he go on; if he still hesitated, the "experimenter" insisted the "teacher" to continue. So how many participants went all of the way to 450 volts labeled XXX? Approximately 65 percent of the participants obeyed and went to the top of the shock board. Recall, Milgram used deception in his experiment; no shocks were actually administered, but the participants thought they were administering painful shocks to someone. So why did they do it? They were obeying an order from an authority figure and the "experimenter" indicted he would be responsible if something harmful happened to the "learner." Milgram's study illustrates two very important factors influencing whether someone will obey another individual: if the person is an authority figure and if that person will claim responsibility if anything bad should happen.

In both Solomon Asch's and Stanley Milgram's studies, people were "pressured" to make a choice between following their own personal standards or beliefs and being responsive to others. For example, in Milgram's study, the participants were torn between hearing the pleas from the "learner" and the commands from the "experimenter." If you think of these findings with respect to social relationships in adolescence, this may help to explain why teenagers engage in antisocial behaviors, when they typically would not. Recall from Chapter 1, there are dominance hierarchies in cliques and the higher-status or "authority" members dictate membership and behavior and keep lower-status members in line. In addition, if all of their other peers are doing something, they are likely to as well.

SELECTIVE SOCIAL INTERACTION THEORY

This theory states that as we get older, we become more selective about our relationships, including friendships. Younger adults tend to have more friends and acquaintances than middle-aged or older adults. Young adults have increased social contacts and are exploring different types of relationships; as they move into middle adulthood, many acquaintance relationships are often gotten rid of. The number of relationships decreases over time as social roles change and other commitments such as work and family take up more of our time. Therefore, as we get older, we tend to focus only on the relationships that mean the most to us and are the most emotionally rewarding. According to Laura Carstensen, the founding director of the Stanford Center on Longevity at Stanford University, reducing the number of relationships is a useful way, as people get older, to regulate their emotional experiences and conserve energy. Carstensen's theory will be further discussed in Chapter 5 when examining social relationships in adulthood.

SOCIAL EXCHANGE THEORY

An important aspect of societies is fairness and equity in our social dealings with people. We expect people to honor a standard of being fair in their dealings with us and with others, and we should repay a favor with a favor. You may have even heard people illustrate this by saying phrases such as "one hand washes the other" or "you scratch my back, I'll scratch yours." Social Exchange Theory proposes that our social behavior is an exchange process. In this exchange process, underlying all behaviors is the desire to maximize our benefits and minimize our costs. We like people when we perceive our interactions with them to be beneficial to us. We often see this in male friendships (see Chapter 5). They tend to focus on making sure the benefits derived from the friendship are equal by doing things for one another (e.g., help one another move or fix something around the house).

This chapter focused on some of the major theories related to socialization. Society has influenced the creation of these theories, and these theories in turn have shaped society. The next chapter focuses on socializing throughout the life span from childhood to late life.

5

When: Socializing throughout the Life Cycle

From a very early age, humans want and need social interaction. After birth, infants and their primary caregiver (usually a parent) begin to engage in synchrony. Synchrony involves a coordinated, rapid, and smooth exchange of responses between a caregiver and an infant. It usually begins with parents imitating the infant and, within the first few months of life, becomes more frequent and elaborate. Synchrony helps infants learn to read others' emotions and to develop the skills of social interaction. For example, a nine-month-old knows that he or she can make his or her father laugh. However, is synchrony crucial for development? The answer is "yes." Dr. Edward Tronick developed a way to study synchrony, called the "still face technique." The "still face technique" is when an adult keeps his or her face unmoving and expressionless in face-to-face interaction with an infant. It turns out that babies become very upset by the still face, display negative emotions, and show signs of stress. For instance, the baby will try to engage the parent, but once that does not work, he or she will become fussy, frown, look away, cry, and so on. Therefore, parents' responsiveness to an infant is important for psychological and biological development. In other words, infants' brains need social interaction to develop to their fullest.

SOCIALIZING IN CHILDHOOD

Young children's primary source of socialization is the family. For most young children, they spend the majority of their time with members of their family (e.g., primary caregiver [such as a parent], siblings, grandparents). According to theorist Albert Bandura (refer to Chapter 4), one of the ways people learn is by simply watching others. At a very young age, children are watching their family members and learning what to do and, in some cases, what not to do (i.e., counterimitation). Through this modeling, children acquire socialization behaviors without any rewards or punishments; they can learn by simply watching and listening to others. Children tend to imitate models who are nurturing, friendly, and powerful and who possess desirable characteristics and skills (e.g., popularity, intelligence). By behaving like these models, children hope to obtain those valued characteristics for themselves when they grow up. This experience gives children a sense of self-efficacy, the belief in one's own ability to succeed in particular situations or accomplish a task.

In addition to modeling, young children also play a direct role in their social environment. As discussed in Chapter 4, according to theorist Lev Vygotsky, the basis for apprenticeship in thinking is guided participation. Through guided participation, children play an active role in their socialization not only by observing but also by participating in organized activities with more mature family members. Children and their parents and/ or older siblings may engage in a variety of activities such as games, play house, pretend cooking, taking care of a doll, and the like. The older family member views the child as simply "playing"; however, the child sees himself or herself as actually performing the task as an active participant. Guided participation is an important part of social development because when adults become joint participants in what children are interested in doing, children achieve more advanced levels of cognitive development and language acquisition, as opposed to when adults only watch a child engage in a particular activity.

Once children reach school age, their primary socialization source still includes the family, but now school becomes an important socialization source as well. A major part of socialization during the early school years is play. What is play? Play is voluntary. It is done for its own sake and not for any outside goal or purpose. Play is fun, and even when it is an imitation of an adult activity or work, it is different because children often exaggerate the adult activities, engage in role reversal, and laugh while playing.

Play is so important to children's development that the UN Convention on the Rights of the Child included play. As illustrated in

Article 31, "States Parties recognize the right of the child to rest and leisure, to engage in play and recreational activities appropriate to the age of the child and to participate freely in cultural life and the arts." In other words, children have the right to relax and play and to join in a wide range of cultural, artistic, and other recreational activities.

Around age three, social relationships are based on companionship, play, and fun. Children at this age are capable of friendship. Friendship at this age is focused on shared activities. Toddlers who spend time together prefer some peers to others and will seek those peers out in order to spend time with them. This is evident to adults, especially parents. Parents are often aware of their children's preferences for certain peers, especially when the child is capable of verbally expressing his or her preference. Toddlers who are friends tend to be similar to one another. They tend to have similar social skills, interaction styles, and activity levels. They can seek each other out, follow each other around, and verbally communicate with one another. At this age, toddlers also take turns imitating one another and are aware that they are being imitated. This process is called coordinated imitation. Take for example, two toddlers on a playground. One toddler jumps down the stairs of the playset and then the other toddler does the same. Then one goes down the slide and the other follows both smiling and laughing the entire time. The fun of this is that each child knows he or she is being copied or imitated. Each behavior is an offer for the other child to imitate. These early interactions with peers help children develop social skills such as learning to play as equals and keeping things interesting enough to allow the fun to continue. Preschool social relationships begin to encompass genuine friendship, which involves trust and endure over time. As preschoolers get older, their view of friendship evolves.

Older preschoolers see friendship as a continuing state and as a stable relationship that has meaning beyond the here and now. These children's friendships show the mutual connection they have for one another by continued efforts to play together and to be close to one another. Older preschoolers also pay more attention to concepts such as support and shared interests. At this age, children's care for one another is shown in a variety of ways. For example, preschoolers who are friends tend to share their emotions with one another, smile at and laugh with one another, and respond if their friend is in distress by attempting to help or comfort him or her (e.g., give him or her a hug or help him or her up after a fall). However, playing together still remains an important part of all preschoolers' friendships.

How do preschoolers play? At the beginning of the preschool years (around age three), children typically engage in functional play—play that involves simple, repetitive activities, or in other words, doing something for the sake of being active. By age four, children typically engage in constructive play—play that involves manipulating objects to make or build something. Constructive play is important for a variety of reasons. It allows children to (1) experiment with their advancing cognitive skills, (2) problem solve, (3) practice their motor skills, and (4) learn to cooperate with one another. How does this translate into play with others at this age? In 1932, Mildred Parten conducted a comprehensive observational study of preschoolers and identified various types of social play: unoccupied behavior, onlooker play, solitary independent play, parallel activity, associative play, and cooperative play. Unoccupied behavior is when a child is actually not playing, rather occupying himself or herself by watching anything that is of interest at the moment. Onlooker play occurs when children simply watch other children play. Solitary independent play is when a child plays alone and independently with toys that are different from those used by other children (within close proximity) and makes no effort to be by those other children. In other words, the child pursues his or her own activity without paying attention to what others are doing. Parallel activity is when children play with similar toys, in a similar manner, but do not interact with each other. Children play independently, with toys that are like those which the children around them are using, but they play with the toys in a manner in which they choose and do not try to influence or modify the activity of the other children near them. These children play *beside* rather than *with* the other children. Associative play involves a child playing and interacting with other children. The conversation concerns the common activity, and there is a sharing or borrowing of play materials and/or toys. All the members engage in similar if not identical activity, and there is no organization of the activity around any material goal. The children do not give up their individual interests to that of the group; instead each child plays as he or she wishes. The primary interest is in relations or associations with other children, not in the activity itself. In cooperative play, children play in an organized group for the purpose of making something, competing with one another to obtain a goal, exaggerate adult behaviors, or play formal games. When children engage in cooperative play, it is easily noticeable who does and who does not belong to the group. Older preschoolers engage more in constructive play than in functional play. As children get older, they also engage in more associative and cooperative play than do younger children, who engage in more parallel activity and onlooker play.

Besides the age of a child, gender and cultural background also influence different styles of play. Most children's social relationships are with other children of the same sex. Friendships are rare between opposite-sex peers. This preference for same-sex friendships is seen throughout the life span. It is not that there are not opposite-sex friendships as children get older; however, the majority of people at any given point in their life tend to have fewer opposite-sex friendships than same-sex friendships. Among children, boys tend to play differently than girls. This tendency to play differently than girls is influenced by their understanding of gender. During the preschool years, children begin to develop expectations about appropriate behavior for girls and boys. Like adults, young children expect males to be more independent, forceful, and competitive and females to be warm, nurturing, and expressive. Therefore, boys' social interactions tend to be constricting, meaning it involves issues of dominance and leadership. They often play in larger groups and public places away from adult observation, whereas girls tend to stay closer to adults. Boys also tend to show interest in blocks, transportation toys (e.g., trucks and airplanes), and objects that can be manipulated. In addition, they often engage in rough-and-tumble play (e.g., wrestling). In contrast to boys, girls generally limit their group sizes to two or three playmates. They also tend to stay closer to adults while playing. Girls' social interaction is enabling, meaning it emphasizes turn taking and equal participation by the group members. In addition, girls prefer to play with dolls, dress-up, and domestic activities such as sewing and cooking and tend to engage in sedentary activities (e.g., reading and drawing).

Play is also an expression of a child's culture. Culture not only influences the type of play children engage in, but it also helps children to become knowledgeable members of their culture. Children begin to learn about cultural values and expectations through play. For example, while children in most cultures engage in pretend play, the content of the pretend play varies (as opposed to the structure of the pretend play). In addition, in some cultures, children's play incorporates music, singing, and dancing as a way to pass along cultural heritage from one generation to the next.

The nature of a child's play is influenced by his or her social experiences. Parents influence young children's peer relationships in a variety of ways. They often have to manage their children's social lives. Parents arrange playdates, choose or suggest certain social activities for the children, often serve as rule providers, step in and enforce the rules when necessary, and supervise the social activities. Parents can model socially competent and incompetent behaviors, indicating how (and how not) to deal with conflicts. Boys whose fathers play with them are better liked by their peers than are boys whose fathers do not; perhaps this is because such play allows boys to learn to interpret others' emotions and regulate their own play. Preschool children tend to be more popular if parents coach them on how to deal with unfamiliar peers.

Just as parents can influence their children's social experiences, children can influence their parents' behaviors. For example, parents of socially competent children are more involved than other parents in teaching their children social skills and providing opportunities for their children to interact with peers. They tend to believe maladaptive behavior results from specific situations. Parents of less socially competent children believe that the child's nature is determinative and cannot be changed—the child was "born that way." These parents are not as likely to help their children solve their social problems with peers.

As children get older, play continues to remain an important aspect of socialization; however, older children's social relationships include social status. Social status is the level of peer acceptance or peer rejection within the peer group—in other words, the degree to which children are liked or disliked by their peers as a group. A comprehensive book entitled *Peer Rejection in Childhood* discusses children's social relationships, specifically social status and factors associated with being accepted or rejected by one's peers. Social status differs from friendship in that friendship is a mutual relationship and social status is not. For example, friendship involves mutual liking (i.e., two people who like each other), whereas that may not be the case regarding someone's social status. A child could like a particular classmate or consider that classmate his or her friend; however, that classmate may not like or consider that child a friend in return. There are five social status categories within a peer group: popular, rejected, neglected, controversial, and average.

Popular children are liked by many peers and disliked by few peers. They are skilled at initiating social interaction with peers and maintaining positive relationships with others. Popular children tend to be physically attractive, friendly, cooperative, helpful, and sensitive to others; do well academically; are good at sports; and are perceived this way by teachers and parents as well as by other children. They are skillful at communicating and at integrating themselves into an ongoing conversation or play session (i.e., they fit in instead of barging into a conversation or activity). Popular children tend to be more assertive than aggressive, getting what they want without fighting with or hurting others.

In contrast to popular children, rejected children are disliked by many peers and liked by few peers. There are two categories of rejected children: rejected aggressive and rejected withdrawn. Rejected aggressive children are prone to hostile and threatening behavior, physical aggression, disruptive behavior, and delinquency. They tend to be hyperactive, socially unskilled, and unable to regulate their emotions (i.e., they have poor self-control). Rejected aggressive children, especially girls, may engage in "relational aggression," spreading rumors about others, withholding friendship, and ignoring or excluding other children. Rejected aggressive children lack social skills and overestimate their social competence. These children seem to view aggression as an end, which peers dislike, instead of using aggression as a means toward other ends, which peers may not actually like but reluctantly respect. Rejected aggressive children are more likely than their peers to be motivated by "getting even" with others or showing them up. They are more likely to attribute malicious intent to others. They have more difficulty finding constructive solutions, such as taking turns. Other rejected children are shy, withdrawn, timid, and, not surprisingly, lonely; they are called rejected withdrawn. Rejected-withdrawn children are socially withdrawn, wary, and timid. They have less confidence in their social skills, are more anxious in peer contexts, and are at risk for bullying.

However, not all withdrawn children are rejected. Some withdrawn children are categorized as "neglected" because they are neither liked nor disliked by their peers. They tend to be neglected primarily because they are not noticed by their peers. "Neglected" children tend to back away from peer interactions that involve aggression. These children often prefer to be by themselves yet have enough social skills to enter a group when they want to be around others.

"Controversial" children are those who are liked by many peers and disliked by many others. They have characteristics of both popular and rejected children. They may be not only aggressive, disruptive, and prone to anger but also cooperative, social, and good at sports. They may be viewed by peers not only as arrogant and snobbish but also socially active and good group leaders.

"Average" children are liked by some peers and disliked by others but without the intensity found for popular, rejected, or controversial children. The majority of children are considered "average."

Predictors of popularity do not seem to change substantially with age. However, overt aggression has a less important role in peer rejection in adolescence than in childhood, and withdrawn behavior seems to become a more important predictor of peer rejection with increasing age. Social isolation may be forced on some children as they progress through school, either through their own disruptive or aggressive behavior or through self-isolation. In addition, there seem to be universal characteristics of popularity: knowing how to get along with others and having good social skills. But there are some differences in popularity based on culture. For example, in China, shy children are not neglected or rejected as are their Western counterparts. They are seen as good leaders and as socially competent. Also, in Israel, popular children are more likely to be direct than in other countries. Even though differences across cultures exist, there are more similarities than differences across cultures in behaviors associated with being liked or disliked by peers.

SOCIALIZING IN ADOLESCENCE

As children reach adolescence, whom they spend their time with changes. During adolescence, the amount of time spent with family decreases and amount of time spent with friends increases. Most adolescents actually spend more time with peers than with their families. Therefore, even though peer relationships are important throughout development, they are especially important during adolescence. Childhood groups are formed for the purpose of play. However, during adolescence, groups become an important feature of social life. The group functions without adult supervision more often in adolescence than childhood. Adolescent groups are more stable and have more well-defined identities. Peers not only play a greater role in providing information about standards of behavior but also become a greater source of pressure for conformity.

Adolescents typically have a wider range of acquaintances; not necessarily more friends, but they are part of a broader social system. In childhood, groups typically consist of a group of three or four friends; however, even though adolescents still have few close friends, they become part of larger network. Two types of groups that are particularly common during adolescence are cliques and crowds. As mentioned in Chapter 1, a clique is made up of a small group of individuals who are good friends and tend to be similar in age, sex, race, and interests. The members of a clique spend time together and often dress alike, act alike, and talk alike. Cliques have a clear-cut status hierarchy. The higher-status members of the clique mock peers who are not part of the clique in addition to low-status members of the clique to keep them in line. High-status members also determine who is permitted to join the clique.

Cliques are often part of a larger group called a crowd. As explained in Chapter 1, a crowd is a larger mixed-sex group of adolescents who have similar values and attitudes and are known by a common label. In contrast to cliques, which get together all of the time, crowds typically get together on weekends or every once in a while. Some crowds have higher status than others. In addition, self-esteem of members often reflects the status of group. Adolescents from high-status crowds tend to have greater self-esteem than those from low-status crowds. Adolescents from lower-status crowds may experience anxiety and unhappiness as a result of belonging to a lower-status crowd. Some of these adolescents may feel put down, may be picked on, or even bullied by some members of higher-status crowds.

So, why do some adolescents become "nerds" while others join the "burnouts"? Adolescents' interests and abilities matter, obviously (i.e., intellectually brighter adolescents who enjoy school gravitate to the "brain" or "nerd" crowds while athletically talented adolescents become part of the "jock" crowd). However, adolescents cannot simply pick and choose among crowds; instead, their peers' perception is important in gaining acceptance into a crowd. Only if peers believe that someone is really a jock, that person will become part of that crowd. Parental influence also plays a role in the type of crowds adolescents are part of. We know that adolescents' social lives are influenced by their home lives. Therefore, the type of parenting style exhibited by an adolescent's parent is important. For example, when parents emphasize achievement, monitor out-of-school behavior, and make decisions jointly, their children are less likely to be in the "druggie" crowd. Diana Baumrind conducted a comprehensive study about parenting. From her and others research about parenting, we know that parents tend to display four different types of parenting styles: authoritarian, authoritative, permissive, and uninvolved. The parenting styles differ on two overall dimensions: the amount of demandingness and control and the amount of warmth and responsiveness exhibited by parents toward their children. Authoritarian parents tend to exhibit a lot of demandingness and control but little warmth or responsiveness toward their children. They value strict, unquestioning obedience from the children and tend to be controlling, punitive, and cold. Authoritative parents display high to moderate levels of demandingness and control and a lot of warmth and responsiveness toward their children. They are firm, setting clear and consistent limits. Although they are relatively strict, they are warm and loving and provide rationale for behaviors; they encourage independence in their children. Permissive parents tend to display little to no demandingness or control but show a lot of affection toward their children. They require little of their children and tend not to assume responsibility for how their children turn out. Uninvolved parents exhibit no demandingness or control or warmth or responsiveness; they practically show no interest in their children. Uninvolved parents are emotionally detached from their children and see their role as nothing more than providing food, clothing, and shelter.

Adolescents whose parents apply authoritative parenting practices tend to do best. They are independent, self-assertive, friendly with their peers, and cooperate well with others. These children tend to join crowds that endorse adult standards of behavior. When a parent's child-rearing style is neglectful or permissive, his or her children are less likely to identify with adult standards or behavior and instead join crowds that reject adult standards (e.g., druggies or burnouts). This seems to be true regardless of racial background. We tend to see these outcomes in African American, Asian American, European American, and Hispanic American families. Therefore, in Western societies, and especially in the United States, parents are more often advised to use authoritative methods. Keep in mind, child-rearing practices that parents are urged to follow reflect cultural perspectives about the nature of children and the role of parents. For instance, the authoritative parenting style is rare in non-Western cultures. Child-rearing practices in Eastern societies are more likely to involve strict control. Such control is seen as a measure of parents' involvement in and concern for the welfare of their children. These parents expect that their authority will be obeyed without question and without requiring an explanation. The role of the parent carries greater inherent authority than it does in Western societies. Parents are not supposed to provide reasons why, which is an important component in the authoritative parenting style. This does not mean that they have an authoritarian parenting style; rather some call it a "traditional" parenting style—a term proposed to describe the kind of parenting typical in traditional cultures. Similar to the authoritative parenting style, this type of parenting style involves high demandingness and high responsiveness; however, these parents' demandingness is different in that it does not encourage discussion or debate. These parents expect their children to comply with their requests.

A common assumption about adolescents is that they are rebellious and have a great deal of conflict with their parents; however, this does not seem to be the case. Although adolescents begin to assert their independence, generally relationships with parents continue to be important and close. Parents and adolescents who have a great deal of conflict also typically had conflict at earlier ages. Most families who have good relationships during childhood continue to have good relationships during adolescence. In fact, most adolescents say they like their parents, feel close to them, and respect them. In addition, adolescents' core values are usually similar to their parents' values in terms of the importance of work, educational and career ambitions, and political and religious views. If there is an increase in conflict with parents, it is typically over issues such as household chores, style of dress, and the adolescent's choice of friends. There may be conflicts involving minor disagreements about parental authority, partly because adolescents and parents may have different ideas about what areas of life should be subjected to parental authority.

Adolescents not only are affected by their parents but also affect their parents and their child-rearing style in return. It is often seen in families with multiple children that parents will display different parenting styles based on their child's birth order, gender, personality, and so forth. This is evident when siblings within the same family are asked about what their parents are like toward them; they often give different accounts of their parents' behaviors. For example, one sibling might say that his or her parents are very strict while another sibling thinks they are lenient. This means that siblings most likely experience a different family environment from one another. This different family environment can be seen in differences in the siblings' behaviors, social relationships, and psychological functioning.

Adolescent social groups whether in school or any other place else typically have a well-defined structure. Most groups have a dominance hierarchy in which there is a leader to whom all other members of the group defer. The other members of the group know their position in the hierarchy. They concede to those members who are above them in the hierarchy and assert themselves over those members who are below them. A dominance hierarchy is useful in social groups because it can reduce the amount of conflict and the resources can be appropriately allocated within the group because every member knows his/her place. What determines where members stand in the hierarchy? It depends on age and gender. For example, with children, especially boys, physical power is often the basis for the dominance hierarchy. The leader is usually the most physically intimidating child. However, among adolescents, hierarchies are often based on individual traits that relate to the group's main function. For example, at summer camp, the leaders most often are those with the greatest camping experience. As a result, leadership based on essential skills is effective because it gives the greatest influence to those with the skills most important to the group's functioning.

Groups establish social norms, and groups may pressure their members to conform to these norms. This "pressure" is often characterized as an irresistible, harmful force. The common belief is that adolescents put immense pressure on each other to behave antisocially; however, not all pressure is bad. In reality, this pressure is not always detrimental. For example, most adolescents resist pressure to behave in ways that are antisocial, such as stealing. In addition, group pressure can be positive; adolescents often urge one another to work hard to try to earn decent grades in school, participate in school activities (e.g., trying out for an athletic team or working on the yearbook), or become involved in community projects (e.g., volunteering at a local food bank). There are many benefits of peer relationships during adolescence. Peer relationships can have positive influence on adolescents' psychological and social adjustment and enhance one's self-esteem. In addition, adolescents can benefit from peer relationships by having fewer behavioral problems and performing better in school.

When do social groups have the most influence? Groups exert pressure primarily where social standards and standards for appropriate behavior are not well defined. For instance, preference in music and how one dresses up are completely subjective, so adolescents conform to the group guidelines. Similarly, standards on smoking, drinking, and using drugs are often unclear. For example, regarding underage drinking, parents and groups such as SADD (Students against Destructive Decisions) may discourage teens from drinking, yet the American culture is filled with young people (many of them celebrities) who drink alcohol, seem to enjoy doing so, and do not suffer any negative consequences because of it. With such contradictory messages, it is not surprising that adolescents look to their peers for answers. Consequently, some adolescents drink (use drugs, or smoke, or have sexual intercourse) to conform to their social group's norms, whereas others refrain from those activities, reflecting their group's norms.

Within each broad social group, adolescents develop friendships. Why do certain adolescents become friends and not others? Similar to children, younger adolescents form friendships with others based on mutual liking, age, gender, and common interests (e.g., school, sports). As adolescents get older, they develop closer, caring relationships that involve sharing their most personal thoughts with one another, affection toward one another, and discussing any problems they may have regarding matters such as family, school, or other relationships. Adolescents are likely to say that they "talk about their problems with best friends" and "a best friend really understands you." This age difference may be due in part because adolescents spend more time with their friends than younger children. Friendships are more significant relationships in adolescence than in childhood. Also, adolescent girls describe their friendships as more intimate than do adolescent boys. This sex difference is seen throughout the life span; adult women tend to have more intimate friendships than adult men.

SOCIALIZING IN EMERGING ADULTHOOD

Emerging adulthood is the distinct period that extends from the late teens through the 20s (approximately ages 18–25). Developmental psychologist Jeffery Arnett proposed this new conception of development. Arnett argues that this period of life is neither adolescence nor young adulthood. For many individuals, it is not simply a time of transition into adulthood, rather a distinct period of life marked by frequent change. It is a time in which many different potential futures remain possible and personal freedom and exploration are higher for most people than at any other time in their lives.

Laura Carstensen's Socioemotional Selectivity Theory provides a great framework for understanding social relationships across adulthood. According to Carstensen, there are three functions of social interaction in adulthood. Social interactions (1) serve as a source of information; (2) provide an avenue for self-development—in other words, help adults develop and maintain sense of self; and 3) are a source of pleasure and emotional well-being. Adults of all ages find out information from one another, develop a sense of who they are from interacting with one another, and benefit emotionally from one another.

A key component of social relationships in adulthood is the social roles of adults. Social roles are expected attitudes and behaviors that come with a person's position in society. Although there is a lot of variability in adults' social roles, there are age-related patterns in these roles. The social roles that most often take place during emerging adulthood are leaving (and returning) home and becoming a partner or spouse.

In years past, it was customary; once a child reached adult age, he or she moved out of his or her parents' house. Even though, the proportion of young adults living at home decreases with age, currently, more young men and women live in their parents' homes than in the past. This may be due to a higher cost of living, certain jobs may require more years of education, parents may have larger homes or less children to support, young adults are not drafted into the military, adult children of recent immigrants from certain countries are traditionally expected to remain in the family home until marriage, or because people tend to get married at a later age than before. Even due to these reasons, it seems as though the process of moving out of one's parents' house has become more complex. Nowadays, we often see young adults move back and forth, from living with their parents, to moving out, to coming back for a time; the reasons for this vary. A few examples are moving out to attend college and then moving back after graduation, moving out to live with a significant other and having to move back if the relationship ends, having to move back if a parent becomes ill to take care of him or her, or moving back home after the loss of a job. Whatever the reason may be, the proportion of young adults living at home has increased.

Another common social role during emerging adulthood is becoming a partner or spouse. When it comes to romantic relationships, you often hear that opposites attract. So, do opposites attract? Not as a rule. Academic studies have found a tendency toward assortative mating. Couples often resemble each other in physical appearance and attractiveness, mental and physical health, intelligence, popularity, warmth, personality (e.g., risk-takers tend to be with risk-takers), and interests. Couples also tend to be similar to the degree in which their parents are happy as individuals and as couples and in such factors as socioeconomic status (SES), race, religion, education, age, and ethnicity. Relationships based on similarity are much more likely to last than those where partners distinctly differ. Besides similarity, where two persons meet (the location) influences the likelihood if they will form a couple. Location contributes to similarity in that people meet at places they have in common. This should make sense since many people in emerging adulthood meet at college or while participating in leisure activities (e.g., risk-takers may meet while rock climbing or bungee jumping).

Once people meet, what happens next? According to psychologist Bernard Murstein, people apply three filters when they meet someone: stimulus, value, and role. The stimulus filter consists of evaluating the potential partners' qualities (e.g., physical characteristics, how he or she dresses, reputation, social standing). A person may ask himself or herself if the other person's physical appearance matches his or her appearance. At this point, relationships are built on superficial, physical characteristics such as the way a person looks. This usually happens when people meet each other for the first time. Next, the value filter consists of evaluating the person's value and beliefs (e.g., sex, religion, and politics). At this point, the relationship is characterized by increasing similarity of values and beliefs and usually represents the second to seventh encounter with one another. Finally, the role filter consists of evaluating compatibility. A person may ask himself or herself if the other person's ideas about the relationship, communication style, and gender roles match his or her ideas. At this point, the relationship is built on specific roles (e.g., they may define themselves as girlfriend-boyfriend). This usually represents eight or more encounters with one another. When applying each filter, the variables pertaining to that filter should be more influential in affecting the encounters than variables from the other filters. For example, during the value filter, similarity among values and beliefs should be more important than the individual's physical appearance (i.e., a stimulus filter). After applying these three filters, if the person answers "yes" to the questions, then this person and the other one are likely to form a couple and become a relatively permanent pair (e.g., they may cohabit or get married).

Cohabitation is living together with a romantic partner without being married. The number of individuals who cohabitate in the United States has increased over the years, and it has been commonplace in other places too such as parts of Europe (e.g., France). The reasons for cohabitation vary. Some partners cohabit to share expenses in order to save money. Other couples, especially those in emerging adulthood, cohabit as a trial marriage. Still others, those stereotypically in middle and late adulthood, cohabit as a substitute to marriage. These adults typically have seen their previous marriages end and are looking for an alternative to marriage or do not want to lose a pension or Social Security benefits from a previous marriage. In addition, nowadays, more women are self-supporting, and there is less social pressure to marry, so couples may opt to cohabit. There has been a shift from a strongly religious society to a secular society, which may contribute to the higher rates of cohabitation as well. Even though the rates of cohabitation have increased over the years, marriage still remains the lifestyle of the vast majority of adults. However, in many industrialized nations, there is a trend toward later marriage (i.e., late 20s) in order to take time to pursue educational and career goals or to explore relationships. Age is an important factor for marital success. For example, divorce statistics indicate that individuals under the age of 20 at the time of their first marriage are three times more likely to get divorced than individuals who marry for the first time in their 20s and six times more likely than individuals who marry for the first time in their early 30s. Why? According to Erik Erikson (refer to Chapter 4), intimacy (which is the primary task of young adulthood) is difficult to achieve unless the person has a strong sense of self (which is the major task in adolescence). Many teenagers are still trying to figure out who they are, and if they get married, they may grow apart as they mature.

Through his research, Robert Levenson has discovered that couples differ in how satisfied they are with their marriages, and how couples deal with conflict seems to be one factor that determines how satisfied they are. All relationships involve conflict some of the time. Both happy and unhappy couples argue; arguments are inevitable. It is the way in which a couple resolves conflicts that appears to be related to marital satisfaction. Effective problem solving and good communication are necessary. Couples who manage conflicts in constructive manner tend to be more satisfied in their marriage. For example, in marriages that succeed, spouses tend to work out their problems together rather than letting them fester. It is interesting to note that some research on same-sex couples suggests they seem to handle conflicts in their relationships more positively than spouses from opposite-sex couples. This ability to deal with conflict may account for one of the reasons why same-sex couples (lesbian couples in particular) typically indicate that they are on average satisfied with their relationships. Same-sex couples also tend to enjoy close relationships associated with greater levels of social support, positive attitudes, and lower anxiety levels than opposite-sex couples.

In general, for most couples, overall marital satisfaction is highest at the beginning of the marriage, falls in the middle (if they have kids), and rises again at the later stage (when their kids leave home). At first, the couple has the capability to do many things together and can be open to new experiences. These first few years of marriage are filled with exploration and evaluation. Then, once the couple has a child, they get into a routine; they have less time for one another and stereotypically engage in more defined gender roles. It is hard work to take care of kids; it requires a lot of energy for the feedings, changing diapers, dealing with sickness, and so forth. This can be very stressful and typically takes a toll on the marital relationship. However, later in life, when the kids are grown up and move out of the house, the couple has more time to spend together and do things of interest to them.

Several studies reveal there are key factors to help have a long, happy marriage. For instance, couples who make time for one another and try new things together; are there for each other and support each other when things are going well, not just in times of need; show interest in each other's lives; communicate constructively about any problems in the relationship; confide in one another; and express gratitude are more likely to stay together for the long term. However, relationship expert John Gottman maintains that the most important factor in a lasting marriage is friendship. He has conducted research for 30 years studying hundreds of couples regarding their relationships. Gottman found that successful couples have "a mutual respect for and enjoyment of each other's company." Couples who stay together know each other; they are well versed in each other's personality idiosyncrasies, likes and dislikes, hopes and dreams. They have an enduring love for each other and express this affection regularly in both big and little ways. According to Gottman, the quality of the friendship determines whether the couple is satisfied with the sex, romance, and passion in their marriage.

Friendship is distinct from other social relationships. The role of a friend is present from early childhood to old age (i.e., throughout life cycle) in contrast to many other social roles that are limited to certain portions of the life span (e.g., spouse, parent, and worker). Friendships are voluntary. They have broad and ambiguous boundaries; therefore, there are varying definitions of what friendship is and what it means to be a friend. Friendships are based in similarity. In other words, friends are usually those of the same age, sex, and background. In addition, liking of common activities and similar interests are key components in friendships. Friendships are primarily oriented toward enjoyment and personal satisfaction, as opposed to the accomplishment of a particular task or goal. Trust is especially important in friendship because of its voluntary nature.

As previously mentioned, preschool and younger elementary-school children's friendships revolve around shared activities. Besides shared activities, older elementary-school children's friendships also consist of trust and helping one another in need. Adolescent friendships involve intimacy, loyalty to one another, and emotional support. Friendships are important throughout adulthood, partly because a person's overall satisfaction with life is related to how often that person keeps in contact with his or her friends as well as the quality of those friendships. For example, college students who have strong ties to their groups of friends adjust better to stressful life events. The importance of maintaining contacts with friends is apparent among ethnic groups as well. For instance, African Americans who have many friends are happier than those with only a few friends. Regardless of one's background, friendships play a major part in determining how much a person enjoys life.

According to social psychologist George Levinger, adult friendships can be viewed as having five stages: (1) acquaintanceship, (2) buildup, (3) continuation, (4) deterioration, and (5) ending. Acquaintanceship is an interest at an early time in a relationship. Then the friendship continues to buildup followed by a continuation period. The continuation stage may be marked by a variety of adjustments, continuing growth of interdependence, friendly but bland coexistence, intense but strong intimacy, or an empty but mutual tolerance. Friendships vary with respect to the degree of how involved individuals are in each other's lives. After a period of time, there may be a deterioration or decline in the friendship; however, not all friendships deteriorate. The ending stage signifies breakup through death or some other form of separation.

Younger adults tend to have more friends and acquaintances than middle-aged or older adults. This trend lessens over time as social roles change and other commitments become more time-consuming (e.g., children, work). Developmental psychologist Brian deVries has uncovered three broad dimensions that underlie adult friendships. The most frequently mentioned dimension is the affective or emotional basis of friendship. This dimension includes self-disclosure and expressions of intimacy, appreciation, affection, and support, all of which are based on trust, loyalty, and commitment. The next dimension is the shared or communal nature of friendship. Friends participate in or support activities of mutual interest such as exercising or attending a charity event. The third dimension of friendship is sociability and compatibility. Our friends keep us entertained and are sources of fun and recreation. These three dimensions are found in friendships among adults of all ages.

There tends to be differences in the types of friendship based on gender. In general, females have more "close" friends and see their friends more often than males. Male friendships tend to be based on shared activities. Their friendships are more group and activity oriented, are more guarded, involve less self-disclosure, and are less intimate than female friendships. Female friendships tend to be based on emotional support. Their friendships are generally described as closer and more intimate than male friendships. Also, females tend to offer more support and are more satisfied with same-sex friendships than males. They tend to be more generous and less self-interested than males. Males tend to prefer to "do something" with a friend and females tend to prefer to "just talk." When males talk with their friends, it is generally about some activity. Female friendships have a more communal or helping orientation, meaning they focus on the needs and well-being of the other person, whereas male friendships have a more exchange orientation, meaning they focus on making sure the benefits derived from the friendship are equal. For example, in a male friendship, one person may help another move to a new apartment or house and in return he helps his friend set up for a party. Female friendships may provide greater nurturance and intimacy but require more commitment and involvement. In contrast, male friendships may expect and get less from one another, but their friendships may be more tolerant of conflict than female friendships. If there is a disagreement among male friends, they argue about it and then everything may be fine in a day or two, whereas in a female friendship, an argument may result in not speaking to one another for weeks or months.

Much of the early literature has focused on same-sex friendships; however, more recently there has been research done by University of Wisconsin–Eau Claire psychologist April Bleske-Rechek and her colleagues on opposite-sex friendships (i.e., male-female friendships). So why do men and women become friends? We can look to evolutionary psychology to help answer this question. Compared with women, men consider sexual attraction and a desire for sex as important reasons for initiating opposite-sex friendships. Therefore, in opposite-sex friendships, males tend to overperceive and females tend to underperceive that friend's sexual interest in them. Women consider physical protection as a more important reason for initiating opposite-sex friendships. Just as in same-sex friendships, in opposite-sex friendships, respect and trust are important. In addition, opposite-sex friendships enhance your self-esteem, provide someone you can talk openly with, and provide companionship. Having a friend who is the opposite sex also allows you to gain information on how to attract a mate. The issue of male-female friendships will be further examined in Part III of this book entitled "Controversies and Debates."

So why are friendships important? Friendships serve many purposes, and these purposes vary by life stages or particular circumstances. Friendships are a means of stimulation. They add interest and opportunities for socializing and can expand our knowledge base, ideas, and perspectives. Friends often serve as confidants and models of coping and can help buffer against stressful life experiences such as a death in the family or a divorce. Friends are useful because they give assistance when needed and provide resources to help us meet our needs or reach our goals. Adults with good friends tend to have higher levels of social support and lower levels of depression than adults without good friends. Overall, friendships contribute positively to our self-esteem and overall life satisfaction.

SOCIALIZING IN MIDDLE ADULTHOOD

Many people believe that during middle adulthood, most people are faced with a "midlife crisis." This term was coined by Elliott Jacques in 1967 and surged into public consciousness in the 1970s to refer to a stressful period when people review and reevaluate their lives. In most cultures, this term has become a catchphrase, which is sometimes used as an explanation for an episode of depression, an extramarital affair, or a career change. According to Jacques, what brings on a midlife crisis is the awareness of one's own mortality. The adult recognizes that the first part of adulthood is over, time has become shorter, and there is a realization of unfulfillment of his or her dreams from when he or she was younger. So, is there a universal midlife crisis? Not really. For the majority of people, middle adulthood is no more traumatic than any other developmental period. Indeed, most adults do go through some transition during adulthood, but it is usually not a "crisis." Adults, however, do question the events that have occurred, are occurring, and are yet to occur in their life. When Daniel Levinson was in middle adulthood wrestling with personal issues, he was curious about this age of midlife. He searched for answers to his questions about what it means to be an adult and the major issues facing adult life. In order to answer these questions, Levinson extensively interviewed middle-aged males (he later explored the lives of middle-aged females as well) and their family members as well as visited their places of work. A key concept that emerged from Levinson's research was that of the "life structure." According to developmental psychologist Daniel Levinson, the "life structure" is an underlying pattern of a person's life at any given time. It is the pattern of life that reflects person's priorities and relationships with others. It is the answer to the question, "What is my life like now/at this point in time?" This pattern is built around whatever a person finds most important. The "life structure" is not permanent; rather, it evolves and is modified throughout one's life.

According to Levinson, early on in adulthood, individuals become independent and begin to take on adult responsibilities. For example, they leave their parents' home and become financially and emotionally independent. They also choose an occupation and begin to form relationships usually leading to cohabitation or marriage and parenthood. During middle adulthood, marriage/family and occupation are the most common central elements of the life structure. Individuals settle down and set goals and time for achieving those goals. They anchor their lives in their family, occupation, and the surrounding community.

How well people handle this transition is called "ego resilience," a term developed by Jack Block in the 1950s. Ego resilience is the part of personality that enables people to handle changes. With respect to middle adulthood, individuals with high ego resilience see this transition as opportunity for change, whereas individuals with low ego resilience see it as time of staying the same or decline.

The social roles from emerging adulthood are redefined and renegotiated in middle adulthood. During middle adulthood, adults tend to be more satisfied with their lives than younger adults. This may be due to the fact that most middle-aged adults with children become "empty nesters," meaning the children move out of the house and on their own. Jobs become more important during middle adulthood.

The role of grandparent is often added during the middle adult years. This is a role that usually brings a lot of joy to most adults' lives. However, for some, the role of grandparent may become one of surrogate parenting—a role assumed by grandparents when parents are not able to raise their own children; in other words, when grandparents become "parents" to their grandchildren. This does not include living with their own children and helping out, but it takes place when a parent is unwilling or unable to take care of his or her own children. The reasons for this may be that the parent became a parent at a very young age, is in prison, addicted to drugs, suffers from a psychological disorder or physical illness, or has died.

Some middle-aged adults may feel a "generational squeeze." These adults are compelled to support their aging parents while still trying to help their maturing/adult children. It is also sometimes called the "sandwich generation" because these adults are "sandwiched" between the obligation to take care of their aging parents, who may be ill or in need of financial support, and their own children, who may also need financial and emotional support. These obligations demand considerable time and money. With the added pressures of managing their own career and personal issues, as well as the need to contribute to retirement, these middle-aged individuals are under a lot of stress. In some cases, these individuals have to postpone their own retirements because of the added financial obligations. As mentioned earlier, some middle-aged adults have the added responsibility of caring for their grandchildren, which can be another added source of stress.

SOCIALIZING DURING THE LATER YEARS

Social roles in late adulthood tend to become more simplified. For instance, older adults may downsize and move into a smaller home or to an active adult community, work part-time or retire, volunteer, or become a great-grandparent.

Friendships play an important role throughout the life span, and later life is no exception. In late adulthood, casual friendships are less common and existing friendships take on added importance. In old age, friendships tend to replace the support that once was received from family members. The fact that people choose their friends may be especially important to older people who often feel control over their lives slipping away. This may help explain why most older adults who have close friends are healthier, happier, and live longer. Important aspects of friendships among older adults include common interests, social involvement, and mutual help. We know that intimacy is a key component in friendships in emerging and middle adulthood; intimacy is also important in later life because these older adults need to know they are still valued and wanted, despite some physical and other age-related decline. Older adults who can confide in friends have someone who is also going through similar changes to talk to about their worries and aches and pains. By doing so, they often deal better with the various changes related to the aging process. Friends can buffer against the impact of stress on older adults' physical and mental health.

We see similar gender differences in friendships in later life as in earlier adulthood. Older women tend to have more friends and more intimate friendships than older men. Also, older women continue to see their friends at least as often as they did in the past. On the other hand, older men see their friends less, see them more in groups than one-on-one, and consider friendship less important than older women.

With the increasing likelihood that a person's spouse will die as they get older, friendships are important in later life to help deal with the loss and replace some of the social functions that were provided by the deceased spouse. Widowhood is an immense emotional challenge; it means loss of a partner and disruption in almost every aspect of the individual's life. Because women tend to live longer than men and tend to be younger than their husbands, they are more likely to be widowed. With widowhood come emotional and practical problems. For instance, the person no longer maintains the role of being a spouse. Family and friends initially are there to lend support after the loss, but after time, they go back to their own lives. His or her social life changes as well. Friends who still have their spouses may feel uncomfortable around the widow(er), or the widow(er) may not want to hang around married couples because they may feel like a "third wheel." People who adjust best to widowhood are those who keep busy, take on new roles (e.g., paid or volunteer work), become more deeply involved in ongoing activities, and see their friends often.

This chapter focused on socialization throughout the life span and, in particular, the important role friendships play throughout one's life. As mentioned earlier, friendship is distinct from other social relationships. The role of a friend is present from early childhood to old age, in contrast to many other social roles that are limited to certain portions of the life span. Socializing tends to change as we get older; however, one thing that remains certain is the significant role of friends in our lives. Our friends are there for us when times are good and give us much-needed support in the bad times. As highlighted in this chapter, while much of socializing and friendships have common elements, not all friendships are the same (e.g., male-male friendship versus female-female friendships). The next chapter discusses the similarities and differences of socializing among various cultures.

6

Where: Socializing around
the World

We are living in an increasingly globally connected world. Not only do we travel more and further than those who came before us, television, film, music, and social media mean that we also share a number of the same cultural referents. Certainly, processes of cultural diffusion (the spread of cultural artifacts and meanings from one group to another) and cultural leveling (the ways that cultures geographically distant from each other become similar to one another) are at highs. Much of this is due to the weight of cultural ideologies and products that flow from the United States. This is evident when we arrive in the Bahamas and see a Wendy's fast-food joint next to a street vendor selling conch fritters, see visitors wear Mickey Mouse gear on our trip to Disneyland Paris, or turn on a TV in a hotel room in Lagos and view Nickelodeon Africa or watch MTV Thailand while on vacation in Bangkok.

Certainly as a country of both indigenous Americans and immigrants—forced and voluntary—our experiences in the United States have always been full of contributions from a host of cultures, as seen in the language, foods, celebrations, and music readily recognized today as uniquely American. More recently, patterns of globalization and immigration mean that a 7-year-old African American boy in Chicago names sushi as his favorite meal, a 14-year-old Latinx girl in Los Angeles listens to K-pop daily, and an Irish American couple runs a yoga studio in their Seattle hometown. Indeed, globalization, immigration, media and technology, and the cultural diffusion and cultural leveling that come from these mean that cultural influences in a number of arenas are melding in ways that make them harder to tease out. This is definitely true when we think of socializing and hanging out. Wherever we look, we are likely to see far more similarities in these patterns than differences. Sports, shopping, sipping drinks, and sharing secrets are all frequently seen in socializing rituals in places from South Carolina to South Africa and from Alabama to Albania. Socializing in other parts of the world would also provide comparable purposes of sociability, social integration, and social support, among others. Still, in this chapter, we look at seven different places around this vast world and note some particularities in each.

NORWAY

Want to be happy? Norway is the place to be. According to the 2017 World Happiness Report, Norway is the "happiest" place on earth. In 2011, the UN General Assembly adopted a resolution that recognized happiness as a "fundamental human goal" and called for "a more inclusive, equitable and balanced approach to economic growth that promotes the happiness and well-being of all peoples." In 2012, the first ever UN conference on happiness took place, and the UN General Assembly adopted a resolution which decreed that the International Day of Happiness would be observed every year on March 20. It was celebrated for the first time in 2013 and provides a focal point for events spreading the influence of global happiness research. Since 2012, each year the United Nations has released the World Happiness Report, which ranks 155 countries by their happiness in terms of life satisfaction. Each year, Norway has consistently ranked among the top four countries compared to the United States, which is usually in the top 20. What makes Norway such a "happy" place to live?

Norway is part of Northern Europe and is situated on the western side of the Scandinavian Peninsula; Sweden is its neighbor to the east and Denmark to the south. The majority of the population of Norway speak the official language, which is Norwegian. The people of Norway abide by cultural rules called Janteloven or Jante Law. Jante Law was formed in 1933 by Danish Norwegian author Aksel Sandemose in his novel entitled *A Fugitive Crosses His Tracks*. According to Commisceo Global, the tenets of Jante Law are (1) you are not to think you are anything special; (2) you are to think you are as good as others; (3) you are not to think you are smarter than others; (4) you are not to think you are wiser than others; (5) you are not to behave as if you are better than others; (6) you shall not believe that you know more than others; (7) you are not to think you are more important than others; (8) you are not to think that you can fix things better than others or are good at anything; (9) you are not to laugh at others; (10) you are not to think that anyone cares about you; and (11) you are not to think that you can teach others anything.

As you can see from Jante Law, an important element of the Norwegian culture is humility. In general, Jante Law says you are not better than anyone else. It is thought that in writing these laws Sandemose was inspired by a belief that existed in ancient Norse culture that in order to preserve one's happiness, one should be cautious and humble. It teaches people to be modest and is shown in most people's refusal to criticize others. Norwegians try to see all people as being equal. They do not flaunt their wealth or financial achievements and question those who do.

Family life in Norway consists mainly of the nuclear family. People do get married; however, marriage is not a prerequisite to starting a family; therefore, many couples live together without being married. Raising a family in Norway has some vast differences compared with raising a family in the United States. We can gain insight on what life is like in Norway from an American photographer Rebecca Zeller, who lives in Oslo, Norway, with her husband and three children. She spoke to Joanna Goddard about her experiences living in Norway. Recall that Chapter 5 discusses the different parenting styles and child-rearing techniques exhibited by parents in the United States; however, that is not the case in Norway. According to Zeller, "There is a sense that there's just one right way to do things and everyone does it that way." For example, in Norway, "all children go to bed at 7pm, all attend the same style of preschool, all wear boots, all eat the same lunch ... that is the Norwegian way." The Norwegian parenting style fosters independence, fresh air and nature, egalitarianism, and modesty. In Norway, parents are focused on promoting independence. Children do things alone early, whether it is walking to school or to the movies.

In Norway, childhood is strongly institutionalized, says Norwegian sociologist and economist Margunn Bjornholt. When children turn one year old, they enter Barnehage, a state-subsidized daycare. Parents pay a small amount of money each month, and their children are cared for while they work. Unlike in the United States, parents in Norway get almost a full year of state-sponsored leave from work. Women or men may take up to one year's "maternity" leave at 80 percent of their pay or 10 months at 100 percent pay. If a woman decides to stay home with preschool children, she receives a monthly stipend from the government. After that, mostly everyone goes back to work.

Because everyone works, there is really no playground culture, unlike in the United States where you see parents and their children having "playdates" by going to the playground or engaging in some other activity. Zeller commented when she and her family moved to Norway, her kids had not gotten into Barnehage yet, so she was alone with them all day from March until August. There was not much to do because all of the parents were working and all of the kids were in Barnehage. There were very few activities for children, kids' museums, or "playdates" like you see in the United States.

Norwegians believe that it is better for children to be in daycare as toddlers. At daycare, methods reflect the country's love of fresh air. In winter, children are bundled up and taken outside to nap in their strollers. According to an article entitled "6 Foreign Parenting Practices Americans Would Call Neglect," if asked, most Nordic parents will tell you that exposing babies to the elements makes them stronger and more resilient. Is this good for them? Researchers do not agree as to whether naps outside are good or bad for babies. Some studies indicate that kids who spend more hours outside (generally, not just for naps) end up taking fewer sick days from school during the year than those who spend most of their time indoors; other studies find there is not a relation in the hours spent outside and number of absences from school. In an article written for BBC magazine, Helena Lee discusses the age-old Nordic tradition of allowing infants and toddlers to nap outside in a stroller. What is the optimal outdoor temperature? According to Marjo Tourula, a research coordinator at the University of Oulu in Finland who has studied children sleeping outdoors, it's 5 degrees Celsius or 23 degrees Fahrenheit. The parents she interviewed said they believed sleeping outside would toughen their children to harsh climates, help them sleep and eat better, and contribute to their overall health. The babies are bundled up (often in wool) in their strollers, and many parents put cream on their faces to protect their skin in very cold weather. According to Tourula, the cold environment makes swaddling possible without the risk of overheating.

As discussed previously, the Norwegian idea of Jante Law values "the group" as opposed to American culture, which values and promotes the concept of "the individual." In Norway, the needs of the individual are subordinate to the good of the collective. To stand out or call attention to yourself is considered impolite. People in Norway do not boast or play up their accomplishments. Norwegians view themselves as egalitarian people whose culture is based on democratic principles of respect and interdependence. They like people for themselves and not for what they do for a living or how much money they earn. Norwegians separate their business and personal lives; therefore, for instance, it is not appropriate to discuss business at a dinner party. They have simple tastes and are not prone to pretentiousness or to show off the possessions they own. They pride themselves on being honest and sincere in their personal relationships.

JAPAN

Japan is an island nation in the Pacific Ocean with dense cities, imperial palaces, mountainous national parks, and thousands of shrines and temples. Almost four-fifths of Japan is covered with mountains. The Japanese Alps runs down the center of the largest island, Honshu. The highest peak is Mount Fuji, a cone-shaped volcano considered sacred by many Japanese. Japan's nearest neighbors are the Siberian region of Russia in the north and Korea and China farther south.

In Japan, being able to greet people (to say "hello" and "good-bye") is a fundamental expectation, so much so that parents use greeting exercises to reinforce this important skill and to teach this to their children in the same way parents in the United States teach their children the ABCs. These greetings serve as a reminder that you need to acknowledge and care for others. Japan is considered a collectivist culture, meaning they put the needs of the others (e.g., family or the company they work for) ahead of their own needs. East Asian Languages and Cultures Professor Matthew Burdelski examined children's socialization in the Japanese culture. For over 10 years, he recorded conversations from households, playgrounds, and a preschool in Japan. Burdelski was looking at the ways Japanese caregivers use the expressions *Gomen ne* and *Gomen-nasai* ([I'm/we're] sorry) when addressing other people and ways they encourage children to say these expressions to others. He found that apology situations are an important aspect through which children learn how to behave in a way that is socially acceptable. According to Burdelski, this happens so often in the Japanese language that Japan has been called a "culture of apology" because speakers often "apologize" or *ayamaru* in a variety of settings.

The Japanese are famous for their willingness to work very hard. Just as they do in Norway, in Japan, they separate work and personal lives; however, socializing is a big part of the Japanese work environment. According to Japan Intercultural Consulting, after-hours socializing is an important part of the business day. Even though socializing is important to business, it does not mean after-work dinners or gatherings are extensions of business meetings, unlike in the United States. These gatherings or dinners are not about business. They are a chance for small talk and for everyone to get to know one another on a personal level. During dinner, the Japanese sip, slurp, chew, chomp and even burp loudly throughout the meal as a polite sign that they are enjoying the dinner; the louder the better. Alcohol is a key part of socializing in Japan, and the custom is for colleagues and friends to keep each other's glasses full; this means that you do not refill your own drink. As a result, there will be a constant flow of refills as everyone tries not to let the other person's glass go empty. The most polite way is to pour using two hands.

In an article written by Rochelle Kopp on "Handling Common Tricky Areas," when socializing with the Japanese, Kopp maintains an important aspect of business socializing in Japan is the *nijikai* or "second stage" of the evening's entertainment. This second stage involves a change of location after dinner is finished. This is in part because restaurants want to discourage their patrons from staying too long, and because getting up and going to a different place tends to refresh everyone's mood. Occasionally, the second location will take place at a coffee house; however, more commonly it takes place at a bar. For example, *nijikai* may be at a karaoke bar where everyone in the group takes turns singing popular songs into a microphone over prerecorded tracks. Some Americans may feel uncomfortable singing in front of others and therefore may not want to take a turn singing karaoke. However, not taking your turn is considered rude by the Japanese. The point of karaoke is not how well you sing; rather it is to connect with the group, even at the risk of looking or sounding silly. In other words, being a good sport is more important than being talented. Spending time with your colleagues in a relaxed situation outside the office —be it eating, drinking, playing golf, singing karaoke, or just simple sightseeing—is extremely important for relationship building. Japanese want to get to know the people they do business with on a personal level. For these reasons, socializing is an essential part of developing relationships.

Family is extremely important in Japanese culture. The word *ie* means household or family. Nowadays, the Japanese family structure tends to resemble that in the United States, a household is comprised of a couple living together with their children (i.e., a nuclear family). Therefore, it may appear that family plays the same kind of role in both societies; however, there is a different sociocultural dynamic in these societies. Recall from Chapter 5, child-rearing practices in Eastern societies are more likely to involve strict control. Such control is seen as a measure of parents' involvement in and concern for the welfare of their children. These parents expect that their authority will be obeyed without question and without requiring an explanation. The roles of the parent and other elder family members carry greater inherent authority than in Western societies. Parents are not supposed to provide reasons why; therefore, some call this type of parenting a "traditional" parenting style. Similar to the authoritative parenting style, this type of parenting style involves high demandingness or control and high responsiveness or warmth; however, these parents' demandingness is different in that it does not encourage discussion or debate. These parents expect their children to comply with their requests.

In the United States, once a couple has a child, they still try to find time for themselves. They usually will try to have a "date night" where they go out without the child, be it to see a movie or to have dinner or both. In Japan, childhood is seen as an important period in one's life. A "date night" with one's spouse is almost nonexistent. Restaurants are expensive, and people tend to work very late. It is extremely rare for middle-class couple to eat out in Japan. It may be just once a year they get a night out without the kids. Typically, women eat dinner early with the children, and as mentioned earlier, since socializing is a big part of the work environment, men tend to eat dinner late with their colleagues from work. Therefore, men and women in traditional Japanese families often live separate lives. Even at night, the couple may not sleep together in the same bed. In Japan, co-sleeping is common. Co-sleeping is the practice where parents sleep in the same bed as their child. It is highly unlikely for children in Japan to sleep alone, even if the family has the space. The practice is considered so important that couples will sleep separately to ensure that all of their children can sleep with an adult. The Japanese respond to their babies' cries immediately and hold them almost constantly. While parents in the United States may worry that this would spoil their children, the Japanese believe that babies who get their needs met and are loved unconditionally as infants become more independent and confident children.

Similar to Norway, Japanese parents are focused on nurturing independence. Parents in Japan allow their kids a lot of independence after a certain age. For example, it is not uncommon for children as young as five years of age to ride the subway by themselves. Christine Gross-Loh, who has a PhD from Harvard University in East Asian History, is a journalist, and is the author of several books, including one titled *Parenting without Borders: Surprising Lessons Parents around the World Can Teach Us*, has lived in Japan, and when she is there, she lets her kids run errands, take the subway, and wander around town without her. However, she would not do the same in the United States. Gross-Loh commented, "If I let them out on their own like that in the U.S., I wouldn't just get strange looks, somebody would call Child Protective Services." You can also see Japanese parents promote independence when their children are not getting along with one another. If the kids are arguing over a toy, or over which part they want to be in a play, the Japanese believe this sort of conflict is actually good for kids because it gives them a chance to experience conflict and resolve it all on their own. The parents may try and guide them or model good techniques to resolve a conflict; however, they usually let the kids work it out by themselves.

If you find yourself wanting or needing to travel to Japan, here are a couple of aspects related to socializing to keep in mind. According to Catherine Forth's article about what not to do in Japan, the Japanese do not touch to greet one another or show public displays of affection. Unlike in Europe or Latin America where hugs and kissing on the cheeks are greetings among casual acquaintances, Japan is more reserved with their public displays of affection. You almost never see people holding hands, walking arm in arm or kissing on the streets. Even couples who are madly in love will rarely do so in public. Therefore, do not expect any physical contact when saying hello or good-bye to even close friends in Japan; you will just make them uncomfortable. What should you do instead? It is best to do a formal bow as a greeting. Just as people do not show affection in public, people in Japan also do not eat or drink when they are walking. It may be due to their cultural respect for food (i.e., most meals begin with an Itadakimasu prayer, which means "I humbly receive"); eating or drinking while walking is generally not done in Japan. Unlike many Western countries where people eat and drink on the go all the time, people in Japan prefer to take the time to stop and consume food and beverages while being still.

BRAZIL

The largest country in South America, Brazil, is home to a multiracial society with roots in indigenous, African, and European cultures and has a growing presence on the world stage, as their recent hosting of the World Cup and the Olympics demonstrates. When many think of Brazil, it is the beaches of Rio de Janeiro, the rainforests along the Amazon, and the sounds of bossa nova that come to mind. Then there is the football (that is soccer to us in the United States) fanaticism and the nightlife immortalized in song, film, and the popular imagination of people around the world. There are other aspects to leisurely pursuits in Brazil, however. If we relocate our attention from the glitz and glamour of Rio de Janeiro to Salvador, a city in the state of Bahia, we would see some other forms of socializing emerge.

Salvador is one of the oldest cities in Brazil and its third largest today, behind Rio de Janeiro and São Paulo. As the first and largest enslavement port in the Americas, Salvador's contemporary culture remains heavily influenced by its African heritage and present. One sign of this past in the present can be found in the lively practice of capoeira and samba there.

Capoeira is a martial art form that was masked as a dance in its blend of Angolan and Brazilian origins that dates back to Salvador in the early 16th century and is seen today in mixed martial arts and as the foundation for break dancing. It has always had social dimensions. Enslaved Africans, kidnapped from Angola and forced into captivity in Brazil, created capoeira with its kicks, spins, and acrobatics in an effort to defend themselves as they fled bondage and escaped slavery. As they were unable to possess or train with weapons, enslaved Brazilians met in secret to teach and train with each other in a collective attempt toward freedom. In order to evade detection, if a slaveholder saw them in practice, they would pretend to be dancing, one of the few leisure activities allowed to them. Though ultimately banned in the early 19th century through the middle of the 20th century, capoeira is a leading form of socialization in Salvador today, attracting not just locals and curious tourists but also dedicated capoeiristas, or practitioners of capoeira, from all over the world. It is a very communal practice. Two capoeiristas face each other within a *roda* or circle of other capoeiristas who sing, rhythmically clap hands, and play percussive instruments during the *jogo* or gameplay. Often performed on Salvadoran beaches, streets, and parks, capoeira players not only use this as a way to improve their craft and be with other capoeiristas, but the play also attracts large crowds of spectators, much as beach volleyball tournaments do in the United States.

Created and sustained out of some of the same repressive circumstances as capoeira is samba—both the music and the dance that accompany it. It too is vital to the maintenance of a distinct Afro-Brazilian cultural, spiritual, and physical presence in Salvador, Bahia, and Brazil. It was and is a way to build and continue shared bonds and community. Indeed, it is not uncommon to see a capoeira roda flow seamlessly into a samba roda and the play turn into a dance. Samba is often thought of as the official dance of Brazil, and it is danced in the streets, at parties, clubs, picnics, family gatherings, wedding receptions, official ceremonies, and just because. Both capoeira and samba are commonly seen throughout the city, state, and country regularly and especially during Carnaval where they are not just social but competitive acts as well. Likewise, both contribute to the continuity of the Afro-Brazilian heritage of the country as well as the vibrancy that is Brazil.

GHANA

Ghana, a middle-income, West African democracy is located in the Gulf of Guinea between the nations of Cote d'Ivoire and Togo. In 1957, it

became the first African nation to wrest itself away from its European col-
onizers, serving as inspiration for other sub-Saharan nations as well as
African Americans and other people of African descent around the world.
Because of its coastal environment, going to the beach is a popular pastime
for Ghanaians and visitors alike. Also due to its coast, Ghana was an
important point in the transatlantic slave trade as many kidnapped West
Africans were marched through the interior of Ghana and other West
African countries to the Ghanaian coast. There, kidnapped and subsequently enslaved, West Africans were held in underground dungeons
in places like Elmina and Cape Coast Castle before being forced through
what was called "the door of no return," marking their last time on
African soil before being exported to the Americas by the thousands on
slave ships. Today, these castles that held kidnapped West Africans serve
as reminders of the atrocities of the enslavement of West African people,
drawing large numbers of Ghanaians, people of African descent from the
Americas and Europe, as well as others who want to remember and respect
those who experienced such cruelty.

  This literal and symbolic homeland for members of the African
American community has meant that a number of African Americans
have spent time and in some cases expatriated to Ghana. These include
both everyday African Americans whose names may not have been
recorded in history books as well as luminaries such as activist Malcolm
X, author Maya Angelou, and author, activist, and founding father of sociology, W.E.B. Du Bois, who expatriated to Ghana, where he died at the
age of 95. Indeed, there is a robust community of African Americans living
in Accra, Ghana, in particular, where they seek their West African roots
while also bringing with them their unique African Americanness. As
the capital and largest city in Ghana, a look at hanging out in Accra is particularly instructive. Just as in the United States, sports, music, and
beaches are go-to activities when it is time to hang out.

  Football—or soccer as we call it in the United States—is the national
pastime of Ghana and is immensely popular in Accra and throughout the
rest of the country. The national team is the Black Stars and is a perennial
standout in Africa and is competitive with teams from around the world.
The team's name shows another connection between Ghana and African
Americans as it is named for the Black Star Line, founded by the
Jamaica-born, U.S.-based pan-African activist Marcus Garvey to further
his mission of expatriating African Americans from the United States to
West Africa during the first part of the 20th century. Whether playing
home in their stadium in Accra or away, Ghana's numerous football fans
organize much of their social life around their team. When there is not a

game, it is not uncommon to see people playing in fields through the city, either as part of a team or just for the sheer pleasure of it. Where there is a football, there is a crowd, meaning that football is a popular choice when it is time for socializing for its participants and its spectators.

Musical innovation is found throughout Ghana's history and its residents spend time enjoying these to be sure. Recently, a new genre has developed out of Accra—hiplife. A mashup of Ghanaian highlife music —an influential musical form that came to life around the middle of the 20th century and spread through West Africa and beyond, highlife is itself a hybrid of traditional Ghanaian music and harmonies and European brass and string instruments—and African American hip hop, hiplife has moved from Accra to iPhones, Spotify playlists, and clubs throughout Africa, the Caribbean, the United States, Canada, and Europe. The music signifies the good time to be had while listening to it as its name is a reference to those living the "high life," going to fancy clubs and high-end restaurants, and having a good time while being envied by those who are missing out. An emerging popular place to have a good time while listening to hiplife and other music is in Accra's growing rooftop lounge scene. An Internet search of "Accra rooftop" will attest to this, as it returns hundreds of thousands of results, many of which are bars, restaurants, and other venues that would each lay claim to it being Ghana's "best place to hang" or "coolest joint."

When one wants a more restful or relaxing place to spend time socializing, a trip to the beach is in order, an easily done feat, given Ghana's coast. One of the most popular beach destinations for Accra's residents is Labadie. There, it is common to find people in groups playing football and beach volleyball, swimming in the lake, shopping at some of the markets, eating fresh seafood, or just relaxing during the day. Labadie's many bars and restaurants make this a desirable place to see and be seen partying at night. Other beaches, like Busua, are more remote and attractive to those looking to backpack, get away from it all, and enjoy the natural beauty of Ghana for a weekend trip.

INDIA

In its colonial past, Mumbai was known as Bombay. Even for those with little knowledge of India, it is often the India of Mumbai they recall when they picture the subcontinent, as it has been often depicted in American film and TV. If we go underneath these portrayals, what might we see of Mumbai? It is one of the most important cities in India, both domestically and internationally, as it is at India's financial, corporate, and cultural center. Mumbai, India's largest city, is a good entrée into the social life of India. Since Mumbai is an expensive, highly populated city with large rates of density like New York or San Francisco, space is hard to come by. While this means privacy may be compromised, the upside is that companionship and its benefits are often close at hand.

Because space is so limited, property is expensive, and the city is quickly growing and attracting India's growing educated classes, many recently built housing developments are incorporating public and communal spaces into their planning. Newer apartment complexes, for example, often have gyms, green spaces like parks and gardens, and other recreational facilities, which in turn facilitate opportunities to connect with others. These spaces also often host frequent get-togethers for their residents, providing them for places and occasions to meet, socialize, and expand their social network. This is significant as Mumbai is growing as a world city; many of its newest inhabitants are newcomers to the city and are building their social lives and circles upon arrival. Perhaps as a result of the city's density, hanging out at parks and the beach is often how Mumbai residents engage in socializing. During monsoon season, it is common to see people out and about at Worli Sea Face while they view waves roll in. At other times of the year, it is one of Mumbai's many popular places to go for an evening stroll. Indeed, an evening stroll is quite popular as a way to pass the time with others in Mumbai. Another place that this occurs is along one of Mumbai's most popular streets, Marine Drive, also known as "the Queen's Necklace" in reference to the illumination provided by a sparkling semicircle of lights as the street ends onto a similarly popular beach. While walking along Marine Drive or the beach with friends or family, one may see vendors selling food, kids enjoying amusement park rides, as well as plenty of other people also out for a walk as the sun sets. Another popular destination, as seen in its large crowds, is Mumbai's largest park —Shivaji Park. There, Mumbai residents can be found gathered together for people watching, playing sports and games, grabbing a snack, or having a conversation on the weekend.

Additionally, just as in other major cities, the arts and festivals are key pillars of socializing. One art associated with Mumbai is certainly film, and with good reason. Film as an industry and a pastime is a vital element of Mumbai's economic and social life. Bollywood—a name hearkening back to Mumbai's colonial past as Bombay—is indeed the Hollywood of India. India's first film was made in Mumbai at the turn of the 20th century, and it remains the center of Indian film culture and production. There are film societies and clubs that people join, and many cultural centers like galleries and museums have spaces within them that are dedicated to film. If you are in Mumbai and want to watch a film, there are copious movie theaters to choose from. Within their walls, patrons meet to watch the latest as well as classics from India and abroad. Going to the movies is such an important practice currently that several developers are pouring large amounts of money into revamping or building movie theater complexes much like the multiplexes so popular throughout the suburban U.S. landscape. Prior to the rise of multiplexes, movie attendance in Mumbai was more intimate, occurring in small cinemas located in nearly every neighborhood of the city. Here is another example of changes in where and how hanging out is shaped by economic and other social transformations. Local and international film festivals also offer chances to connect with other cinephiles.

Additionally, there is no shortage of celebrations to mark in Mumbai, and each provides plenty of opportunities to socialize in public and in more intimate settings. In its cosmopolitanism, Mumbai residents celebrate both Western and Indian festivals, some of which are secular and some of which are religious, encompassing Muslim, Hindu, and Christian faith traditions. One popular festival is Ganesh Chaturthi, which marks the birthday of Ganesha, the Hindu god represented as an elephant. Ganesh Chaturthi takes place annually between August and September and was established in the late 19th century to bridge caste differences and unite Indians to fight off British colonial rule. As Ganesha is revered as the god of all and the remover of obstacles, it makes sense that this celebration continues more than 100 years later as a ritual to mark the success and promise of unification. Not only does socializing happen in the duration of the festival, but it occurs in the preparation for it as well. Teams of people work together, bonding as they come up with designs and projects to create the biggest and most impressive displays, gaining bragging rights for them and their communities. It culminates in an extravagant, large, and joyful parade.

MEXICO

Mexico is a country between the United States and Central America and is known for its Pacific and Gulf of Mexico beaches and its diverse landscape of mountains, deserts, and jungles. The social atmosphere tends to be fairly laid-back in Mexico; however, when meeting someone, you should avoid using his or her first name until that person invites you to do so. According to Commisceo Global, Mexicans tend to emphasize hierarchical relationships. They place a high value on hierarchy and structure in business and family matters. People respect authority and look to those above them for guidance. Rank is important, and those who are above you in rank must always be treated with respect; therefore, it is important to know who is in charge. Mexicans are aware of how each individual fits into the hierarchy whether it is a family, friend, or business hierarchy. It is considered disrespectful not to follow the hierarchy.

In Mexico, it is customary for people to be polite, courteous, and patient. Therefore, keep in mind if you travel to Mexico, it would be wise to display politeness and patience in social situations; otherwise, you may find yourself getting nowhere. Individuals who display impatience or lack of general respect for others will typically not experience overt conflict; however, people may just ignore you, and therefore, you may wait a long time for what you asked for or may not get it at all.

The family is at the center of the social structure in Mexico. The World Values Survey is a global network of social scientists studying changing values and their impact on social and political life. They distribute a questionnaire to assess the beliefs and values of individuals in nearly 100 different countries. In a report published in 2016 about the country of Mexico, when asked to rate how important your family and friends are in your life, 97.6 percent of Mexicans answered that family was "very important" in their lives compared to only 38.6 percent who responded that friends are "very important." Familismo means to value family needs over the needs of the individual. Mexicans are very aware of their responsibilities to immediate and extended family members such as cousins and even close friends. The extended family is as important as the nuclear family since it provides a sense of stability. Mexicans consider it their duty and responsibility to help family members. For example, they may help them find a job or buy a house. Hosting parties at their homes is an important aspect of Mexican life and making people feel comfortable is a large part of the values and customs of the country.

There is a sense of devotion to one's family and respect for one's parents and grandparents. Adult children tend to keep close relationships with their parents. Although extended families typically do not live together in the same household in Mexico today, family is still the number one priority among many Mexicans. Multigenerational families spend a lot of time together. Extended family members may live by each other, or if families live farther apart, members regularly make trips to visit each other. A weekly lunch or dinner where all the family gets together is a common occurrence. Also, grandparents typically help care for their grandchildren. As parents age, they often move in with their adult children, or the adult children move in with their parents. Adult children try to take care of their parents for as long as possible and only resort to a care facility if the parent needs medical assistance.

According to columnist Judit Covarrubias Garcia, Mexico has traditionally had a patriarchal family structure, meaning the father or male figure is head of the household. He is the authority figure and person who
makes the decisions. Fathers are in charge of family decisions, and their
authority is rarely challenged by either their wife or children. Mothers
are greatly admired, but their role may be perceived as subordinate to that
of their respective husbands. Mothers are the heart of the family. They
cook, clean, and take care of the children. Thus, females typically portray
a submissive and dependent role in the marriage relationship, and males
are given the "leader of everything" role. There are defined roles for mothers, fathers, and children in Mexican families. "Machismo" is the term for
the traditional role of males expected to be strong and powerful.
Machismo means "masculinity." These manly attitudes are expected from
Mexican males almost from birth, and machismo plays a pervasive role in
shaping Mexican culture. According to Commisceo Global, there are different outward behaviors to display machismo. For example, making
remarks to females is a stereotypical sign of machismo and should not be
seen as harassment. Mexican males generally believe that nothing should
be allowed that would tarnish their image as a man. When Mexican males
reach adolescence, they are expected to take an interest in females and to
talk and act in a particular manner to demonstrate their masculinity.
There are females whom the males exploit for sexual purposes to show
their machismo.

"Marianismo" is the term for the role of females in Mexican family culture. The importance of modesty is highly emphasized. Children, especially girls, are socialized to value conformity to social norms. Daughters
learn how to be a woman from their mother. Rebelliousness and delinquency are rare. Mexican adolescents will be reluctant to engage in any
activity that might bring shame to their families.

Nowadays, the head of the household is called *jefe de familia* and is used
for the person be it a woman or man who is in charge. Today, parenting
roles in Mexico are a bit more egalitarian, but it really depends on the
upbringing of both parents and the roles they agree to take on within their
family. The major changes seen in family structure over the past 50 years
mainly come from the empowerment of Mexican women. Although gender inequality is still an issue, the fact that many women are now household leaders is evidence of progress. Some changes that made this new
empowerment possible include increased opportunities in education and
the need of the workforce to make use of its women. While the country
still has a lot of "machismo" attitudes, women dropped the "marianismo"
attitude when it was no longer feasible. Up until about the 1980s, it was

fairly common for women with means to attend a university without a serious intention of joining the workforce. However, the major economic crisis of the early 1990s moved more women into the workforce as couples tried to earn enough to support their families. This revolutionized how people perceived education. According to the Organisation for Economic Co-operation and Development (OECD), since then, 40–50 percent of Mexican women, from both rural and urban backgrounds, have increasingly earned their degrees and actively pursued their profession of choice.

Columnist Judit Covarrubias Garcia explains, while some Mexican families still follow the traditional family structure, many others follow family trends similar to those in the United States and Europe. For instance, there has been a shift from extended families to nuclear families, an increase of female-headed households, and more varied structure of families (including same-sex couples and their children). She talks about the daily life of young adults in Mexico. According to Garcia, due to the fact that education is expensive and there is a high cost of living typically, only young adults from upper middle-class families leave their homes to go to college. Therefore, it is less common for young adults from rural areas to leave their families in pursuit of an education; if they do, it is more of a sacrifice. Most young adults with access to local colleges and universities continue living with their parents while attending school, and many continue to do so even after they graduate and join the workforce. In Mexico, there is not a stigma for living with your parents as there might be in other countries. Many children live with their parents until they get married or have enough money to cover the expenses of living on their own.

Although the modern Mexican family does not follow all long-established customs, there are many traditions that are still an important part of the culture to this day. For instance, many young Mexican females are honored on their 15th birthday with a quinceañera celebration. During the celebration, the girl's father ceremoniously exchanges her flat, childish-style shoes for a demure pair of modestly high-heeled shoes to denote her passage into womanhood. The event is full of sentiment as the young woman dances with her father as the guests look on. Likewise, even though it is celebrated in the United States more so than Mexico, Cinco de Mayo or the "Fifth of May" is a holiday celebrated in some parts of Mexico in honor of the Mexican army's 1862 victory over France at the Battle of Puebla during the Franco-Mexican War. In the United States, Cinco de Mayo has evolved into a commemoration of Mexican culture and heritage, particularly in areas with large number of Mexican Americans.

There are also many religious festivities still celebrated in Mexico. For instance, the Feast of Our Lady of Guadalupe is observed on

December 12. It is a holiday celebrating the appearance of the Virgin Mary to a Mexican man named Juan Diego in 1531 who was a simple farmer and laborer. She is considered the patron saint of the country. People travel not only to the main cathedral built in her honor but also to any church or temple dedicated to her. Additionally, Dia de los Muertos or Day of the Dead is celebrated on November 2, which is a day set aside to remember and honor those who have died. Families place an altar at home for their deceased loved ones and go clean and dress their tombs. The families get together to reminisce about those who have passed. They often tell stories or share fond memories about the deceased. Finally, just like several towns in Mexico, many of the people in Mexico have been named after a saint. Consequently, when it is that saint's anniversary, the person is likely to receive phone calls, get text messages, and an occasional treat to celebrate the day.

SAUDI ARABIA

Saudi Arabia, known for its wealth derived from oil, is considered the cradle of Islam, and as such much of the public display of socializing in Saudi Arabia is organized around its practice. The traditional institutions of religion, monarchy, and family intersect and shape much of social life in Saudi Arabia.

Whereas in most cultures alcohol consumption (for those of legal drinking age) is a common part of social life, alcohol is forbidden in Saudi culture, so going wine tasting with coworkers, unwinding with buddies with beers at a local pub, or celebrating one's 21st birthday with a bar crawl is not happening in places like Riyadh, Saudi Arabia's capital city. This is vastly different from the Japanese culture mentioned earlier where socializing after work usually involves drinking especially in *nijikai*, or "second stage" of the evening's entertainment, which often takes place at a bar. In Saudi Arabia, alcohol is available in establishments that serve clientele from the West, but it does not play the same role in having a good time there that it might here. What, then, can we expect socializing in Saudi Arabia to look like?

Men in Saudi Arabia express more physical closeness with each other while socializing across the board than their American counterparts. Upon encountering each other, men exchange greetings that include handshakes and kisses upon each cheek. There is also less physical distance between Saudi men interacting together. If men in casual situations in the United States have between 18 inches and 4 feet between them as they walk down the street, it is not uncommon to see men in Saudi Arabia walking arm in arm as a reflection of their warm—but not sexual, as same-sex relationships are illegal and punishable by death there—relationship.

Because of the primacy of the family, many socializing activities take place within extended family arrangements, eased by shared or close living arrangements. That socializing with family is important is shown when housing construction in Saudi Arabia is examined. Even among relatively new construction in the increasingly wealthy and suburbanizing Saudi Arabia, personal dwellings are often built with courtyards, areas for men and women to receive their same-sex guests, family gathering spaces, and accommodations for multiple generations. New homes replicate old traditions, rituals, and patterns of entertaining so that even as new communities spring up, they are inhabited by familiar people and customs. Indeed, the social connectedness, attachments, and systems of obligations are strong and deep due to overlapping shared familial, religious, communal, and household ties.

Customarily, men and women do not socialize with each other in public. Indeed, Saudi women are largely relegated to live their social lives in private, with other women or men to whom they are related. When Saudi women are in public, it is with a male relative as their escort. When Saudi women are in a car, it is with a male relative as their driver since women are forbidden to drive. In public spaces like shopping malls, zoos, spas, restaurants, and mosques, there is strict gender segregation, with men having far more access, freedom, and opportunities for socializing than women. When they do share the same space, there are physical barriers separating women and men. In other cases, there are sex-segregated separate days, facilities, or spaces, such as doors and floors dividing nonrelated men and women. In some locations, the lines are drawn between family and men-only sections. In these cases, women must use only the family section.

These gender divisions in socializing that exist in public also exist in private throughout Saudi culture. As a result, there are several both semipublic (open to family in residence, visiting relations, and guests) and semiprivate spaces (generally open only to family) within the home. In some homes, this means that women do all of their socializing with women relatives within private quarters and men control the less private areas where they host any male guests they have.

In some family living arrangements that extend across multiple buildings, passageways completely hidden from external view allow women family members to move between houses as they use rooftops, alleys, inner courtyards, and backdoors. In this way, women have greater freedom and control of their own movements and can spend time talking, laughing, applying makeup, trying on new clothing, and visiting each other without fear of rebuke or reprisal from male relatives or religious officials. Children living in these conditions also have more ability to play and engage their imaginations with others. As women and children in Saudi society have limited access to public life, if these housing arrangements are unavailable, they are forced to have far more limited social ties and lives as they must stay within the confines of apartments and small homes.

As economic and social shifts come to Saudi Arabia, though, some changes are afoot. In Jeddah, a relatively liberal coastal city, it is becoming more common to see men and women sharing meals together at local dining establishments, even as they break the law in doing so. More women are working in the paid labor force, and while they often are forced to use separate elevators and office spaces, that too is changing and is no longer universal in Saudi work environments. For the first time, in 2015, women—councilmembers and advisors to the Saudi king—attended and interacted with nonrelated men in the royal court.

This chapter has emphasized the various ways socializing occurs around the world. If you recall from the section on Norway, the 2017 World Happiness Report ranked Norway number 1 out of 155 countries in terms of "happiness." What about the other countries touched on throughout this chapter? Brazil was ranked 22, Mexico 25, Saudi Arabia 37, Japan 51, India 122, and Ghana 131. Think about the similarities and differences in socializing in each culture highlighted in this chapter. What possible factors may contribute to their "happiness" ranking or more specifically life satisfaction? What contributes to your overall life satisfaction based on the culture in which you live?

Part II

Scenarios

In this section, five different scenarios are presented about various aspects of socializing. The scenarios are related to the topics discussed throughout this book. After each scenario, an interpretation of that particular situation is given.

 ## Jake Doesn't Want to Go to School

Jake is a happy but timid six-year-old boy. He lives with his mother, father, and older sister who is nine years of age. It is the first day of school, and he is a bit nervous yet excited to start first grade. This year Jake gets to go to school all day long, just like his big sister who is starting third grade. Jake is happy because going to school all day means that he gets to eat lunch at school and even has a second recess period, unlike in kindergarten when he only went to school for half the day. When Jake gets to school, he meets his new teacher and finds out that many of his classmates who were in his kindergarten class last year, as well as some new kids, are in his first-grade class this year. Jake is glad to see so many of his classmates from last year.

The day begins with the children introducing themselves to each other and revealing one fun thing they did over the summer. He is excited to hear all of the fun things his classmates did this past summer. When it is Jake's turn to introduce himself, he is a bit nervous, but he tells the class his name and that he had fun swimming at the pool over the summer. While at recess, Jake does not play

*with anyone but instead plays by himself. At lunch, he sits with some of his class-
mates (at his assigned lunch table) but does not say very much to any of them.
When a classmate next to Jake tries to talk with him by asking him a question,
Jake politely answers with a quick response. Finally, the first day of school comes
to an end, and when Jake's mom asks him how it went, he replies, "Okay."*

*A few weeks pass and Jake finds himself more and more alone. He is not con-
fident in his ability to play sports well like some of the other boys in class during
gym, and he tends to be anxious during recess because he rarely has someone
who wants to play with him. To make matters worse, Jake is beginning to get
teased by a couple of the other kids in the class because he is so quiet. One morning before school, Jake asks his mom if he can stay home. His mom asks him if he
is not feeling well or if anything is bothering him, and Jake simply replies, "I just
don't want to go to school."*

The story of Jake touches on socializing in childhood. Recall from
Chapter 5, as children get older, their social relationships begin to include
social status (i.e., the degree to which they are liked or disliked by their peers
as a group). There are five social status categories within a peer group: popular, rejected (aggressive or withdrawn), neglected, controversial, and average.
Rejected-withdrawn children are socially withdrawn, wary, and timid. They
have less confidence in their social skills, are more anxious in situations with
their peers, and are at risk for bullying. In many cultures, as children get
older, there is less tolerance among the peer group for withdrawn behavior.
This behavior is seen as negative, and these children are at risk for being disliked and bullied by their peers. As a result, social isolation may be forced on
some children as they advance in school, either through their own disruptive
or aggressive behavior or through self-isolation.

Jake is at risk of becoming rejected-withdrawn among his peers. This is
evident due to the fact that he gets anxious in various social situations
with his peers (e.g., at recess or the lunch table) and lacks confidence in
his ability to play sports. Jake often plays by himself at recess because he
most likely lacks the social skills to be able to initiate a social interaction (
e.g., asking another peer to play with him). He is also beginning to get
teased by some of the kids in his class. The bullying may get worse as he
gets older if he continues along this path of social withdrawal. Children
who grow up as social outsiders are more likely to feel depressed, have
low self-esteem, and do poorly in school.

So what can be done to help a child like Jake make friends? As discussed
in Chapter 4, Albert Bandura believed that learning occurs by simply
watching others' behaviors. We learn new behaviors by observing and imitating the behavior of others, especially people who are nurturing and

powerful and those we admire. Therefore, modeling appropriate social skills is important for these children. Another effective method is to coach or teach these children how to initiate appropriate interactions with others (e.g., asking someone to play). Once the child learns to do this, reinforcing that appropriate behavior is key. When a child does something constructive, reinforce or encourage that positive behavior so that the child continues to behave in that manner. Some children may act inappropriately in a social situation simply because they do not know how to behave. Therefore, role playing can be an effective way to help children learn to make friends. Have the child act out the part of a specific peer so he or she can understand a different point of view or socially acceptable alternatives in a particular social situation. Lastly, it is helpful to plan structured (as opposed to unstructured) activities with other children (refer to Chapter 1 for more information about structured versus unstructured socializing). For children who feel socially inadequate, just hanging out with other kids can be stressful. Therefore, it is better to have a planned structured activity, such as going to a movie or the zoo, making a craft project, or playing a sport. This takes the pressure off the child to have to think of something to do with his or her peers and reduces the need for frequent conversation.

Maria Is Offered Drugs

It is Friday afternoon. Maria is sitting in her science class, waiting for the school bell to ring. At last, it rings and school is out. Maria is excited as most teenagers are since it is the end of the school week. As Maria walks back to her locker to get her things before heading to the bus to go home, she runs into a fellow classmate, Joe, whom she thinks is cute and has secretly liked for a few months. He asks Maria, "Are you going to the party this weekend"?

Maria replies, "Maybe. How about you?"

Joe says, "Yeah. I hope to see you there."

Maria smiles and proceeds to walk to her bus. On the way home, still excited from her conversation with Joe, she tells her good friend about her encounter. Her friend is happy for her and agrees to go with her to the party. While getting ready for the party, Maria wonders if she will see Joe there and if they will have a chance to hang out. Her friend drives over to Maria's house to pick her up, and they head off to the party. The party is at one of their classmate's house whom they know but are not friends with; his parents are out of town for the weekend. When they arrive, they see some friends of theirs, some classmates they know from school, and other teenagers they do not know.

The party is in full force. There is music playing, people dancing, a basketball game being played outside, and the majority of partygoers are drinking alcohol. Maria and her friend walk through the house looking for Joe. As they maneuver their way through the crowd, Maria is offered a beer, which she accepts. Maria and her friend find a spot in the living room where they can listen to music and dance. After a while, Maria spots Joe talking with some of his friends. He sees her from across the room and goes over to her. They begin to talk about school, their favorite music, and the high school football team winning the big game the other night. After a while, Joe asks Maria if she would like to go somewhere quiet to talk some more. Maria really likes Joe, so she agrees, and he leads her to one of the bedrooms in the house. While in the bedroom, Maria and Joe continue to talk. Maria is hoping that Joe will kiss her but instead he pulls a bag of pills out of his pocket and takes one. He then asks her if she would like one. Maria asks, "What are they"?

Joe replies, "I'm not sure; some pills from my parents' medicine cabinet. I like to take one every once in a while because it makes me feel good. Go ahead and try it, they're harmless."

Maria is not sure what to do; she really likes Joe but is afraid of what might be in those pills.

As highlighted in Chapter 5, most adolescents spend more time with peers than with their families. Therefore, peer relationships are especially important during adolescence. Groups become an important feature of social life during adolescence, and the group often functions without adult supervision. As illustrated in Maria's story, she attends a party at her class-mate's house whose parents are out of town for the weekend. Adolescent peer groups exert "pressure" primarily where social standards and standards for appropriate behavior are not well defined. For example, standards on smoking, drinking, and using drugs are often unclear. Parents may discour-age their teens from drinking or doing drugs, yet society is filled with young people (many of them celebrities) who drink alcohol and do drugs, seem to enjoy doing so, and do not suffer any negative consequences because of it. With such contradictory messages, it is not surprising that adolescents look to their peers for answers. Peers not only play a greater role in providing information about standards of behavior but also become a greater source of pressure for conformity.

Unfortunately, Maria's situation is not uncommon among teens. They attend a party or some other unsupervised function where drinking and drug use are taking place and often they are invited to take part in those activities. According to the National Institute on Drug Abuse (NIDA) for Teens, prescription drugs are the third most commonly misused substance by Americans age 14 and older, marijuana being the number one misused substance, and alcohol number two. Prescription drug misuse has become a public health problem, because misuse can lead to addiction and even death due to overdose. For teenagers, this is a growing problem; you cannot turn on the television without seeing a news report about a teenager who died from an accidental drug overdose or after a night of binge drinking.

The NIDA for Teens states that teenagers misuse prescription drugs due to a variety of reasons. For instance, they may want to get high, to decrease pain they are experiencing, or because they think it will help them with their school work. Many teens get the prescription drugs they misuse from friends or relatives, sometimes even without the person knowing, as was the case with Joe who got them from his parents' medicine cabinet.

The NIDA for Teens reminds teenagers that prescription drugs are often strong medications, which is why they require a prescription from a qualified physician. Every medication has some risk for harmful effects, sometimes serious ones. Physicians consider the potential benefits and risks to each patient before prescribing medications and take into account a variety of different factors such as the person's weight, other medications the person is taking, and the side effects of the drug. When prescription drugs are misused, they can be just as dangerous as illegal drugs.

So, what is Maria to do? "Just saying no" is a good start, but it is also helpful for parents to have teens engage in role plays where they can practice what to say when someone offers them drugs. Children and teens should be taught respect for their body. Taking these substances can jeopardize their physical and psychological health. Keep in mind, knowledge is key. Maria should be aware of the consequences of taking something when she does not know what it is. She may experience a side effect from the drug especially if she is using it in combination with another substance such as alcohol. There are a variety of useful resources such as the NIDA for Teens and the Addiction Education Society for teens to learn more about the dangers of substance abuse.

Chris's Neighborhood

Chris, 17, lives in a low-income, African American neighborhood where his family has lived since the 1950s. Neighborhoods like his are often described as "bad." It is true that the unemployment, crime, and violence rates are higher there and that there are more visible signs of disorder, like abandoned buildings, people hanging out on corners, and trash on the streets. Chris gets angry when he hears people only focus on these things. They ignore the people who organize Easter egg hunts, throw back-to-school parties for all the kids in the neighborhood, hold barbeques in the park every summer, and make sure that all the senior citizens have their snow shoveled each winter. Chris knows his community as a good place, full of good people. He thinks that some things could be better, though.

He wishes that schools were better, there were more jobs, and that jobs paid more. He also wishes that it was calmer and quieter sometimes, especially in the summer when more people are around. He gets concerned about the older people there, people like his grandmother and her friends who are increasingly afraid to come outside. Last summer, his grandmother refused to even sit on her front porch or work in her garden past the late afternoon—things he knows that she loves to do. These elders used to be active in the neighborhood, but that has declined due to some moving away, some dying, and those who remain being too fearful.

Still, it is home. Chris often says he knows everybody in his neighborhood. He knows who is cool to be around and who he should avoid. If he is at least cool with people there, he thinks they will look out for him and not really bother him. He speaks to them when he sees them but does not hang out with them much anymore since he learned from his parents and other relatives that "birds of a feather flock together" and "you're known by the company you keep." Some of the kids he grew up with are involved with gangs, and some have been in and out of jail. He feels bad for them, especially since he knows the lack of employment and high-quality educational opportunities contributes to this. He also knows that the way people are seen and treated in his community is different than the way people in other communities are.

Chris's favorite cousin, Pierre, lives in an affluent suburb. Chris observes these differences during his visits. He sees the doctors', dentists', and psychologists' offices. He sees the big houses and nice cars. He notes the grocery stores and shopping plazas. There, people are not as close-knit, but there are so many more activities and opportunities available, from the new playground equipment, the well-maintained pool and ice-skating rink, and all of the help-wanted signs everywhere. Some of Pierre's classmates in high school used and sold marijuana, and when they were caught, they were issued warnings at the least and citations at the most. When Chris's high school friends were caught with weed, they were expelled and arrested. As Chris goes back and forth between his house and Pierre's, he wonders how life can be so different three miles away.

Looking at Chris's life reveals the importance of geographical location in social networks and the assets and opportunities available through these. In low-income communities, particularly low-income communities of color, there are limited resources, including activities for young people to cultivate their interests and have safe spaces to spend time. Those that are available are in short supply and often not able to serve all who want them as the presence of long waiting lists for summer and after-school programs at libraries, parks, and community centers indicate. These are places that may be rich in people with a host of abilities and knowledge who care for and about each other but not when it comes to the financial, social, and cultural capital valued by society overall. There are connections but just not enough of the sort of connections that lead to upward social mobility.

A long body of research by sociologist William Julius Wilson points to strong, healthy, and safe urban communities depending on three interrelated processes: the presence of strong, well-integrated social networks, residents who cooperatively monitor and ensure neighborhood safety and other measures of well-being, and residents' participation in formal and voluntary neighborhood associations. In the absence of these and in the presence of high levels of neighborhood poverty, social disorganization—a community's lack of ability to achieve communal safety, social norms, and other goals—arises. It is clear that Chris's neighborhood has the first, but as the other two processes are in decline and when taken with increased poverty and other structural barriers like access to jobs, employment, stores, mental and physical health care, and safe recreational activities, it is no wonder that Chris has the concerns about where he lives. This is a concern expressed far beyond Chris—as people in the neighborhood would tell you. There is also a narrative around this in popular cultural, academic, and news media and political discourse. Chris's concerns are also echoed in what we know about social isolation, as we discuss in the first three chapters.

Some initiatives have been shown to turn these tides. These include the Harlem Childrens' Zone (HCZ) in New York and the Becoming a Man program in Chicago. In the HCZ, led by activist and educator Geoffrey Canada since 1990, investments of time, money, and hope have been leveraged to address the structural, institutional, and personal issues that people of communities like Chris's face. Currently serving thousands of people in a 100-block area, the community connectedness that HCZ provides shows such positive outcomes that during the presidential administration of Barack Obama, there was a major federal and private push to replicate their model in what were termed "Promise Neighborhoods" in cities around the nation. This model involves access to services that have been shown to reduce the kinds of social ills associated with poor neighborhoods of color such as involvement with crime, drugs, and gangs while increasing test scores, grades, college attendance, neighborhood satisfaction, and other positive measures. In the Chicago program, which as its name suggests focuses on young men, students in schools in some of the city's most marginalized communities receive both group and cognitive behavioral therapy, mentoring, tutoring, as well as career and college preparation. The benefits have been demonstrated at both individual and communal levels through the data that show lower arrest rates, lower violent crime rates, and higher high school graduation rates. Programs like these have been touted as models and are being replicated as they are designed to bridge the social, cultural, human, and financial capital gaps between what Chris sees and experiences when he is in his community and when he is in his cousin Pierre's.

 ## Jessie Doesn't Call Me Anymore

Rosa met Jessie when they were first-year college students. As they made eye contact during the getting-to-know-you exercise as their teaching assistant made the first of many corny jokes, they knew they would become friends. Rosa and Jessie were inseparable from that moment on. As they spent time studying, partying, and eating together, they learned that they had much in common. They shared musical interests, political outlooks, preferences for veggie pizza, and clothing. In their sophomore year, they became roommates. Rosa and Jessie went on spring break trips together each year until they graduated, promising each other that this would become their ritual, their thing, even after their real lives, complete with careers, partners, and children, began.

After graduation, Jessie went to graduate school in New York and Rosa got a job teaching fourth grade in Phoenix. They stayed in contact with each other consistently, yet the amount of time they spent on the phone, texting, or tweeting each other started to decline after their first year in different cities. When they did talk, they were still excited to hear about both the major and the minor things the other had going on. These conversations, though, did not happen frequently enough for Rosa's tastes.

Initially, Rosa assumed that Jessie was busy with school, learning about the new city she was living in and trying to meet new people. Rosa wondered if something was wrong. When she asked, Jessie assured her that everything was fine between them. It was time for Rosa's school to go on spring break, and she decided it would be fun to recreate the old days with Jessie. Jessie seemed enthusiastic when Rosa suggested that she come to New York for a few days to catch up and create new memories. Rosa had figured that she would have to find ways to keep her busy during the time Jessie was in class. What she did not anticipate was that though Jessie only had class on Mondays and Tuesdays, she had made plans with her new friends for Wednesday and Thursday, leaving Rosa alone. Again. When they were together, it was never just the two of them—instead it was always Rosa, Jessie, and Jessie's new friends.

Rosa had expected that Jessie would have made new friends and started new chapters in her life, but she was still stunned at how different Jessie was acting and even more stunned that her friend did not show the warmth, care, and interest in their relationship that she had come to count on. Rosa was hurt when she got back to Arizona Sunday afternoon, so she decided to take a few days to cool off before confronting Jessie about the way she felt. When she called that Friday evening, her call went directly to voice mail. She called again Friday night and again only got Jessie's voice mail. Rosa thought that was odd but decided to go to bed. She woke up Saturday hoping that Jessie had called or at least texted. When Rosa saw that she had not, she texted Jessie. Jessie did not respond to her text. Rosa logged into Facebook to reach out to her friend that way only to learn that Jessie had unfriended her. Rosa opened up Twitter and typed in Jessie's name and got a message saying that Jessie had blocked her. Sliding down the wall and curling herself into a ball as she sobbed, Rosa was literally floored when she grasped that Jessie had turned her back on her and their six-year friendship.

There are plenty of books that talk about how to heal after a breakup. There is a script that we can follow after we are dumped by a person we were dating as anyone who has watched commercials, TV shows, or films in the United States can tell you. There are fewer road maps for recovering from the broken heart that losing a close friend brings. No longer being able to recount shared memories and plans for the future is painful, something that is often not acknowledged when friendships dissolve. The ebb and flow goes through cycles and sometimes dissolves. When a friendship ends, whether mutual or not, there may be hard feelings. When a friendship ends, due to one friend's unilateral decision, there is acute pain that the lack of closure only exacerbates.

A friendship between two people is known as a dyad. A dyad, a relationship between two people, is the smallest social group that can form. It is also the most unstable social group that can form, as it can end, at any time, for any reason, as Jessie and Rosa's relationship shows us. Even if only one person makes the decision and even if the other person objects, the social group—in this case, a friend relationship—is done. This is different from a triad, or a relationship of three people, which can remain a social group upon the exit of a group member.

What happened between Jessie and Rosa, though painful, is not too uncommon. As we discussed in Chapter 3, there are rhythms to all social relationships, and this certainly includes friendships. The stages we experience in life certainly affect the maintenance and stability of our friendships. We often leave our high school friends behind when we go to college. Jessie left her college friend behind when she started graduate school. It is likely that at least some of her friends from her period in graduate school will not make the cut when she starts her career or moves to yet another city. Jessie will likely have more changes in her social circle if and when she gets married, and these may change further still should she have children. Other life course reasons that friendships may end include divorce. It is often said that in divorces, not only are assets redistributed but friends are too and that in addition to fighting over custody of pets or children, former spouses may fight over who gets to keep which friends. People report losing friends after changing or losing jobs or retirement. Despite promises to stay in touch and period Facebook or Instagram posts, friendships that were work based may not survive the job change. There is also evidence that people experience contractions in their social circles after the death of their spouse. That old friends stop calling or inviting the surviving spouse for parties or to dinner compounds their grief.

What can Rosa do about these feelings? She can note that she is not alone. Rosa should also realize that though she is the one in pain, she is not at fault for the dissolution of her friendship with Jessie. If the emotional turmoil becomes too unbearable or is long lasting, Rosa might seek the services of a counselor.

 ### Betty Is the Last One Left

As Betty was about to blow out the candles on her birthday cake, she looked around the room at all of the people who were there to help celebrate her 80th birthday. She was surrounded by her sister and her sister's husband, her own children, grandchildren, great-grandchildren, and a few neighbors who lived nearby. Her great-granddaughter asked (as people usually do when someone is about to blow out the candles on a birthday cake), "Granny, what are you going to wish for?" In that moment, Betty began to think about her life. She was now 80 years old and what would be her birthday wish? Some people may wish for monetary things such as a car, a new piece of jewelry, or a pet of their very own. Betty thought about it and decided she does not need any more possessions. Others may wish for an advancement, be it a promotion at work or a job with better pay, a bigger house, or to move to a nicer neighborhood. Betty thought about that; however, she is retired from her job as an accountant, and she and her husband downsized their home after their children were grown and moved out. Still

others may wish for a long healthy life, but Betty has already lived one. Sure she has experienced some of the age-related ailments that most people do, who live to be her age, but overall she has lived a fairly healthy life. None of those were Betty's wish. What Betty wished for was someone to talk to, a friend. Someone who was her own age, someone who would understand the age-related issues she was dealing with at this point in her life.

Betty grew up in a house with her parents and her three siblings, a sister and two brothers. Her two brothers both passed away many years ago. Her sister is still alive, is married, and lives about an hour away. Betty was happily married to her husband for almost 50 years before he died a few years ago. She had had many friends throughout her life. Up until recently, she would regularly get together with her friends from high school for lunch or dinner or to play cards. However, all of her friends have passed away, with the last one being a year ago. Betty's children, grandchildren, and even great-grandchildren stop by on a regular basis to visit or to take her out for a bite to eat. Her one granddaughter even takes her to play bingo once a month. Betty is surrounded by people; she not alone, but she is lonely. Even though she socializes with people on a some-what regular basis, be it her children, grandchildren, or great-grandchildren, she really does not have anyone her age with whom to socialize. Betty is the last one left.

When people live long enough to reach late adulthood, their social roles change. As mentioned in Chapter 5, older adults may downsize and move into a smaller home or to an active adult community, work part-time or retire, volunteer, or become a great-grandparent. Betty has experienced most of these things already. She and her husband moved to a smaller home after their children moved out, she is retired from her careers as an accountant, and she has been blessed with a number of great-grandchildren.

As people get older, they often find themselves spending more and more time at home alone. This social isolation is not good for older adults' over-all health; it may lead to depression and increases the likelihood of death. Surprisingly, the feeling of loneliness negatively affects us as much as actually being alone. Therefore, it is important for Betty to become socially active. As mentioned throughout this book, friendships play an important role from the time we are little kids to late life. The fact that people choose their friends may be especially important to older people who often feel control over their lives is slipping away. This may help explain why older adults who have friends are healthier, happier, and live longer. Older adults tend to benefit from confiding in others who are also going through similar changes. What about Betty? She does not have any friends who are still alive. She does not have friends to talk with who are dealing with similar age-related changes. How can she deal with this social loss? Having her children, grandchildren, and great-grandchildren visit and spend time with her is wonderful; however, Betty should also consider becoming a volunteer at a local school or library in her community or adding a social activity to her routine. As highlighted in Chapter 3, doing the same thing day after day is not good for the brain, especially as we get older; it is beneficial to try something new. In Betty's case, she may want to join a class at the local park district or senior center, serve meals or organize clothing donations at a place for the homeless, help an organization send care packages to soldiers stationed overseas, care for animals at a local shelter, or help with gardening at a community garden or park. Any one of these activities would be a great way for Betty to try something new and maybe connect with people her own age.

Part III

Controversies and Debates

In this section, three issues related to socializing are debated. An introduction to each controversy is provided, and then each issue is debated by professional scholars who take opposing viewpoints. Keep in mind that the scholars may agree with one another on certain aspects of the issue but disagree on other aspects. It is important to read opposing viewpoints and critically evaluate information in order to gain a better understanding of that information. The first controversy examines interracial friendships. The second controversy explores whether men and women can just be friends. The third debate considers whether technology has made present-day socializing easier or more difficult.

 Controversy #1: Interracial Friendships: Do Race and Ethnicity Matter?

INTRODUCTION

Race, through the history of the United States, has been a hot-button issue. Though the heat of the conversation around race in the United States may raise or lower, there are certainly always flames around it. Still, through the history of the United States, friendships across racial and ethnic lines—lines that themselves change and morph based on social, political, migration, and other factors—have existed. Certainly, intimate interracial relationships—romantic and platonic—on these are rooted in colonial times. Indeed, one grouping of Blacks and Whites that included enslaved people, farmers, and indentured servants banded together in colonial Virginia in 1676 to overthrow their colonial rulers for, in part, dispossessing them of land and pay and failing to protect them from Native Americans who were attempting to get their land back from those who had taken it from them in the first place. In the wake of the ultimately unsuccessful Bacon's Rebellion, legal codes were established that created rules that cemented race and racial division in the United States. These rules prohibited interracial marriages and gatherings and established a firm racial hierarchy that granted privilege to Whites, such as the ability to own land, vote, and avoid servitude, and oppression to Blacks, including the lifelong and inheritable condition of enslavement. Violating these laws could mean harsh beatings, brutal physical and psychological punishments, and loss of life. For Whites, it could also mean loss of status and freedom. In this moment, a social structure built upon social and cultural segregation of Blacks and Whites began in Virginia and spread like wildfire through the colonies. Undeniably, powerful incentives against the formation of interracial friendships became enshrined in policy and law, and this has continued impact on such relationships today.

If we look at interracial friendships, we can observe a lot about who and what the United States is today. In early 2009, former U.S. Attorney General Eric Holder caused a stir for some and agreement for others when he said that Americans were cowards when it came to talking about race. He went on to say that the country had made strides in reducing segregation in the workplace and indeed "we work with one another, lunch together and, when the event is at the workplace during work hours or shortly thereafter, we socialize with one another fairly well, irrespective of race." Yet, according to Holder, these interactions often treat race as the elephant in the room—everyone knows that it is there, yet no one mentions it, preferring to pretend that it is absent. Furthermore, according to Holder, after work and on the weekends, these interactions largely disappear as we ourselves disappear into our racially and ethnically segregated personal communities. Though controversial, Holder was right. We do live largely segregated lives as evidenced through our segregated social circles.

As we saw in Chapter 1, most friendships occur within race. We also saw that Whites are least likely to have a friend of another race. Recall that data from the Public Religion Research Institute (PRRI) show that when it comes to one's intimates, 75 percent of Whites have no racial or ethnic diversity in their networks, as is the case for 65 percent of African Americans and 46 percent of Latinx people. There is even more network homogeneity when it comes to those whom one is closest to. For these people, perhaps it is not that interracial friendships cannot exist but that they do not.

Though data show that interracial friendships are not the norm for most of us in the United States, many express openness to and desire for these relationships. Why, then, do they not occur more frequently? Part of the answer lies in where we live, work, and are educated, as noted in Chapter 1. Though struck down in the 1954 Supreme Court decision in the *Brown v. Board of Education* case, segregation abounds in the United States. Residential segregation means that most of us will live in communities with others who share our racial and ethnic heritage. As most of us attend schools—at least before college—close to home, school then becomes another site of segregation. If most of whom we are close to emotionally is based on who we are close to geographically, then we see few opportunities to even have cross-racial and cross-ethnic encounters, let alone friendships. By the time we are in circumstances where we are more likely to see those who do not share our race and ethnicity, such as in college, the military, and at work, the barriers for connecting across these differences have been raised. These, though, are not insurmountable, and plenty of people do have racially and ethnically diverse networks of associates, acquaintances, and friends.

What, then, about those who do have more inclusive friend networks? They certainly do exist. However, they face a set of issues that those with networks comprised of social ties with others with whom they share racial and ethnic identities do not. As racial and ethnic tensions become more publicly visible again, demarcations also become visible within friendships across racial and ethnic boundaries as people who have spent time together laughing, crying, and all points in between realize that they have quite different perspectives on what a Trump presidency, the #BlackLivesMatter movement, a wall between the United States and Mexico, the Dakota Access Pipeline, and a ban on Muslim entry into the country mean. For friendships with people who have different racial and ethnic backgrounds to work, all parties need to be frank about their stances and receptive to those of their friends'. Part of this will mean discussing, facing, and conquering prejudices, stereotypes, and conscious and unconscious biases and racism, a difficult task to be sure. Though it may be a true challenge, avoiding these issues is not the route as this will cause the type of unresolved tension and conflict that strains and ends friendships. As these are interracial and interethnic relationships, the fallout may extend beyond the individual to the entire group, creating even more prejudice and discrimination.

In the following two essays, two scholars debate the topic of interracial friendships. The first essay takes the stance that race and ethnicity matter in friendships, whereas the second essay takes the stance that race and ethnicity do not matter when it comes to friends with someone. As you read each essay, think about your own friendships and what has contributed to you becoming friends with someone (e.g. where you live or go to school, common interests you have, similar beliefs and values).

RESPONSE 1: YES, RACE AND ETHNICITY MATTER IN FRIENDSHIPS

I don't see color, I just see people.

I don't care if someone is green or purple, I like them for who they are, not what they look like.

It was destiny for us to be BFFs.

While those who make such statements may mean well, they don't reflect the reality of the historical and current interpersonal patterns of interaction in the United States. Imagine if we made statements like this regarding sex/gender? "I don't see men or women; I just see people." Does that sound remotely possible? Sociologists refer to race as a "master status" because it is a primary part of a person's life—it influences your identity, and it is one of the first things someone else notices about you. Saying you don't notice race or that it doesn't matter denies a primary piece of your friend's cultural history, identity, and "who they are." Maybe you may feel that your identity is made up more by your ethnicity (your cultural practices, beliefs, and traditions) than your race. However, persons of color don't have a choice whether to identify or not as a member of a particular group because "you are what others see you as."

In the United States, where our history includes the institution of slavery and acts of genocide, your "race" (combined with social class and gender) has always had a major role influencing if you have advantages or disadvantages in society. While race is not real in a genetic sense (DNA tests show the geographic history of where in the world your ancestors came from), it is very real in its everyday consequences. Choosing a friend is not just a matter of having shared interests; it is also having the opportunity to meet, spend time together, and develop a sense of belonging together. Those opportunities to meet are impacted by the neighborhood where you live, school you attend, and activities you can afford to participate in. The history of racially segregated housing continues to impact the diversity in our schools. In fact, educational segregation in K–12 schools is higher now than in the late 1960s during the Civil Rights Movement.

In addition, the racial attitudes of your parents impact your own beliefs and frame how you see the world. When you are a child, your ability to build friendships is influenced by who is welcomed into your home and whose home you are allowed to visit. As we grow older, interracial friendships are even harder to foster or maintain. A 2013 survey found that 40 percent of White Americans and 25 percent of Americans of color stated that their entire friendship network consisted of people with the same racial identity as themselves. As we age and our lives get more complicated with work, family responsibilities, more entrenched political views, and perhaps the desire to be comfortable (and safe) in our friendships, the probability of maintaining interracial friendships becomes more challenging and less likely unless we make a commitment to do so. In a moving personal essay by Professor Brittney Cooper, she argues that interracial friendships "require a level of risk and vulnerability that many of us would rather simply not deal with."

I am not saying that interracial friendships can't happen and be wonderful, but we need to consider that persons in the friendship may experience it differently. Acknowledging different experiences, dealing with the perceptions of others, and personal struggles are things that you should be able to share with a best friend. However, if your best friend is often perceived as either superior or inferior to you (because that's what happens in a racially stratified society when prejudiced thinking and racist actions are institutionalized and normalized), it puts a definite strain on a relationship. When one of the friends is White, the issue of White privilege has to be acknowledged and dealt with. Being considered "American" without a racial identifier in front (such as African American or Native American) provides advantages and is indeed a privilege—even if that person is not personally racist toward persons of color. We must actively work toward a society in which all persons will equally have the power to define themselves, to confront stereotypes and stigmatizing images, and have their cultural practices and beliefs considered normal and valid. While that struggle continues, as a White person married to a person of color, I have to remind myself to do more listening than talking. I still have a lot to learn.

Carlene Sipma-Dysico

RESPONSE 2: RACE AND ETHNICITY DON'T MATTER

No, race and ethnicity do not matter in friendship. Second to marriage, friendship is one of the most intimate societal connections. Generally speaking, friendship is a chosen tie that people enter based on trust, so we as friends often embark in these relationships as a result of a connection with the whole person.

Race has no biological basis. It is recognized as having a long history of attempts to organize groups of people based on similar skin color and physical appearance. Race is often difficult to define and classify because racial categories in society are unstable, shift often, and are significantly connected to other social categories, social forces, and social structures. Ethnicity refers to a shared culture and way of life. Language, religion, material culture such as clothing and food, and cultural products (e.g., music and art) are reflections of ethnicity. The way in which one self-identifies ultimately determines their race and ethnicity in spite of the socially constructed categories determined by governmental entities.

Instead of race and ethnicity mattering in friendship, factors such as social location, social class, and status influence friendships, whereas they are socially patterned and socially constructed. Friendships are inherently social as opposed to personal in that they are patterned based on social conventions rooted in social and economic milieus. Dyadic constructions do not shape friendship, rather biographic and historic characteristics alter friendships that are maintained. Structural influences such as privatization continue to negatively alter friendship and solidarity.

Chung, a female Asian adoptee, writes about her "complicity in racism," how she "aspired to friendship" with her then White peers during her early years in school, and knowing her place among her White friends. During her college career, she recounts a moment in which her view of herself began to shift. A shift in her level of comfort in talks about race occurred, going against how she was raised. As she transitioned into adulthood, she began to question her friendships as she often found herself being the only person of color and wondered if she was a token. In an interaction regarding race, relationships, and changing views, Chung recounts her dialogue with Rohin Guha, an editor of color. Chung and Guha exchanged methods for self-preservation and asserting values in friendships with the hope of avoiding stereotypes from those who are not of the same race and who are White. As such, Chung indicates that patience is a necessary part of friendship. Guha points out honesty as a cornerstone of lasting friendships, and equally important, he believes in the ability to listen: "The fear of being my group's Yellow Power Ranger/Asian sidekick was always a fear I had back then, a fear I didn't know how to vocalize."

Acknowledging and accepting one's race and ethnicity is essential; however, in friendship, race and ethnicity are irrelevant when love and virtuous goodness are at the core. In other words, when individuals who are engaged in the friendship are completely and totally immersed in unearthing a world greater than their own, race and ethnicity become secondary. This is not to say individuals need to ignore their race and ethnicity or that of their friend. Instead, going beyond the physical (i.e., race) and tapping into what is unseen are equally important. One's race and ethnicity contributes to the authenticity, richness, and educational components of the friendship.

When we go beyond the definitional parameters of friend, race, and ethnicity, we find that there is one race, the human race. The human race is made up of people from a variety of ancestries that are ultimately tied together. Human beings as a whole have more in common than uncommon. These commonalities are shaped differently and by differing factors and should be used as a means to learn from one another rather than divide. Race and ethnicity certainly play a part in friendship, but they do not matter and do not ultimately determine the success or the failure of friendship.

It is hard to claim and even embrace the thought that race and ethnicity do matter in friendship. Often, one does not get to choose what shapes their world because on the macro level there are institutions in place that use race and ethnicity divisively, but one does get to choose what stabilizes it and interracial friendship can.

Kristi Kelly

 Controversy #2: Can Men and Women Just Be Friends?

INTRODUCTION

In Chapter 5, we learned that from the time we are born, we want and need social interaction. When children are little, their primary source of socialization is the family. They spend the majority of their time with family members such as their parents, siblings, and grandparents. Once children are school age, school becomes an important source of socialization. A major part of socialization during the early school years is play. During these years, most of children's social relationships are with other children of the same sex (i.e., girls play with girls and boys play with boys). Friendships are rare between opposite-sex peers. Same-sex play during childhood seems to be universal; it is seen in most cultures throughout the world. This preference for same-sex friendships is also seen over the course of one's life. It is not that there are not opposite-sex friendships as we get older; however, the majority of people at any given point in their life tend to have fewer opposite-sex friends than same-sex friends. As we reach adolescence, whom we spend our time with changes. During adolescence, the amount of time spent with family decreases and amount of time spent with friends increases. Most adolescents actually spend more time with peers than with their families.

From the time we are children to older adults, friendships play a major role in socialization. Friendships are distinct from other social relationships; they are voluntary. In other words, while you may not get to choose your family, you get to choose your friends. Most friendships tend to be based in similarity. In other words, friends are usually individuals of the same age, sex, and background. In addition, liking of common activities and similar interests are key components in friendships. Friendships are primarily oriented toward enjoyment and personal satisfaction, as opposed to the accomplishment of a particular task or goal. Trust is especially important in friendship because of its voluntary nature. Friendships are important in adulthood, partly because a person's overall satisfaction with life is related to how often that person keeps in contact with his or her friends as well as the quality of those friendships.

There tends to be gender differences in friendship. Male friendships tend to be based on shared activities, whereas female friendships tend to be based on emotional support. Males tend to prefer to "do something" with a friend, and females tend to prefer to "just talk" with a friend. When males talk with their friends, it is generally about some activity they are going to do or have done (e.g., play golf or attend a sporting event). Female friendships focus on the needs and well-being of the other person. In contrast, male friendships focus on making sure the benefits received from the friendship are equal. Female friendships provide greater nurturance and intimacy but require more commitment and involvement. Conversely, male friendships may expect and get less from one another, but their friendships may be more tolerant of conflict than female friendships.

If these differences in same-sex friendships exist, why do men and women become friends with each other? According to research conducted by April Bleske-Rechek and David Buss on opposite-sex friendships, compared with women, men consider sexual attraction and a desire for sex as important reasons for initiating an opposite-sex friendship and lack of sex as a reason for ending one. Therefore, in opposite-sex friendships, males tend to overperceive and females tend to underperceive that friend's sexual interest in them. Women consider physical protection as a more important reason for initiating an opposite-sex friendship and lack of physical protection as a reason for ending one. There are benefits and costs to having a friendship with the opposite sex. Many of the benefits and costs are similar for both women and men. For example, for both men and women, benefits of opposite-sex friendships include companionship, enhancing one's self-esteem, having someone to talk openly with, and the sharing of resources. In addition, by having a friend who is the opposite sex, you can gain information about the opposite sex and help in attracting a mate. For both women and men, the costs of opposite-sex friendships are that there may be confusion about the status or nature of the relationship (e.g., one person may be romantically attracted to the other), jealousy, and not being as attractive to other potential daters because of the friendship. Even though these similarities exist, men and women may sometimes have different goals in opposite-sex friendships. For instance, as mentioned previously, men consider sexual attraction as a reason for initiating an opposite-sex friendship and as a result are more likely to see sex and romantic potential in an opposite-sex friend as a benefit, whereas women see it as a cost.

So why debate if men and women can be just friends? The reason is, because we know friendships are important. Friendships are a means of stimulation. They add interest and opportunities for socializing and can expand our knowledge, ideas, and perspectives. Friends often serve as confidants, as models of coping, and can help safeguard against stressful life experiences. Friends are useful because they give us assistance when needed and provide resources to help us meet our needs or reach our goals. Overall, friendships contribute positively to our self-esteem and overall life satisfaction.

So, can men and women just be friends? Although both men and women may sometimes be looking for a companion or friend and nothing more, in other circumstances, matters may differ. Below, two scholars debate the issue of opposite-sex friendships. First essay discusses evidence pertaining to men and women not being able to be just friends. The second essay examines evidence about men and women being able to just be friends.

RESPONSE 1: WHY WOMEN AND MEN CAN'T BE FRIENDS

> Eww, don't play with her, girls have cooties!
> You can't wear that, pink is a girl color!
> Why do you want to play ball with the boys, you're a girl!
> Ok, children, line up. Boys on this side, girls on that side.

From a very young age, we are given the message that boys and girls are different and should be separated. This is what social scientists call "gender socialization." Socialization is the process by which we learn what is expected of us in our society. Gender socialization refers to the ways that messages about socially expected behaviors for boys and girls (and ulti- mately men and women) influence us. At early ages, we are given the mes- sage that gender is a significant difference between us. This may be at home, where sons and daughters are given different chores, may be disci- plined differently, or may be separated by our parents—that is, girls stay with mom, and boys go with dad. Or it may be at school, where teachers may interact differently with students based on their gender, may have dif- ferent expectations, or may tolerate different types of behaviors from boys versus girls.

This early gender socialization causes a social distance between boys and girls that follows us to adulthood. Fairly quickly, children pick up on the adult messages, even when they are subtle and perhaps only implied. We begin segregating ourselves by gender in the early years of school. In the comments previously, only the last one is a direct message from an author- ity figure. The first three are examples of the ways that children separate themselves by gender. Well before middle school, boys and girls are much more likely to have same-sex friends and only cross that gender boundary when puberty hits and romantic interests arise.

So why does this early gender socialization process mean that women and men can't be friends? First, friendships are generally based on shared experiences or shared interests. Since we are socialized from a young age to play separately from one another and to engage in different activities, this foundation for friendships between girls and boys is usually missing. By the time we reach adulthood, women have been developing friendships with other women for years, and men have been developing friendships with other men for years. We become more comfortable with same-sex pla- tonic relationships.

Second, even if we were able to overcome this early gender socialization and cultivate opposite-gender friendships, there are still obstacles. We are also socialized to expect heterosexual romantic relationships (heteronorma- tivity). This means that opposite-gender friendships can be confusing. Heterosexual individuals may be concerned about mixed messages in a way that they are not with their same-sex friends. LGBT individuals may find opposite-gender friendships equally challenging as a result of the social or cul- tural expectations of who may be seen as a friend and who may be seen as a love interest. Because we segregate by gender so early in life, most people do not have a model for an opposite-gender relationship that is not romantic in nature. Think about a heterosexual married couple, for example. What would be your reaction if one spouse had lunch every day at work with an opposite-gender coworker or if he or she made plans to go for drinks after work or go to the movies? Many people would see this as a form of cheating, even if there was no sex involved. Why? The combination of our gender socialization and our assumptions of heteronormativity result in the expectation that intimate relationships between women and men are only appropriate between romantically involved couples. Thus, opposite-gender friendships are discouraged, and many people may avoid them either intentionally or unconsciously because they are unfamiliar and confusing.

Thus, women and men cannot be friends in our society. Not because we are inherently incapable of such friendships. We are not, as some observers suggest, from different planets or different worlds. The reason we cannot be friends is because we have been socialized not to be. The cultural messages we receive from a very young age encourage same-gender friendships and discourage opposite-gender friendships. Gender segregation limits our interactions with opposite-gender peers. So, by the time we reach adulthood, we have experience with and feel more comfortable in same-gender friendships. Furthermore, opposite-gender relationships are perceived as romantic or potentially romantic at all times. This makes same-gender friendships for adults difficult to manage and to explain to romantic partners. And so, we generally stay within our comfort zone by avoiding opposite-gender friendships.

Jennifer Tello Buntin

RESPONSE 2: YES, MEN AND WOMEN CAN BE FRIENDS

Many people's experiences, as well as published research on the topic, have suggested that it is difficult for men and women to be "just friends." We often hear stories about male-female friendships that took a turn for the worse when one person in the friendship developed feelings for the other. In circumstances where romantic feelings are not mutually shared, one friend is often pained by rejection, while the other is burdened by the discomfort of rejecting (and possibly losing) a cherished companion. On the other hand, we sometimes hear about people who developed romantic feelings for a close friend, and after finding that such feelings were mutual, the friendship blossomed into a passionate romance. These are two very different outcomes, but they share a common message: when romantic feelings enter an opposite-sex friendship, the "friendship" might not exist for much longer.

But is it possible for men and women to be close friends? The answer is yes—men and women can, and often do, engage in mutually satisfying friendships. Research shows that most people have a close friendship with a person of the opposite sex, and opposite-sex friendships are especially common among people aged 18–24. The ubiquity of male-female friendships is understandable, given the fact that people commonly form opposite-sex friendships for many of the same reasons that they form same-sex friendships: perceived similarity, trust, interdependence, mutual acceptance, enjoyment of the other's company, engaging in shared activities, and social support. Male-female friendships can even provide unique advantages that are not typically found in same-sex friendships, such as shared information about the opposite sex, honest feedback from the other gender's perspective, and access to a wider social network, which could allow for increased status and more opportunities to meet potential dating partners. Among males and females whose personalities do not match gender role stereotypes (e.g., men who are more emotionally expressive, and women who are more independent/assertive), opposite-sex friendships can be more rewarding than same-sex friendships, since they allow for greater feelings of perceived similarity. Not all male-female friendships are based on the expectation of an eventual romance.

Of course, opposite-sex relationships are threatened by a particular danger that is not typically found in opposite-sex friendships: romantic attraction. The implication behind the question of whether men and women can be close friends is that opposite-sex friendships will dissolve when one friend eventually develops unrequited feelings for the other. But just because this outcome is possible does not mean that it is *inevitable*. Research shows that most opposite-sex friends do not become romantically involved. Even among male-female friends who have sex (the so-called friends with benefits), friendships often continue—even if one or both individuals decide to stop having sex. This is especially seen among partners who truly view each other as friends and who did not build their relationship on sexual attraction alone. When sex becomes part of a friendship, it does not always lead the relationship to demise. In many reported cases, it can have the opposite effect. The majority of men and women in one study who reported having sex with a friend stated that it was actually beneficial for their friendship, serving as a way of enhancing closeness without changing the relationship into an unwanted romance. It therefore seems entirely possible for men and women to maintain close friendships, even when one considers the crucially important variable of sexuality. Perhaps instead of asking *whether* men and women can be close friends, we should question *what* must men and women do to maximize their chances of forming and maintaining opposite-sex relationships.

Male-female relationships are perhaps more likely to succeed when a few basic ground rules are followed. First, it would not be a good idea to enter a platonic friendship with an opposite-sex person who you are romantically attracted to. Ask yourself if you would feel jealous if your potential companion started dating someone. If the answer is yes, do not start a friendship with that person because you are unlikely to provide genuine companionship. Second, be honest about what you want from an opposite-sex friendship, and make your intentions known quickly. If you realize your needs are different from your companion's, it might be better to cut ties and move on. Using the guise of friendship with the hope that a friend will one day be willing to fulfill other needs (sexuality, long-term romantic commitment) can start a sequence of experiences that require you to deny your own needs in order to fulfill someone else's. This dynamic is unlikely to work for long, and it sets the course for unhappiness and heartache as the friendship continues and nothing changes. Opposite-sex friendships are most satisfying to both individuals when each friend has the same needs, and such needs are clearly communicated.

One final takeaway point is that there are several ways that opposite-sex relationships can form. Many of these friendships are strictly platonic, while others combine genuine friendship with sexuality, but without commitment, and still others are based solely around hookups and sexual enjoyment. But even among within these categories, there is room for infinite variation. As a relationship develops, each person forges his or her own unique arrangement of personality traits, values, desires, and idiosyncrasies into a behavioral dynamic that characterizes how the dyad will communicate needs, make compromises, and manage conflicts. No two relationships are identical, which makes absolute questions about whether certain relationships will work out difficult to answer with much certainty. Whether men and women can be close friends depends on countless factors, but the basic point is that such friendships do exist and are perhaps more multifaceted and durable than we might initially assume.

Matthew Domico

 Controversy #3: Has Technology Made Socializing Easier or More Difficult in the 21st Century?

INTRODUCTION

Throughout the course of history, humans have mainly socialized through face-to-face communication—that is, until the written word was discovered. People no longer had to socialize through face-to-face interaction. For example, in the 18th century, they could send someone a written letter via the U.S. Postal Service (USPS) or, in the 19th century, send someone a telegram or call someone on a landline telephone. In the 20th century, socializing once again changed with the invention of the Internet. Socializing has always been a reflection of the prevailing technology. The adoption of new technology usually begins with the younger generations' fascination with contemporary gadgets or gizmos and with new skills. This latest technology usually leads to a new form of behavior that will eventually impact their daily lives (e.g., Internet, cell phone) and forever change the way something is done. If we take the cell phone as an example, many adolescents and adults own one and carry it with them at all times. However, it was not long ago that people traveled to and from places without a cell phone. For instance, teenagers would have to call their parents to let them know they arrived safely when they got to their friend's house from the landline telephone at that house.

Recall from Chapter 1, the emergence of new technologies, such as cell phones, the Internet, and various social media channels, has forever changed the way that we connect with others. We used to think of socializing as only occurring in physical places with others (e.g., attending a sporting event, going to dinner, seeing a movie); however, nowadays, socializing can also occur in electronic spaces (e.g., live-tweeting events, Google Hangouts, Facebook Live). We are no longer bound by where we live and those we live around when it comes to socializing. While during much of the 20th century, hanging out in front of the television and watching a movie with a group of friends meant that one was sharing a room with those they were watching with, watching a movie with friends in the second decade of the 21st century might be one in which each friend is in a different house, state, or even a different country streaming the latest movie through their computers at the same time while group-chatting with each other to share their thoughts about that movie. In the past, socialization involved physical places where people would meet and engage in a shared purpose, goal, or behavior. However, over the years with various technological advances, these places include electronic and virtual spaces like social media platforms where one can connect and socialize with someone they may never meet face-to-face. Nowadays, shared spaces are not confined to a physical place. According to the book, *Dimensions of Leisure for Life*, overcoming a sense of isolation is probably one of the best aspects of online communities and virtual worlds. Someone who feels like an outsider in his or her own community or family could find someone online with similar hobbies, interests, or experiences. Think about someone who enjoys singing; this person is able to share that passion with people all over the world by using the Internet. Now famous,

Justin Bieber was discovered from posting videos of himself singing on YouTube. Due to these technological advances, people may not have the need to leave their homes. They can work, socialize with others, and order almost anything they want or need, including food or groceries and have them delivered all from the comforts of their own home. However, this lack of face-to-face interaction and by simply sharing common interests with people through technology may not have a positive effect on social skills and social development.

Technology has had a profound impact on what it means to be social. In the 1960s as the television began to become popular in homes across the United States, the poet T. S. Elliot stated, "[Television] permits millions of people to listen to the same joke at the same time, and yet remain lonesome." Fast-forward 40 years later, and what T. S. Elliot warned about the television may also be true of online socialization. In 2000, Norman Nie, director of the Stanford Institute for the Quantitative Study of Society (SIQSS), conducted a study about Internet usage. He found that increased Internet use was associated with spending less time with family and friends. In other words, the more time people spent on the Internet, the less time they spent interacting with people in the "real world." In contrast to these suggested negative impacts of technology on socializing, because of technology, you can find a long-lost friend and reconnect with that person through a social networking site. In addition, if your family and friends do not live near you, technology makes it possible for you to keep in touch with them on a regular basis. Technology allows us to share our lives with those we care about and with others by the use of photos, videos, text, posts, and so on. As a result, has technology made socializing easier or more difficult in the 21st century? The following two scholars will answer this question, each taking opposing viewpoints. They will share their thoughts about whether technology has made socializing easier or more difficult. As you read these essays, think about your own life and how technology has impacted how you socialize with others. Has it made easier or more difficult for you to socialize? While each essay acknowledges the other side, the first essay focuses on evidence in support of technology making socializing easier in the 21st century. The second essay discusses evidence of technology making socializing more difficult.

RESPONSE 1: WHY TECHNOLOGY HAS MADE SOCIALIZING EASIER IN THE 21ST CENTURY

It's no question that technology provides countless time-consuming distractions. After all, selecting the best selfie for Instagram, keeping up with endless Snapchat messages, or thinking of the wittiest hashtag to use on Twitter takes time, leaving us fewer opportunities for, you know, actually talking to people face-to-face. Smartphones, portable video games, and virtual reality have already started to shape our culture in profound ways. But is technology transforming us into a society of asocial screen-gazers who have little interest in the world around us? Has compulsive smartphone checking damaged our ability to socialize with others? No. A more likely alternative is that 21st-century technology has not changed our ability to relate to others—it has only changed *how* we choose to socialize with others.

The whole "smartphones are inherently ruining our ability to relate to each other" narrative is misguided, but it's easy to see where the idea comes from. Smartphones and social networks can take away from time that could be spent speaking with others face-to-face. And even when we find ourselves around groups of other people, our mobile devices can distract us from our in-person conversations and may lead us right back in to our personal bubble.

But don't let these ideas fool you. New technologies are not making us less social, and they are not replacing human connection. These fears are surprisingly older than you might expect. In 1909, America's leading sociologist at the time, Charles Cooley, warned about morning newspapers replacing American breakfast conversation and how such a change could undermine family sociability. Fortunately, it seems that families have found a way to maintain interpersonal connectedness, even with all the pesky newspapers threatening to destroy our ability to relate to each other.

Socialization has been threatened by older technologies long before the invention of the smartphone. Reading a printed newspaper on the subway is more preferable than blankly staring into space, especially when you find yourself sitting among groups of strangers whom you would not want to speak to anyway, regardless of your social aptitude. Before the age of Google, it was common to see groups of people waiting at a bus stop, holding newspapers in front of their noses. Today, the smartphone provides a similar escape, not necessarily from human connection but from boredom. And although the lone commuter busily fumbling on his cell phone looks disconnected from the social world, there is likely much more socializing happening than can be seen by the casual observer. This person could be sharing a music playlist, chatting with a friend in Thailand, or organizing a local church group outing through Facebook. In fact, some research suggests that Internet and cell phone users tend to have larger numbers of friends and more diverse social networks. Other research shows that people who use sites like Facebook have closer interpersonal relationships and are more engaged in political and civic activities. So maybe smartphone use is not such a socially isolating activity as it seems.

The technology through which we communicate does not impair our ability to socialize—it reflects and magnifies it. Few can deny the power of technology to make social relationships easier to maintain over time. Online social networks have made it possible for people to remain close to us, no matter where we find ourselves geographically in the world. High school acquaintances, college drinking buddies, distant relatives, and former coworkers are all accessible at a moment's notice, as are catalogs of their semipublic information shares—such as photos of their pets, musings about the storylines of their favorite television dramas, and even endorsements of potentially taboo topics such as political affiliation or religious persuasion. Social media technology provides unlimited opportunities for conversation starters with a great number of people in our lives, even as time moves them to different corners of the globe.

Technology also allows for a variety of benefits for younger people that simply were not present in previous decades. For example, some socially anxious teens and young adults find extended sessions of face-to-face interaction intimidating and uncomfortable. Text and Internet messaging provides the ability to have a conversation that is not pressured by the requirement of rapid responses, encouraging a potentially more deliberate, thoughtful exchange of ideas. Similarly, text messaging and social media technology provide a medium for teens to gain social support from and practice interaction with the other sex. Social media aside, the Internet also provides a knowledge and resource base for virtually every question about sex and sexuality, preventing the need for teens to bring up embarrassing topics in conversation or figure things out on their own. And finally, technology helps teens discover their sense of identity. Exposure to a wider network of people and information can help them expand their likes, interests, and perspectives beyond those in their limited peer group or community.

We all know of individual cases of technology use that might be detrimental, such as the woman who buries her face in a smartphone while on dates or the man whose obsession with online games leads him to avoid other types of interpersonal connection. But for most of us, technology does not impair our ability to socialize. It's pretty simple: if you begin having less face-to-face conversations and simply rely on technology to send information, then you have to take responsibility for your own role in damaging your social life. The problem is not technology—it's the choice about how frequently and appropriately technology should be used and whether it comes at the expense of sustaining healthy interpersonal relationships.

At the same time, there have always been people who are not all that socially inclined—and such, their interests lead them to more singular pursuits such as books, television, or Internet use. Technology did not impair their social skills—genetics, environment, and social learning are the more likely culprits. But in cases like these, it is not that greater technology use leads to poor social skills, but rather that *poor social skills lead to a greater use of technology*. This "directionality problem" can give us a skewed impression of the role that technology has in our lives. After all, the awkward, tech-loving geek featured in many popular TV shows and movies is a more memorable character than the socially well-adjusted person who spends a good part of his or her day responding to notifications on his or her mobile device.

Every generation looks at the generations before them and recalls a simpler time, when things just seemed to work better, without the stresses and complications of the present day. For some of us, technology is feared, misunderstood, or misused. But for most people, most of the time, technology offers more social benefits than detriments, especially to those who are invested in the lives of their friends, families, and communities. We have never lived in a world with so much opportunity to remain so richly connected with those around us.

Matthew Domico

RESPONSE 2: TECHNOLOGY OFFERS BOTH BENEFITS AND DRAWBACKS

As humans, we naturally desire physical intimacy, even if it is short lived. However, is that social interaction a thing of the past? Has technology made socializing difficult on a profound and tangible level? In a simple answer, it depends. For people who do not want, need, or desire to know more than what digital manipulation creates, social engagement over the Internet is a perfect virtual island getaway; however, new conduits for personal exploits can also make social engagement and relationship building a task in futility.

The Internet makes camouflaging flaws and identities easier than it has ever been, with individuals maintaining their anonymity with fancy names like *sxybabe25* or voicing their truest thoughts in posts, blogs, and on web pages. Technology not only makes it easier to know about people from around the world, of different races, ages, and classes, but it also makes it easier to create nameless selves, void of physical intimacy. These immaterial communal environments have led to a decrease in closeness and an increase in powerlessness. From acts of microaggression to full-on bullying, individuals can say or be whomever they want without question. People, young and old, create identities they believe are appealing to electronic voyeurs, reinforcing exaggerated ideas of social norm and devaluing their very existence. Computerized platforms, with endless possibilities, are staging grounds where individuals erect identities that go viral for committing social faux pas. Unfortunately, this digital stage fosters a need to create virtual identities that constrict the growth of healthy lived experiences and manifests in social disengagement through an unrealistic presentation of self, especially for young and older individuals.

Technology has not only made learning and socializing easier, but it has also made growing up and growing older more difficult. For older individuals, technology reinforces ageist desires to not be old, harboring desires for a time when the adult physical development was in its infancy, evolving newly out of puberty. This assumption of the inadequacy of being old works against the healthy development of an aging image. Individuals' presence on the web is in continuous contact with images of younger, beautifully staged images that are juxtaposed with those of older individuals' images. The illusion of attaining a socially acceptable identity in the shadow of assumed perfection increases the presence of damaging social images for individuals young and old. Youthful images and behavior are used as a universal representation of virility, strength, and beauty, existing in opposition to those that do not fit within those parameters. Individuals who participate in social networks such as Instagram or Facebook are in daily, sometimes hourly, contact with images that can isolate them socially by marginalizing their participation.

Individuals who covet images and disengage from positive feelings toward themselves, or have low self-esteem, increase the likelihood of a loss of power through the emulation or internalization of such images as norms. When individuals emulate others' dress, mannerism, language, and makeup, they reinforce ideals that their individuality is not socially acceptable. Individuals who accept the idea that idealized images on the web equate to beauty, power is freely taken from them. This is when teens, children, and young adults self-harm or adapt other destructive habits. Individuals who present themselves in distorted ways over the Internet to appear present, attempting to avoid judgement, manifest the opposite effect.

Social definitions of beauty are spelled out through commercials that use words like "be a man," "get your girls," or "be ageless," implying that those who are not those things are flawed. The accentuation and creation of popular culture bolstered by technology can decrease personal feelings of positive social value. With technological advancements occurring every day, some individuals are left behind socially, emotionally, and economically because it is an invisible playground for bullies, a new media platform for advertisers, a platter of variable goodies for perversion, and a lonely place for those who are alone. Technology is a powerful tool for hyphenation—it can bring together groups and create new social interactions; however, it is also a way to delineate social groups by defining who is and who is not acceptable. Unfortunately for some individuals, the relinquishing of power, virtual and real, has consequences on self-definition and social presence.

Jacquelyn Manning-Dantis

Directory of Resources

ACADEMIC JOURNALS

American Journal of Sociology (AJS)

Established in 1895 as the first U.S. scholarly journal in its field, it remains a leading voice for analysis and research in the social sciences. The journal presents pathbreaking work from all areas of sociology, with an emphasis on theory building and innovative methods. AJS strives to speak to the general sociological reader and is open to sociologically informed contributions from anthropologists, statisticians, economists, educators, historians, and political scientists.

Cognition

An international journal that publishes theoretical and experimental papers on the study of the mind. It covers a wide variety of subjects concerning all the different aspects of cognition, ranging from biological and experimental studies to formal analysis. Contributions are from a variety of fields such as psychology, neuroscience, linguistics, computer science, mathematics, ethology, and philosophy. In addition, the journal serves as a forum for discussion of social and political aspects of cognitive science.

Developmental Psychology

Publishes articles that significantly advance knowledge and theory about development across the life span. The journal focuses on seminal empirical contributions. The journal occasionally publishes exceptionally strong scholarly reviews and theoretical or methodological articles.

BOOKS

Asher, Steven, and John Cole, eds. *Peer Rejection in Childhood*. Cambridge, UK: Cambridge University Press, 1990.

Since we know friendships are an important aspect of socializing, this book discusses research on children who encounter difficulty in gaining acceptance and having friendships among their peers. The volume's contributors, development and clinical psychologists who have been involved in research in this area for over a decade, seek to advance the study of peer rejection by giving careful attention to the psychological processes that create and maintain peer rejection in childhood. Topics addressed include how certain children come to be disliked by their peers, the factors that maintain their rejection, the consequences of poor peer relations, and the results of intervention with various subgroups of rejected children. The volume describes the many advances that have been made in the study of peer rejection and provides organizing models that point to avenues for future inquiry.

boyd, danah. *It's Complicated: The Social Lives of Networked Teens*. New Haven, CT: Yale University Press, 2015.

What is new about how teenagers communicate through services such as Facebook, Twitter, and Instagram? Do social media affect the quality of teens' lives? In this eye-opening book, youth culture and technology expert danah boyd uncovers some of the major myths regarding teens' use of social media. She explores tropes about identity, privacy, safety, danger, and bullying. Ultimately, boyd argues that society fails young people when paternalism and protectionism hinder teenagers' ability to become informed, thoughtful, and engaged citizens through their online interactions. Yet despite an environment of rampant fear-mongering, boyd finds that teens often find ways to engage and to develop a sense of identity.

Domínguez, Silvia. *Getting Ahead: Social Mobility, Public Housing, and Immigrant Networks*. New York: NYU Press, 2013.

Getting Ahead tells the compelling stories of Latin American immigrant women living in public housing in two Boston-area neighborhoods. Silvia Domínguez argues that these immigrant women parlay social ties that provide support and leverage to develop networks and achieve social positioning to get ahead. Through a rich ethnographic account and in-depth interviews, the strong voices of these women demonstrate how they successfully negotiate the world and achieve social mobility through their own individual agency, skillfully navigating both constraints and opportunities.

Gottman, John, and Nan Silver. *The Seven Principles for Making Marriage Work: A Practical Guide from the Country's Foremost Relationship Expert.* New York: Harmony, 2015.

John Gottman's unprecedented study of couples over a period of years has allowed him to observe the habits that can make—and break—a marriage. Here is the culmination of that work: the seven principles that guide couples on a path toward a harmonious and long-lasting relationship. These principles teach partners new approaches for resolving conflicts, creating new common ground, and achieving greater levels of intimacy. Gottman offers strategies and resources to help couples collaborate more effectively to resolve any problem, whether dealing with issues related to sex, money, religion, work, family, or anything else.

McCabe, Janice M. *Connecting in College: How Friendship Networks Matter for Academic and Social Success.* Chicago: University of Chicago Press, 2016.

We all know that good study habits, supportive parents, and engaged instructors are all keys to getting good grades in college. But as Janice M. McCabe shows in this illuminating study, there is one crucial factor determining a student's academic success that most of us tend to overlook: who they hang out with. Surveying a range of different kinds of college friendships, *Connecting in College* details the fascinatingly complex ways students' social and academic lives intertwine and how students attempt to balance the two in their pursuit of straight As, good times, or both.

Seefeldt, Kristin S. *Abandoned Families: Social Isolation in the Twenty-First Century.* New York: Russell Sage Foundation, 2016.

Education, employment, and home ownership have long been considered stepping-stones to the middle class. But in *Abandoned Families*, social policy expert Kristin Seefeldt shows how many working families have access only to a separate but unequal set of poor-quality jobs, low-performing schools, and declining housing markets, which offer few chances for upward mobility. Through in-depth interviews over a six-year period with women in Detroit, Seefeldt charts the increasing social isolation of many low-income workers, particularly African Americans, and analyzes how economic and residential segregation keeps them from achieving the American Dream of upward mobility.

Small, Mario Luis. *Unanticipated Gains: Origins of Network Inequality in Everyday Life*. Oxford: Oxford University Press, 2010.
   Social capital theorists have shown that some people do better than others in part because they enjoy larger, more supportive, or otherwise more useful networks. But why do some people have better networks than others? *Unanticipated Gains* argues that the practice and structure of the churches, colleges, firms, gyms, childcare centers, and schools in which people happen to participate routinely matter more than their deliberate "networking."

Turkle, Sherry. *Alone Together: Why We Expect More from Technology and Less from Each Other*. New York: Basic Books, 2012.
   Technology has become the architect of our intimacies. Online, we fall prey to the illusion of companionship, gathering thousands of Twitter and Facebook friends and confusing tweets and wall posts with authentic communication. But this relentless connection leads to a deep solitude. MIT professor Sherry Turkle argues that as technology ramps up, our emotional lives ramp down. Based on hundreds of interviews and with a new introduction taking us to the present day, *Alone Together* describes changing, unsettling relationships between friends, lovers, and families.

Watts, Duncan. *Six Degrees: The Science of a Connected Age*. New York: Norton, 2002.
   From epidemics of disease to outbreaks of market madness, from people searching for information to firms surviving crisis and change, from the structure of personal relationships to the technological and social choices of entire societies, Watts weaves together a network of discoveries across an array of disciplines to tell the story of an explosive new field of knowledge, the people who are building it, and his own peculiar path in forging this new science.

Way, Niobe. *Deep Secrets: Boys' Friendships and the Crisis of Connection*. Cambridge, MA: Harvard University Press, 2013.
   Drawing from hundreds of interviews conducted throughout adolescence with Black, Latino, White, and Asian American boys, *Deep Secrets* reveals the ways in which we have been telling ourselves a false story about boys, friendships, and human nature. Boys' descriptions of their male friendships sound more like "something out of *Love Story*

than Lord of the Flies." Yet in late adolescence, boys feel they have to "man up" by becoming stoic and independent. Vulnerable emotions and intimate friendships are for girls and gay men. "No homo" becomes their mantra.

VIDEOS

"The Hidden Influence of Social Networks" (2008)
http://www.ted.com/talks/nicholas_christakis_the_hidden_influence_of_social_networks

We're all embedded in vast social networks of friends, family, coworkers, and more. Nicholas Christakis tracks how a wide variety of traits—from happiness to obesity—can spread from person to person, showing how your location in the network might impact your life in ways you don't even know.

"How to Live to Be 100+," Dan Buettner (2009)
https://www.ted.com/talks/dan_buettner_how_to_live_to_be_100#t-8043

To find the path to long life and health, Dan Buettner and his team study the world's Blue Zones, communities whose elders live with vim and vigor to record-setting age. In his talk, he shares the nine common diet and lifestyle habits that keep them spry past age 100.

"It's Our City. Let's Fix It" (2014)
https://www.ted.com/talks/alessandra_orofino_it_s_our_city_let_s_fix_it

Too often, people feel checked out of politics—even at the level of their own city. But urban activist Alessandra Orofino thinks that can change, using a mix of tech and old-fashioned human connection. Sharing examples from her hometown of Rio, she says, "It is up to us to decide whether we want schools or parking lots, recycling projects or construction sites, cars or buses, loneliness or solidarity."

"The Mothers Who Found Forgiveness, Friendship" (2010)
https://www.ted.com/talks/9_11_healing_the_mothers_who_found_forgiveness_friendship

Phyllis Rodriguez and Aicha el-Wafi have a powerful friendship born of unthinkable loss. Rodriguez's son was killed in the World Trade Center attacks on September 11, 2001; el-Wafi's son, Zacarias Moussaoui, was convicted of a role in those attacks and is serving a life sentence. In hoping to find peace, these two moms have come to understand and respect one another.

"Remember to Say Thank You" (2008)
https://www.ted.com/talks/laura_trice_suggests_we_all_say_thank_you
   In this deceptively simple three-minute talk, Dr. Laura Trice muses on the power of the magic words "thank you"—to deepen a friendship, to repair a bond, to make sure another person knows what they mean to you. Try it.

"Social Inequality and Network Effects," Filiz Garip (2016)
https://www.youtube.com/watch?v=PJmFKv5Ys4A&list=PLZapTuSHtu-CeejcJGLVBLqNT-ipS0Idh&index=49
   Part of Stanford Center on Poverty and Inequality's America's Course on Poverty

"Social Media and the Strength of Weak Ties" (2015)
https://www.youtube.com/watch?v=xhPgam5jAsY
   How many degrees of separation are between sociologist and textbook author Dalton Conley and comedian Louis C.K. In this video, part of Conley's "Sociology on Street" video series, he demonstrates how social media has affected the number and strength of our weak ties and asks students to conduct a similar experiment.

"Social Networks and Getting a Job," Mark Granovetter (2016)
https://www.youtube.com/watch?v=g3bBajcR5fE&index=32&list=PLZapTuSHtu-CeejcJGLVBLqNT-ipS0Idh&t=11s
   Part of Stanford Center on Poverty and Inequality's America's Course on Poverty

"What Makes a Good Life? Lessons from the Longest Study on Happiness" (2015)
https://www.ted.com/talks/robert_waldinger_what_makes_a_good_life_lessons_from_the_longest_study_on_happiness
   What keeps us happy and healthy as we go through life? If you think it's fame and money, you're not alone—but, according to psychiatrist Robert Waldinger, you're mistaken. As the director of a 75-year-old study on adult development, Waldinger has unprecedented access to data on true happiness and satisfaction. In this talk, he shares three important lessons learned from the study as well as some practical, old-as-the-hills wisdom on how to build a fulfilling, long life.

"Why Friends Make All the Difference" (2012)
https://www.youtube.com/watch?v=OoAcOt47gws

In this video published by Big Think in 2012, a developmental psychologist explains the surprising cognitive effect of having friends near.

"Why You Should Talk to Strangers" (2016)

https://www.ted.com/talks/kio_stark_why_you_should_talk_to_strangers

"When you talk to strangers, you're making beautiful interruptions into the expected narrative of your daily life—and theirs," says Kio Stark. In this delightful talk, Stark explores the overlooked benefits of pushing past our default discomfort when it comes to strangers and embracing those fleeting but profoundly beautiful moments of genuine connection.

WEBSITES

Friendship Day

http://www.friendshipday.org/

Friendship Day is a revered occasion for friends all over the world. It is a day when people express love and heartfelt feelings for their best friends and buddies and promise to stand by them at all times in all circumstances. It is celebrated on the first Sunday in August each year.

International Day of Happiness

http://www.dayofhappiness.net/about/

A global celebration to mark the UN International Day of Happiness. It is coordinated by Action for Happiness, a nonprofit movement of people from 160 countries, supported by a partnership of like-minded organizations.

KidsHealth

https://kidshealth.org/

The most-visited site on the web for information about health, behavior, and development from before birth through the teen years. There are sections for parents, for kids, for teens, and for educators. KidsHealth is more than just the facts about health. As part of the Nemours Foundation's Center for Children's Health Media, KidsHealth also provides families with perspective, advice, and comfort about a wide range of physical, emotional, and behavioral issues that affect children and teens.

National Institute on Aging (NIA)

https://www.nia.nih.gov/

National Institute on Aging is one of the 27 institutes and centers of National Institute of Health (NIH) that leads the federal government in conducting and supporting research on aging and the health and well-being of older people. The institute seeks to understand the nature of aging and the aging process, and diseases and conditions associated with growing older, in order to extend the healthy, active years of life.

Psychology Today
https://www.psychologytoday.com/

A website in which renowned psychologists, academics, psychiatrists, and writers contribute their thoughts and ideas on what makes us tick.

World Health Organization
http://www.who.int/en/

Working through offices in more than 150 countries, WHO staff work side by side with governments and other partners to ensure the highest attainable level of health for all people.

World Values Survey
http://www.worldvaluessurvey.org/WVSContents.jsp

A global network of social scientists studying changing values and their impact on social and political life, led by an international team of scholars, with the WVS Association and WVSA Secretariat headquartered in Vienna, Austria.

Glossary

Anomie: A sense of despair and normlessness due to a lack of accountability to others.

Apprenticeship in thinking: Knowledge and new ways of thinking are acquired through interactions with more mature members of society.

Assortative mating: Tendency for people to fall in love with and marry someone much like themselves.

Authoritative parenting: A type of parenting style that consists of high levels of warmth and control.

Bonding ties: Close and intimate social ties.

Classical conditioning: Learning that two stimuli go together.

Clique: A group of four to six individuals who are good friends and consequently tend to be similar in age, sex, race, and interests.

Cognitive vulnerability: A strong risk factor for depression has been found to exist in places where there is a dense, shared living space.

Cohort: People born at the same point in time.

Companionate love: Deep commitment to another based on shared interests, passions, and values.

Constricting social interaction: Involves one person trying to emerge as the victor by threatening or contradicting the other person.

Constructive play: Play that involves manipulating objects to make or build something.

Coordinated imitation: Interaction in which young children take turns imitating one another and are aware they are being imitated.

Counterimitation: Learning what not to do by watching others.

Crowd: A large mixed-sex group that has similar values and attitudes and is known by a common label.

Cultural diffusion: The spread of cultural artifacts and meanings from one group to another.

Cultural leveling: The ways that cultures geographically distant from each other become similar to one another.

Dementia: Progressive loss of cognitive function marked by memory problems and confused thinking.

Digital dualism: A fallacy or a bias that supposes that things and relationships that occur in real life are more real or valuable or authentic than those that occur online and through social media.

Dominance hierarchy: A group consisting of a leader to whom all other members of the group defer.

Ego resilience: The part of personality that enables people to handle changes.

Embedded tie: Someone we share a number of indirect paths with, who we are connected to through each of our parents, our siblings, our cousins, our neighbors, and the like.

Emetic drug: A drug that makes the person vomit when drinking alcohol.

Enabling social interaction: Involves actions and remarks that tend to support others and sustain the interaction.

Expressive: Term for relationships that are focused on feelings of affection, caring, and supportiveness.

Functional play: Play that involves simple, repetitive activities.

Generational squeeze: Term for what middle-aged adults may feel when they are compelled to support their aging parents while still trying to help their adult children.

Guided participation: When a skilled tutor or mentor engages the learner in a joint activity.

Homophily: Tendency to prefer people who share what we see as important social statuses.

Informal social control: The ability of a social group to create, maintain, and enforce social norms, order, and regulations from within, without external groups or institutions.

Instrumental: Term for relationships that are focused on achieving specific goals and accomplishing specific actions.

Liaisons: Individuals who have friends from several different cliques but do not belong to one.

Loneliness: The negative emotional state caused when one yearns for connection yet feels disconnected.

Longitudinal study: Research in which the same group of people are studied over a long period of time.

Machismo: The Mexican term for the traditional role of males expected to be strong and powerful.

Marginalized: To treat (a person, group, or concept) as insignificant or peripheral.

Marianismo: The Mexican term for the traditional role of females expected to be modest.

Norms: Standards of behavior that apply to all group members.

Primary social connections: Connections to close family and close friends.

Psychosocial: The interaction between thought and social factors.

Psychosocial moratorium: A period of experimentation when adult responsibilities are postponed as young people explore various aspects of themselves.

Reciprocal determinism: A person's behavior both influences and is influenced by personal factors and the social environment.

Relational aggression: Form of covert aggression by spreading rumors about others, withholding friendship, and ignoring or excluding others.

Residential mobility: Moving from place to place.

Secondary social connections: Connections to people we know through work, school, religious, political, or professional memberships, clubs, or hobbies.

Self-efficacy: Confidence in one's ability to perform a particular behavior.

Self-esteem: Refers to a person's overall sense of self-worth and well-being.

Sociability: The desire to associate with others for the sake of enjoying another's company.

Social capital: Valued resources, experiences, and opportunities.

Social cohesion: The extent to which a community's or group's members are bonded.

Social disintegration: When a person does not achieve social integration.

Social disorganization: A social group's lack of solidarity, cohesion, and interaction.

Social distance: The level to which members of social groups have a preference to interact as close friends, neighbors, relatives through marriage, and within other social relationships with members of other groups.

Social integration: How well incorporated one is to and within his or her social group.

Social isolation: The lack of a sustained connection with others.

Social network: A set of social relations that exists through ties between individuals.

Social roles: Expected behaviors and attitudes that come with one's position in society.

Socialization: The ways through which people learn and internalize the values, beliefs, and norms of a culture or society they belong to.

Sociogenomics: The complex interplay between genetics and social environments, contexts, behaviors, and interactions.

Structural hole: A gap between at least two members of a focal person's social network who could benefit if the gap were closed.

Surrogate parenting: A role assumed by grandparents when parents are not able to raise their own children.

Synchrony: Coordinated, rapid, and smooth exchange of responses between a caregiver and an infant.

Temporoparietal junction: An area of the brain associated with empathy.

Token: The one person in a group who represents something specific.

Ventral striatum: Part of the brain that is associated with reward, reinforcement, and the progression from just experiencing something rewarding to compulsively seeking it out.

Vicarious reinforcement/punishment: Learning from observing the positive or negative consequences of another person's behavior.

Zone of proximal development: The difference between what a person can do alone or with assistance; range of skills a person can exercise only with assistance.

Bibliography

Algoe, Sara B., Shelly L. Gable, and Natalya C. Maisel. "It's the Little Things: Everyday Gratitude as a Booster Shot for Romantic Relationships." *Personal Relationships* 17, no. 2 (2010): 217–233.

Al-Naim, Mashary A. *The Home Environment in Saudi Arabia and Gulf States Vol. II: The Dilemma of Cultural Resistance. Identity in Transition. Vol. 2.* Milan, Italy: EDUCatt-Ente per il diritto allo studio universitario dell'Università Cattolica, 2014.

Alzheimer's Association. "What Is Alzheimer's?" http://www.alz.org/alzheimers_disease_what_is_alzheimers.asp.

Alzheimer's Association. "What Is Dementia?" http://www.alz.org/what-is-dementia.asp.

American Psychiatric Association. "What Is Depression?" 2017. https://www.psychiatry.org/patients-families/depression/what-is-depression.

Anjaria, Jonathan Shapiro. "Is There a Culture of the Indian Street?" *Seminar* 636 (2012): 21–27.

Arabindoo, Pushpa. " 'City of Sand': Stately Re-Imagination of Marina Beach in Chennai." *International Journal of Urban and Regional Research* 35, no. 2 (2011): 379–401.

Arnett, Jeffery Jensen. "Emerging Adulthood: A Theory of Development from the Late Teens through the Twenties." *The American Psychologist* 55, no. 5 (2000): 469–480. doi: 10.1037/0003-066X.55.5.469.

Aron, Arthur, Christina C. Norman, Elaine N. Aron, Colin McKenna, and Richard E. Heyman. "Couples' Shared Participation in Novel and Arousing Activities and Experienced Relationship Quality." *Journal of Personality and Social Psychology* 78, no. 2 (2000): 273–284.

Asch, Solomon E. "Effects of Group Pressure upon the Modification and Distortion of Judgments." In *Groups, Leadership, and Men,* edited by Harold Guetzkow, 222–236. Pittsburgh, PA: Carnegie Press, 1951.

Asher, Steven, and John Coie, eds. *Peer Rejection in Childhood.* Cambridge: Cambridge University Press, 1990.

"Associated Press/MTV Youth Happiness Study." *Associated Press.* Accessed June 9, 2017. http://surveys.ap.org/data/KnowledgeNetworks/2007-08-20%20AP-MTV%20Youth%20Happiness.pdf.

Baker, Billy. "The Biggest Threat Facing Middle-Age Men Isn't Smoking or Obesity. It's Loneliness." *The Boston Globe,* March 9, 2017. www.bostonglobe.com/magazine/2017/03/09/the-biggest-threat-facing-middle-age-men-isn-smoking-obesity-loneliness/k6saC9FnnHQCUbf5mJ8okL/story.html.

Bandura, Albert. "Influence of Models' Reinforcement Contingencies on the Acquisition of Imitative Responses." *Journal of Personality and Social Psychology* 1, no. 6 (1965): 589–595.

Bandura, Albert, Dorothea Ross, and Sheila Ross. "Imitation of Film-Mediated Aggressive Models." *The Journal of Abnormal and Social Psychology* 66, no. 1 (1963): 3–11.

Bandura, Albert, Dorothea Ross, and Sheila Ross. "Transmission of Aggression through Imitation of Aggressive Models." *Journal of Abnormal and Social Psychology* 63 (1961): 575–582.

Baum, Isadora. "11 Things That Could Happen to Your Mind & Body If You Don't Socialize for a Long Period of Time, According to Science." November 29, 2016. https://www.bustle.com/articles/196816-11-things-that-can-happen-to-your-mind-body-if-you-dont-socialize-for-a.

Baumrind, Diana. "New Directions in Socialization Research." *American Psychologist* 35, no. 7 (1980): 639–652.

Beck, Julie. "How Friendships Change in Adulthood." *The Atlantic,* October 12, 2015. https://www.theatlantic.com/health/archive/2015/10/how-friendships-change-over-time-in-adulthood/411466/.

Berndt, Thomas. "Friendship and Friends' Influence in Adolescence." *Current Directions in Psychological Science* 1 (1992): 156–159.

Bleske-Rechek, April, and David Buss. "Can Men and Women Be Just Friends?" *Personal Relationships* 7, no. 2 (2000): 131–151. doi: 10.1111/j.1475-6811.2000.tb00008.x.

Bleske-Rechek, April, and David Buss. "Opposite-Sex Friendship: Sex Differences and Similarities in Initiation, Selection, and Dissolution." *Personality & Social Psychology Bulletin* 27 (2001): 1310–1323. doi: 10.1177/01461672012710007.

Bleske-Rechek, April, Erin Somers, Cierra Micke, Leah Erickson, Lindsay Matteson, Corey Stocco, Brittany Schumacher, and Laura Ritchie. "Benefit or Burden? Attraction in Cross-Sex Friendship." *Journal of Social and Personal Relationships* 29, no. 5 (2012): 569–596.

Bleske-Rechek, April, Mark W. Remiker, and Jonathan P. Baker. "Similar from the Start: Assortment in Young Adult Dating Couples and Its Link to Relationship Stability over Time." *Individual Differences Research* 7, no. 3 (2009): 142–158.

Block, Jeanne, and Jack Block. "The Role of Ego-Control and Ego Resiliency in the Organization of Behavior." In *Minnesota Symposia on Child Psychology*, edited by W. A. Collins, 39–101. Hillsdale, NJ: Erlbaum, 1980.

Bogardus, Emory S. "A Social Distance Scale." *Sociology and Social Research* 22 (1933): 265–271.

Botwin, Michael D., David M. Buss, and Todd K. Shackelford. "Personality and Mate Preferences: Five Factors in Mate Selection and Marital Satisfaction." *Journal of Personality* 65, no. 1 (1997): 107–136.

Boundless. "Applications of Classical Conditioning to Human Behavior." *Boundless Psychology Boundless*. Accessed May 17, 2017. https://www.boundless.com/psychology/textbooks/boundless-psychology-textbook/learning-7/classical-conditioning-46/applications-of-classical-conditioning-to-human-behavior-194-12729/.

Bourdieu, Pierre. *The Field of Cultural Production: Essays on Art and Literature*. New York: Columbia University Press, 1993.

Briggs, Xavier de Souza. "'Some of My Best Friends Are. . .': Interracial Friendships, Class, and Segregation in America." *City & Community* 6, no. 4 (2007): 263–290.

Brissette, Ian, Michael Scheier, and Charles Carver. "Brown Kids in White Suburbs: Housing Mobility and the Many Faces of Social Capital." *Housing Policy Debate* 9, no. 1 (1998): 177–221.

Brissette, Ian, Michael Scheier, and Charles Carver. "The Role of Optimism in Social Network Development, Coping, and Psychological Adjustment during a Life Transition." *Journal of Personality and Social Psychology* 82 (2002): 102–111. doi: 10.1037/0022-3514.82.1.102.

Buettner, Dan. "How to Live to Be 100+." Filmed September 2009 at TEDxTC. https://www.ted.com/talks/dan_buettner_how_to_live_to_be_100#t-8043.

Burdelski, Matthew. "I'm Sorry Flower: Socializing Apology, Relationships, and Empathy in Japan." *Pragmatics and Society* 4, no. 1 (2013): 54–81. doi 10.1075/ps.4.1.03bur.

Burgess, Ernest W. "The Growth of the City: An Introduction to a Research Project." In *The City*, edited by Robert E. Park and Ernest W. Burgess, 47–62. Chicago: University of Chicago Press, 1984. First published 1925.

Burt, Ronald S. *Structural Holes: The Social Structure of Competition.* Cambridge, MA: Harvard University Press, 2009.

Cacioppo, John, Catherine Norris, Jean Decety, George Monteleone, and Howard Nusbaum. "In the Eye of the Beholder: Individual Differences in Perceived Social Isolation Predict Regional Brain Activation to Social Stimuli." *Journal of Cognitive Neuroscience* 21, no. 1 (2009): 83–92. doi: 10.1162/jocn.2009.21007.

Cacioppo, John T., and William Patrick. *Loneliness: Human Nature and the Need for Social Connection.* New York: WW Norton & Company, 2008.

Capoeira, Nestor. *A Street-Smart Song: Capoeira Philosophy and Inner Life.* Berkeley, CA: Blue Snake Books, 2006.

Carstensen, Laura L. "Evidence for a Life-Span Theory of Socioemotional Selectivity." *Current Directions in Psychological Science* 4, no. 5 (1995): 151–156.

Carstensen, Laura L. "The Influence of a Sense of Time on Human Development." *Science* 312, no. 5782 (2006): 1913–1915.

Carstensen, Laura L. "Social and Emotional Patterns in Adulthood: Support for Socioemotional Selectivity Theory." *Psychology and Aging* 7, no. 3 (1992): 331–338.

Castaneda Valle, Rodrigo, and Cuauhtemoc Rebolledo Gómez. "MEXICO—Country Note." *Education at a Glance 2013: OECD Indicators.* https://www.oecd.org/edu/Mexico_EAG2013%20Country%20Note.pdf.

Clifton, Jon. "Latin Americans Most Positive in the World." *Gallup*, December 19, 2012. www.gallup.com/poll/159254/latin-americans-positive-world.aspx.

Cole, Steven W. "Human Social Genomics." *PLOSGenet* 10, no. 8 (2014): e1004601.

Commisceo Global Consultancy Ltd. "Mexico Guide: A Look at Mexican Language, Culture, Customs, and Etiquette." http://www.commisceo-global.com/country-guides/mexico-guide.

Commisceo Global Consultancy Ltd. "Norway Guide: A Look at Norwegian Culture and Etiquette." http://www.commisceo-global.com/country-guides/norway-guide.

Côté, Stéphane, Michael W. Kraus, Paul K. Piff, Ursula Beermann, and Dacher J. Keltner. "Social Class Clash: A Dyadic Model of Social Affiliation in Cross-Class and Same-Class Interactions." *Journal of Experimental Psychology General* 146, no. 2 (2014): 269–285.

Cox, Daniel, Juhem Rivera, and Robert P. Jones. "Race, Religion, and Political Affiliation of Americans' Core Social Networks."*Public Religion Research Institute*, August 3, 2016. http://www.prri.org/research/poll-race-religion-politics-americans-social-networks/.

Crisp, Roger, ed. *Aristotle: Nicomachean Ethics*. Cambridge: Cambridge University Press, 2014.

deVries, Brian. "The Understanding of Friendship: An Adult Life Course Perspective." In *Handbook of Emotion, Adult Development, and Aging*, edited by Carol Malatesta-Magai and Susan McFadden, 249–268. New York: Academic, 1996.

Dominguez, Silvia, and Celeste Watkins. "Creating Networks for Survival and Mobility: Social Capital among African-American and Latin-American Low-Income Mothers." *Social Problems* 50, no. 1 (2003): 111–135.

Downey, Greg. *Learning Capoeira: Lessons in Cunning from an Afro-Brazilian Art*. Oxford: Oxford University Press, 2005.

Drake, St. Clair, and Horace R. Cayton. *Black Metropolis*. New York: Harcourt Brace, 1945.

Du Bois, W. E. B. *The Souls of Black Folk*. New York: Knopf, 1993. First published 1903.

Duggan, Maeve. "Mobile Messaging and Social Media 2015." *Pew Research Center*, August 19, 2015. www.pewinternet.org/2015/08/19/mobile-messaging-and-social-media-2015/.

Dunphy, Dexter. "The Social Structure of Urban Adolescent Peer Groups." *Sociometry* 26 (1963): 230–246.

Durkheim, Emile. *Suicide: A Study in Sociology, Reissue Edition*. New York: The Free Press, 1997. First published 1897.

Edmonds, Molly. "What Are the Effects of Isolation in the Mind?" *HowStuffWorks.com*, April 6, 2010. Accessed June 14, 2017. http://science.howstuffworks.com/life/inside-the-mind/emotions/isolation-effects.htm.

Eisenberger, Naomi I. "Social Bain and the Brain: Controversies, Questions, and Where to Go from Here." *Annual Review of Psychology* 66 (2015): 601–629.

Elstad, Jon Ivar, and Kari Stefansen. "Social Variations in Perceived Parenting Styles among Norwegian Adolescents." *Child Indicators Research* 7 (2014): 649–670. doi: 10.1007/s12187-014-9239-5.

Ennett, Susan T., and Karl E. Bauman. "Adolescent Social Networks School, Demographic, and Longitudinal Considerations." *Journal of Adolescent Research* 11, no. 2 (1996): 194–215.

Erikson, Erik H. *Identity and the Life Cycle.* New York: W. W. Norton & Company, 1980.

Ertel, Karen, Maria Glymour, and Lisa Berkman. "Effects of Social Integration on Preserving Memory Function in a Nationally Representative US Elderly Population." *American Journal of Public Health* 98, no. 7 (2008): 1215–1220.

Fehr, Beverley. "Friendship Formation." In *Handbook of Relationship Initiation,* edited by Susan Sprecher, 29–54. Hoboken, NJ: Psychology Press, 2008.

Forth, Catherine. "19 Things Not to Do in Japan." November 12, 2014. http://www.destinationtips.com/destinations/19-things-not-to-do-in-japan/10/.

Frank, Kenneth A., Chandra Muller, and Anna S. Mueller. "The Embeddedness of Adolescent Friendship Nominations: The Formation of Social Capital in Emergent Network Structures." *American Journal of Sociology* 119, no. 1 (2013): 216–253.

Fratiglioni, Laura, Stephanie Paillard-Borg, and Bengt Winblad. "An Active and Socially Integrated Lifestyle in Late Life Might Protect against Dementia." *The Lancet Neurology* 3, no. 6 (2004): 343–353. doi: 10.1016/S1474-4422(04)00767-7.

Frazier, E. Franklin. *The Negro in the United States.* New York: Macmillan, 1957.

"Friendships: Enrich Your Life and Improve Your Health." *Mayo Clinic,* September 28, 2016. http://www.mayoclinic.org/healthy-lifestyle/adult-health/in-depth/friendships/art-20044860.

Gable, Shelly L., Harry T. Reis, Emily A. Impett, and Evan R. Asher. "What Do You Do When Things Go Right? The Intrapersonal and Interpersonal Benefits of Sharing Positive Events." *Journal of Personality and Social Psychology* 87, no. 2 (2004): 228–245.

Garcia, Judit Covarrubias. "Mexican Family Culture." (n.d.) http://family.lovetoknow.com/family-values/mexican-family-culture.

Gillath, Omri, and Lucas A. Keefer. "Generalizing Disposability: Residential Mobility and the Willingness to Dissolve Social Ties." *Personal Relationships* 23, no. 2 (2016): 186–198.

Goddard, Joanna. "10 Surprising Things about Parenting in Norway." July 15, 2013. https://cupofjo.com/2013/07/10-surprising-things-about-parenting-in-norway/.

Goleman, Daniel. "Researchers Add Sounds of Silence to the Growing List of Health Risks." *New York Times*, August 4, 1988. http://www.nytimes.com/1988/08/04/us/health-psychology-researchers-add-sounds-silence-growing-list-health-risks.html.

Gottman, John. "Psychology and the Study of Marital Processes." *Annual Review of Psychology* 49, no. 1 (1998): 169–197. doi:10.1146/annurev.psych.49.1.169.

Granovetter, Mark. "The Strength of Weak Ties: A Network Theory Revisited." *Sociological Theory* 1 (1983): 201–233.

Grant, Richard. *Globalizing City: The Urban and Economic Transformation of Accra, Ghana.* Syracuse, NY: Syracuse University Press, 2009.

Gunn, Dwyer. "Breaking the Code of the Streets: What Can Science Tell Us about How to Reduce Youth Violence?" *Psychology Today*. Last modified July 5, 2016. http://www.psychologytoday.com/articles/201607/breaking-the-code-the-streets.

Haeffel, Gerald J., and Jennifer L. Hames. "Cognitive Vulnerability to Depression Can Be Contagious." *Clinical Psychological Science* 2, no. 1 (2014): 75–85.

Henderson, Tim. "Growing Number of People Living Solo Can Pose Challenges." *The Pew Charitable Trusts*, September 11, 2014. www.pewtrusts.org/en/research-and-analysis/blogs/stateline/2014/09/11/growing-number-of-people-living-solo-can-pose-challenges.

Hill, Edward M., France E. Griffiths, and Thomas House. "Spreading of Healthy Mood in Adolescent Social Networks." *Royal Society Proceedings B* 282, no. 1813 (2015): 20151180.

Hobson, Katherine. "Feeling Lonely? Too Much Time on Social Media May Be Why." NPR, March 6, 2017. http://www.npr.org/sections/health-shots/2017/03/06/518362255/feeling-lonely-too-much-time-on-social-media-may-be-why.

Human Kinetics. "Dimensions of Leisure for Life: Individuals and Society." 2010. http://www.humankinetics.com/excerpts/excerpts/technology-can-have-positive-and-negative-impact-on-social-interactions.

Hurston, Zora Neale. *Their Eyes Were Watching God.* New York: Harper and Row, 1990.

Ibarra-Rovillard, M. Sol, and Nicholas A. Kuiper. "Social Support and Social Negativity Findings in Depression: Perceived Responsiveness to Basic Psychological Needs." *Clinical Psychology Review* 31, no. 3 (2011): 342–352.

"Interracial Couple Denied Marriage License in Tangipahoa Parish." *The New Orleans Times-Picayune*, October 16, 2009. http://www.nola.com/crime/index.ssf/2009/10/interracial_couple_denied_marr.html.

Japan Intercultural Consulting. "Let Your Hair Down—Socializing with Japanese." http://www.japanintercultural.com/en/japanesebusiness etiquetteguide/letYourHairDownSocializingWithJapanese.aspx.

Jurgenson, Nathan. "Digital Dualism and the Fallacy of Web Objectivity." *The Society Pages*, February 24, 2011. http://thesocietypages.org/cyborgology/2011/02/24/digital-dualism-versus-augmented-reality/.

Knapp, Mark, and Eric Taylor. "Commitment and Its Communication in Romantic Relationships." In *Perspectives on Close Relationships*, edited by Ann Weber and John Harvey, 153–175. Boston: Allyn & Bacon, 1994.

Kopp, Rochelle. "Socializing in Japan—Handling Common Tricky Areas." November 15, 2012. http://japanintercultural.com/en/news/default.aspx?newsID=225.

Kurdek, Lawrence A. "Relationship Quality of Gay and Lesbian Cohabiting Couples." *Journal of Homosexuality* 15, no. 3–4 (1988): 93–118.

Kurdek, Lawrence A. "Relationship Quality in Gay and Lesbian Cohabiting Couples: A 1-Year Follow-Up Study." *Journal of Social and Personal Relationships* 6, no. 1 (1989): 39–59.

Latané, Bibb, Kipling Williams, and Stephen Harkins. "Many Hands Make Light the Work: The Causes and Consequences of Social Loafing." *Journal of Personality and Social Psychology* 37, no. 6 (1979): 822–832.

Lee, Helena. "The Babies Who Nap in Sub-Zero Temperatures." February 22, 2013. http://www.bbc.com/news/magazine-21537988.

Levenson, Robert W., Laura L. Carstensen, and John M. Gottman. "Long-Term Marriage: Age, Gender, and Satisfaction." *Psychology and Aging* 8, no. 2 (1993): 301–313.

Levinger, George. "Toward the Analysis of Close Relationships." *Journal of Experimental Social Psychology* 16, no. 6 (1980): 510–544.

Levinson, Daniel J. "A Conception of Adult Development." *American Psychologist* 41, no. 1 (1986): 3–13.

Lim, Chaeyoon, and Robert D. Putnam. "Religion, Social Networks, and Life Satisfaction." *American Sociological Review* 75, no. 6 (2010): 914–933.

Lincoln, Karen D., Linda M. Chatters, and Robert Joseph Taylor. "Psychological Distress among Black and White Americans: Differential Effects of Social Support, Negative Interaction and

Personal Control." *Journal of Health and Social Behavior* 44, no. 3 (2003): 390–407.

Maccoby, Eleanor E., and John A. Martin. "Socialization in the Context of the Family: Parent-Child Interaction." In *Handbook of Child Psychology: Formerly Carmichael's Manual of Child Psychology*, edited by Paul H. Mussen, 1–101. New York: Wiley, 1983.

Madden, Thomas, Pamela Ellen, and Icek Ajzen. "A Comparison of the Theory of Planned Behavior and the Theory of Reasoned Action." *Personality and Social Psychology Bulletin* 18, no. 1 (1992): 3–9. doi: 10.1177/0146167292181001.

Madeline. "Bronfenbrenner's Bioecological Model of Development (Bronfenbrenner)." In Learning Theories. May 15, 2017. https://www.learning-theories.com/bronfenbrenners-bioecological-model-bronfenbrenner.html.

Mahmud, Shihabuddin. "Identity Crisis Due to Transformation of Home Environment: The Case for Two Muslim Cities, Dhaka and Hofuf." *METU: Journal of the Faculty of Architecture* 24, no. 2 (2007): 37–56.

Matheson, Catherine, Rebecca J. Olsen, and Thomas Weisner. "A Good Friend Is Hard to Find: Friendship among Adolescents with Disabilities." *American Journal on Mental Retardation* 112, no. 5 (2007): 319–329.

Matthews, Cate. "This Is What Happens in a Depressed Person's Brain." August 31, 2014. http://www.huffingtonpost.com/2014/08/20/science-depression-asapscience_n_5696226.html.

McDermott, John. "Why Friends Leave a 'Buffer Seat' between Them at the Movies." *MEL*, June 2, 2016. http://melmagazine.com/why-straight-men-leave-a-buffer-seat-between-them-at-the-movies-a8ae43d53324.

McLeod, Saul A. "Classical Conditioning." *Simply Psychology*. Last modified 2014. www.simplypsychology.org/classical-conditioning.html.

McPherson, Miller, Lynn Smith-Lovin, and James M. Cook. "Birds of a Feather: Homophily in Social Networks." *Annual Review of Sociology* 27, no. 1 (2001): 415–444.

Metz, Michael E., B. R. Simon Rosser, and Nancy Strapko. "Differences in Conflict-Resolution Styles among Heterosexual, Gay, and Lesbian Couples." *Journal of Sex Research* 31, no. 4 (1994): 293–308.

Milgram, Stanley. "Behavioral Study of Obedience." *The Journal of Abnormal and Social Psychology* 67, no. 4 (1963): 371–378.

Morley, Carol. "Joyce Carol Vincent: How Could This Young Woman Lie Dead and Undiscovered for Almost Three Years?" *The Guardian*, October 9, 2011. http://www.theguardian.com/film/2011/oct/09/joyce-vincent-death-mystery-documentary.

Murstein, Bernard. "A Clarification and Extension of the SVR Theory of Dyadic Pairing." *Journal of Marriage and Family* 49, no. 4 (1987): 929–933.

Murthy, Vivek H. "Emotional Well-Being Is the Missing Key to Better Health." *TedMed*, October 4, 2016. http://blog.tedmed.com/emotional-well-missing-key-better-health.

Nahapiet, Janine, and Sumantra Ghoshal. "Social Capital, Intellectual Capital, and the Organizational Advantage." *Academy of Management Review* 23, no. 2 (1998): 242–266.

National Institute on Drug Abuse (NIDA) for Teens. "What Is Prescription Drug Misuse?" https://teens.drugabuse.gov/drug-facts/prescription-drugs.

Neuroscientifically Challenged. "Know Your Brain: Striatum." February 15, 2015. http://www.neuroscientificallychallenged.com/blog/know-your-brain-striatum.

Oetting, Eugene R., and Fred Beauvais. "Peer Cluster Theory, Socialization Characteristics, and Adolescent Drug Use: A Path Analysis." *Journal of Counseling Psychology* 34, no. 2 (1987): 205–213.

Oetting, Eugene R., Joseph F. Donnermeyer, Joseph E. Trimble, and Fred Beauvais. "Primary Socialization Theory: Culture, Ethnicity, and Cultural Identification. The Links between Culture and Substance Use. IV." *Substance Use & Misuse* 33, no. 10 (1998): 2075–2107.

Office of the New York City Comptroller, Bureau of Fiscal and Budget Studies. *New York City Economic Brief.* New York, March 2015. http://comptroller.nyc.gov/wp-content/uploads/documents/Longest_Work_Weeks_March_2015.pdf.

Oishi, Shigehiro. "The Psychology of Residential Mobility Implications for the Self, Social Relationships, and Well-Being." *Perspectives on Psychological Science* 5, no. 1 (2010): 5–21.

Osumare, Halifu. *The Hiplife in Ghana: West African Indigenization of Hip-Hop.* New York: Springer, 2012.

Oswald, Andrew J., and Stephen Wu. "Objective Confirmation of Subjective Measures of Human Well-Being: Evidence from the USA." *Science* 327, no. 5965 (2010): 576–579.

Page-Gould, Elizabeth, Rodolfo Mendoza-Denton, and Linda R. Tropp. "With a Little Help from My Cross-Group Friend: Reducing Anxiety in Intergroup Contexts through Cross-Group Friendship." *Journal of Personality and Social Psychology* 95, no. 5 (2008): 1080–1094.

Park, Robert E. "The City: Suggestions for the Investigation of Human Behavior in the Urban Environment." In *The City*, edited by Robert

E. Park and Ernest W. Burgess, 1–46. Chicago: University of Chicago Press, 1984. First published 1925.

Parker-Pope, Tara. "Socializing Appears to Delay Memory Problems." June 4, 2008. https://well.blogs.nytimes.com/2008/06/04/socializing-appears-to-delay-memory-problems/?_r=1.

Parten, Mildred. "Social Participation among Pre-School Children." *The Journal of Abnormal and Social Psychology* 27, no. 3 (1932): 243–269.

Phillips, Julie A. "A Changing Epidemiology of Suicide? The Influence of Birth Cohorts on Suicide Rates in the United States." *Social Science & Medicine* 114 (2014): 151–160.

Plaut, Shayna. "The Dangers of Drinking Coffee Alone: The Precarity and Isolation of Social Justice Work." *Praxis Center*, May 31, 2017. http://www.kzoo.edu/praxis/isolation/#more-11150.

Polgreen, Lydia. "Ghana's Uneasy Embrace of Slavery's Diaspora." *The New York Times*, December 12, 2005. http://www.nytimes.com/2005/12/27/world/africa/ghanas-uneasy-embrace-of-slaverys-diaspora.html.

Prinstein, Mitchell, and Kenneth Dodge, eds. *Understanding Peer Influence in Children and Adolescents.* New York: Guilford Press, 2008.

Putnam, Robert D. *Bowling Alone: The Collapse and Revival of American Community.* New York: Simon and Schuster, 2001.

Quayson, Ato. *Oxford Street, Accra: City Life and the Itineraries of Transnationalism.* Durham, NC: Duke University Press, 2014.

Rao, Shakuntala. "The Globalization of Bollywood: An Ethnography of Non-Elite Audiences in India." *The Communication Review* 10, no. 1 (2007): 57–76.

Ray, Carina E. *Crossing the Color Line: Race, Sex, and the Contested Politics of Colonialism in Ghana.* Athens: Ohio University Press, 2015.

Reiss, Ira L. "Toward a Sociology of the Heterosexual Love Relationship." *Marriage and Family Living* 22, no. 2 (1960): 139–145.

Robins, Richard, and Kali Trzesniewski. "Self-Esteem across the Lifespan." *Current Directions in Psychological Science* 14, no. 3 (2005): 158–162.

Rosenquist, J. Niels, James H. Fowler, and Nicholas A. Christakis. "Social Network Determinants of Depression." *Molecular Psychiatry* 16, no. 3 (2011): 273–281.

Rubin, Kenneth H., William M. Bukowski, and Jeffrey G. Parker. "Peer Interactions, Relationships, and Groups." In *Handbook of Child Psychology*, edited by Nancy Eisenberg, 619–700. New York: Wiley, 1998.

"Sandwich Generation." http://www.investopedia.com/terms/s/sandwichgeneration.asp.

Sansone, Livio. "The New Blacks from Bahia: Local and Global in Afro-Bahia." *Identities: Global Studies in Culture and Power* 3, no. 4 (1997): 457–493.

"Segregation in Saudi Arabia: No Men Allowed." *The Economist*, February 25, 2015. http://www.economist.com/news/middle-east-and-africa/21645231-more-public-places-are-catering-women-only-no-men-allowed.

Seligman, Katherine. "Social Isolation a Significant Health Issue." *San Francisco Chronicle*, March 2, 2009. www.sfgate.com/health/article/Social-isolation-a-significant-health-issue-3249234.php.

Seligson, Hannah. "Facebook's Last Taboo: The Unhappy Marriage." *The New York Times*, December 24, 2014. http://www.nytimes.com/2014/12/28/fashion/facebook-last-taboo-the-unhappy-marriage.html.

Shakya, Holly B., and Nicholas A. Christakis. "Association of Facebook Use with Compromised Well-Being: A Longitudinal Study." *American Journal of Epidemiology* 185, no. 3 (2017): 203–211.

Sherman, Aurora M., Brian deVries, and Jennifer E. Lansford. "Friendship in Childhood and Adulthood: Lessons across the Life Span." *The International Journal of Aging and Human Development* 51, no. 1 (2000): 31–51.

Shulevitz, Judith. "The Lethality of Loneliness." *The New Republic*, May 12, 2013. http://newrepublic.com/article/113176/science-loneliness-how-isolation-can-kill-you.

Simmel, Georg. *The Sociology of Georg Simmel.* New York: Simon and Schuster, 1950.

Skolnick, Arlene. "Married, Lives: Longitudinal Perspectives on Marriage." In *Present and Past in Middle Life*, edited by Dorothy H. Eichorn, John A. Clausen, and Norma Haan, 269–298. New York: Academic Press, 1981.

Smilansky, Sara. "The Effects of Sociodramatic Play on Disadvantaged Preschool Children." New York: Wiley, 1968.

Smith, Aaron. "Older Adults and Technology Use." *Pew Research Center*, April 3, 2014. http://www.pewinternet.org/2014/04/03/older-adults-and-technology-use/.

Sprinthall, Richard C., and Norman A. Sprinthall. *Educational Psychology: A Developmental Approach.* 2nd ed. New York: Addison-Wesley, 1977.

Stack, Carol, B. *All Our Kin: Strategies for Survival in an Urban Black Community.* New York: Harper and Row, 1974.

Stanford Institute for the Quantitative Study of Society (SIQSS). "Stanford SIQSS Study." http://cs.stanford.edu/people/eroberts/cs201/projects/personal-lives/stanford.html#Results.

Sternberg, R. J. "A Triangular Theory of Love." *Psychological Review* 93, no. 2 (1986): 119–135.

Tannen, Deborah. *Gender and Discourse.* Oxford: Oxford University Press, 1994.

Time Out: Mumbai and Goa. London: Time Out Guides Ltd., 2011.

Tourula Marjo, Isola Arja, and Juhani Hassi. "Children Sleeping Outdoors in Winter: Parents' Experiences of a Culturally Bound Childcare Practice." *International Journal of Circumpolar Health* 67, no. 2–3 (2008): 269–278.

United Nations Human Rights. "Convention on the Rights of the Child, Article 31," 1990. http://www.ohchr.org/en/professionalinterest/pages/crc.aspx.

United States Bureau of Labor Statistics. *2015 American Time Use Survey.* Washington, DC. http://www.bls.gov/news.release/archives/atus_06242016.pdf.

University of Chicago. "Loneliness Affects How the Brain Operates." *ScienceDaily*, February 17, 2009. http://www.sciencedaily.com/releases/2009/02/090215151800.htm.

University of Chicago Medical Center. "Social Isolation Worsens Cancer, Mouse Study Suggests." *ScienceDaily*, September 29, 2009. http://www.sciencedaily.com/releases/2009/09/090929133115.htm.

University of Michigan. "Social Isolation May Have a Negative Effect on Intellectual Abilities." *Medical News Today*, October 30, 2007. http://www.medicalnewstoday.com/articles/87087.php.

Vygotsky, Lev. "Interaction between Learning and Development." *Readings on the Development of Children* 23, no. 3 (1978): 34–41.

Wade, Lisa. "American Men's Hidden Crisis: They Need More Friends!" *Salon*, December 7, 2013. www.salon.com/2013/12/08/american_mens_hidden_crisis_they_need_more_friends/.

Wang, Hui-Xin, Anita Karp, Bengt Winblad, and Laura Fratiglioni. "Late-Life Engagement in Social and Leisure Activities is Associated with a Decreased Risk of Dementia: A Longitudinal Study from the Kungsholmen Project." *American Journal of Epidemiology* 155, no. 12 (2002): 1081–1087.

Watson, John B. Behaviorism. New York: People's Institute Publishing Company, 1924.

Way, Niobe. *Deep Secrets.* Cambridge, MA: Harvard University Press, 2011.

Wellman, Barry. "The Community Question: The Intimate Networks of East Yorkers." *American Journal of Sociology* 84, no. 5 (1979): 1201–1231.

WHO. "Basic Documents (45th ed., Supplement)." Geneva, Switzerland: WHO, 2006. http://www.who.int/governance/eb/who_constitution_en.pdf.

Wilson, C., and B. Moulton. "Loneliness among Older Adults: A National Survey of Adults 45+." *Knowledge Networks and Insight Policy Research*, 2010. Washington, DC. http://assets.aarporg/rgcenter/general/loneliness_2010.pdf.

Wilson, William Julius. *The Truly Disadvantaged: The Inner City, the Underclass, and Public Policy.* Chicago: University of Chicago Press, 2012.

Wilson, William Julius. *When Work Disappears: The World of the New Urban Poor.* New York, Vintage. 2011.

Wolfinger, Nicholas H. "Want to Avoid Divorce? Wait to Get Married, But Not Too Long." July 16, 2015. https://ifstudies.org/blog/want-to-avoid-divorce-wait-to-get-married-but-not-too-long/.

Wong, Paul T. P., and Lisa M. Watt. "What Types of Reminiscence Are Associated with Successful Aging." *Psychology and Aging* 6, no. 2 (1991): 272–279.

Woolcock, Michael. "The Place of Social Capital in Understanding Social and Economic Outcomes." *Canadian Journal of Policy Research* 2, no. 1 (2001): 11–17.

World Happiness Report. 2017. http://worldhappiness.report/wp-content/uploads/sites/2/2017/03/HR17.pdf.

World Health Organization. "About WHO: Who We Are and What We Do." http://www.who.int/about/en/.

World Values Survey. "Mexico." 2016. http://www.worldvaluessurvey.org/WVSDocumentationWV6.jsp.

Yang, Yang Claire, Courtney Boen, Karen Gerken, Ting Li, Kristen Schorpp, and Kathleen Mullan Harris. "Social Relationships and Physiological Determinants of Longevity across the Human Life Span." *Proceedings of the National Academy of Sciences* 113, no. 3 (2016): 578–583.

Yosomono, Eric, Rev. Les Crowley, and Ryan Menezes. "6 Foreign Parenting Practices Americans Would Call Neglect." September 16, 2013. http://www.cracked.com/article_20621_6-foreign-parenting-practices-americans-would-call-neglect.html.

Zhong, Chen-Bo, and Geoffrey J. Leonardelli. "Cold and Lonely Does Social Exclusion Literally Feel Cold?" *Psychological Science* 19, no. 9 (2008): 838–842.

About the Authors and Contributors

Tennille Nicole Allen, PhD, is an associate professor at Lewis University, Romeoville, Illinois, where she chairs the Department of Sociology and directs the African American and Ethnic and Cultural Studies programs. Her scholarly interests include the ways that African American girls and women understand and navigate their identities while resisting the images and perceptions crafted by others. She is also interested in perceptions and meanings of social relationships as well as processes of and challenges in building community among African American girls and women.

Valerie Hill, PhD, is an associate professor and the undergraduate program director in the Department of Psychology at Lewis University, Romeoville, Illinois. Her scholarly interests include social cognition, in particular children and adolescents' understanding of social relationships, as well as college student learning and best teaching practices.

Jennifer Tello Buntin, PhD, is an assistant professor of sociology and director of the Latin American and Latina/o Studies program at Lewis University, Romeoville, Illinois. Her research and teaching interests focus on the Latinx experience in the United States, international migration, and the intersectionality of race, class, and gender. Before starting her position at Lewis University, she was a visiting assistant professor at the Julian Samora Research Institute at Michigan State University and held teaching positions at North Central College and the University of Illinois–Chicago. She received her PhD from the Department of Sociology at the University of Chicago in 2010.

Matthew Domico, PsyD, is an assistant professor at Lewis University, Romeoville, Illinois, where he teaches a variety of graduate and undergraduate courses related to clinical psychology, research, and behavioral neuroscience. He has experience in providing psychotherapy and assessment services to adults, teens, and children and has worked in hospital, college counseling, and community mental healthcare settings.

Kristi Kelly is a higher education administrator, which began well over a decade ago. Her work and experience include career services and workforce development where she has focused on relationship building and access to higher education. Most recently, she has engaged more intentionally in multicultural, intercultural, and diversity inclusion work where she currently directs the multicultural student services office and teaches a cultural diversity and intergroup relations course at Lewis University. Her research entails the experiences of Black women (both students and personnel) in the collegiate setting. Kelly attended Johnson C. Smith University, a private, historically Black, four-year research university in the heart of Charlotte, North Carolina, and earned a bachelor of arts in sociology. She then went on to attend Lewis University in Romeoville to earn her master of arts in organizational leadership and a doctorate in educational leadership.

Jacquelyn Manning-Dantis, PhD, is an adjunct professor at Lewis University, Romeoville, Illinois. She has been teaching in the field of sociology for seven years. She holds a master's degree in sociology from Roosevelt University, Chicago, Illinois. She obtained her doctorate in social gerontology with a certificate in women's studies from Miami University in Oxford, Ohio.

Carlene Sipma-Dysico, PhD, is an assistant professor of sociology at Lewis University, Romeoville, Illinois. She holds a PhD from Loyola University Chicago. Her research interests include race, poverty, and place; structural impediments to reentry and stigmatization of formerly incarcerated persons; and the labor migration experiences and familial outcomes of Guatemalan Maya.

Index